LANDRU'S SECRET

For Hannah and Tess

LANDRU'S SECRET

The Deadly Seductions of France's Lonely Hearts Serial Killer

Richard Tomlinson

PEN & SWORD
HISTORY

AN IMPRINT OF PEN & SWORD BOOKS LTD.
YORKSHIRE – PHILADELPHIA

First published in Great Britain in 2018 by
Pen & Sword History
An imprint of
Pen & Sword Books Ltd
Yorkshire - Philadelphia

ISBN 978 1 52671 529 6

Typeset in Times New Roman 11/13.5 by
Aura Technology and Software Services, India

Printed and bound in the UK by
TJ International Ltd, Padstow, Cornwall

Pen & Sword Books Limited incorporates the imprints of Atlas, Archaeology,
Aviation, Discovery, Family History, Fiction, History, Maritime, Military,
Military Classics, Politics, Select, Transport,
True Crime, Air World, Frontline Publishing, Leo Cooper,
Remember When, Seaforth Publishing, The Praetorian Press,
Wharncliffe Local History, Wharncliffe Transport,
Wharncliffe True Crime and White Owl.

For a complete list of Pen & Sword titles please contact
PEN & SWORD BOOKS LIMITED
47 Church Street, Barnsley, South Yorkshire, S70 2AS, England
E-mail: enquiries@pen-and-sword.co.uk
Website: www.pen-and-sword.co.uk

or

PEN AND SWORD BOOKS
1950 Lawrence Rd, Havertown, PA 19083, USA
E-mail: uspen-and-sword@casematepublishers.com
Website: www.penandswordbooks.com

Contents

List of Characters

The Accused

Henri Désiré Landru: inventor, swindler, romancer, born Paris, 1869

His principal aliases
Raymond Diard: an engineer from German-occupied Lille
Raoul Dupont: an automobile trader from Rouen
Lucien Forest: an industrialist from German-occupied Rocroi
Georges Frémyet: a manufacturer from German-occupied Lille
Lucien Guillet: a factory owner from German-occupied Ardennes
Georges Petit: a manufacturer from German-occupied Lille
Georges Petit: a colonial entrepreneur fromTunis

His wife
Marie-Catherine Landru, née Rémy: laundress, forger, born Mutzig, Alsace, 1868

Their children
Marie Landru: born, Paris, 1891
Maurice Landru: born, Paris, 1894
Suzanne Landru: born, Paris, 1896
Charles Landru: born, Paris, 1900

His mistress
Fernande Segret: born, Paris, 1892

The Missing Women*

(*Age at time of disappearance)

Jeanne Cuchet (39): seamstress, mother of *André Cuchet* (17), who also disappears
Thérèse Laborde-Line (46): unemployed
Marie-Angélique Guillin (52): retired housekeeper
Berthe Héon (55): cleaner
Anna Collomb (44): typist
Andrée Babelay (19): nanny
Célestine Buisson (47): housekeeper
Louise Jaume (38): dress shop assistant
Anne-Marie ('Annette') Pascal (37): seamstress
Marie-Thérèse Marchadier (37): prostitute

The Investigation

Gabriel Bonin: investigating magistrate, Paris
Jules Belin: detective, Paris police
Amédée Dautel: detective, Paris police
Louis Riboulet: detective, Paris police
Dr Charles Paul: forensic pathologist, director of the Paris police laboratory

The Trial

Maurice Gilbert: presiding judge
Robert Godefroy: chief prosecuting attorney
Vincent de Moro Giafferri: chief defence counsel
Auguste Navières du Treuil: assistant defence counsel

Note on Money

In 1913, when this story begins, 1 old French franc had the purchasing power of just below 3.1 euros in 2017. I have used this rate for all conversions into modern money.

Prologue: Alas, I Have Little Hope

On Sunday, 12 January 1919, a housemaid in Paris, 32, single and poorly educated, sent a letter to a village mayor in the best French she could muster.

"I am writing a few words to ask you for some information, unfortunately very serious," Marie Lacoste began. In her despair, Marie forgot her full stops, as she raced on:

"You have in your commune a house at about 100 metres from the church, which is called the *Maison Tric*, the name of the owner, I do not know him, but the house was rented in 1917, to a gentleman around 40 years old, who had a long brown beard and who has as his name Monsieur Frémyet. Therefore this gentleman lived in this house for a good part of the summer of 1917 with a woman of about 45 to 50, or more exactly 47, with blue eyes and chestnut hair, medium height."

The woman was Marie's widowed elder sister Célestine Buisson, who had vanished that summer at Gambais, a village 50 kilometres south-west of Paris, and never been seen again.

"Since then the gentleman has disappeared, but one sees him with other women and this woman who was with him, has not reappeared to her family since the end of August 1917, at Gambais, in the house in question, I know the house and the area."

Marie also knew enough about men and how they disregarded humble women like her to keep her letter short, for she wanted the mayor's full attention. She did not tell the mayor how she and Célestine had huddled together on the man's cot bed, beneath his picture of the wolf in sheep's clothing, while he slept across the corridor. She did not describe how she had peered through the keyhole of his locked garden shed and glimpsed strange shapes, almost like bundles, piled in a heap.

Instead, Marie got to the point. Could the mayor please check "whether my sister has not been officially buried in your area?" If not, "would you have the kindness to make a visit to the house in question and in the garden and question the inhabitants of the area if there is nothing mysterious, but alas I have little hope, for it is too long since that happened."

The mayor of Gambais asked the village schoolmaster, who acted as his secretary, to send Marie a careful reply. No one called Célestine Buisson had been buried in Gambais, the teacher wrote, and no one called Frémyet lived at the *Maison Tric*. Given these facts, the mayor did not have the authority to investigate the house and the garden.

The mayor and the schoolteacher had not lied. Like everyone else in Gambais, they knew the man who rented the Villa Tric (its correct name) as Monsieur Dupont. He described himself as an automobile trader and had been seen coming and going with a series of women ever since his arrival at the house three years before. As far as the mayor was concerned, Dupont's business with these women was his private affair.

Yet something about Marie's letter – perhaps a sense that she would not be put off so easily – pricked the mayor's conscience. He told the teacher to add another line. It so happened that another young woman had written to the *mairie* a while ago with a similar enquiry concerning her own sister, the teacher wrote. Mlle Lacoste might want to compare notes with this correspondent. Here was her address.

***

This is the story of Henri Désiré Landru, the most notorious serial killer in French criminal history, who would never have been arrested without the detective work of Marie Lacoste and the woman to whom she now wrote. When the police finally caught up with Landru at a dingy apartment near Paris's Gare du Nord, they found a short, bald, bearded 50-year-old with a mistress half his age, and a roomful of clutter that included a bust of Beethoven, a volume of romantic poetry, and a patent application for a revolutionary new automobile radiator.

Eventually, the police concluded that Landru had made romantic contact with 283 women during and immediately after the First World War. They were wrong. The true figure was certainly higher, while the official number of Landru's victims – ten fiancées and one young man – was almost certainly too low. The horror unleashed by Landru at two country houses outside Paris transfixed the French public to the point where one newspaper speculated that the entire story had been concocted by the government to distract attention from its hapless performance at the 1919 peace talks.

Landru's trial, held in Versailles in November 1921, was the hottest ticket that autumn in Paris, less than an hour away by train. Celebrities fought to get special passes, including the novelist Colette, the singer Maurice Chevalier, and Rudyard Kipling, who was passing through Paris to collect an honorary degree. Landru was a showstopper, firing off caustic barbs at the judge and the prosecuting attorney as he insisted on his innocence. "My only regret is that I have just the one head to offer you," he sneered at the court, while he mocked the "elegant ladies" in the audience who came each day to gawp at him.

This is also the story of the women who brought Landru to justice in the hope of some kind of vengeance. They were the female relatives and friends of his victims, who tracked him down and confronted him in court, determined to send the killer of their loved ones to the guillotine.

In the beginning Landru was the hunter, at large in a wartime Paris stripped bare of eligible men. He preyed on women via lonely hearts adverts and matrimonial agencies, on trams, buses and metro trains, in public parks and at the apartments and houses he rented in the city and nearby countryside.

When women became his pursuers, Landru still held the advantage of being a man. Parisian detectives and village constables, cobblers, coachmen, and shopkeepers all declined to enquire about this promiscuous *monsieur* who was entitled, in his words, to a "wall" around his private life.

Landru clung to all his presumed rights over women at his trial, secure in the knowledge that the men in the court shared his views about the "feeble sex". The judge disparaged Landru's ten missing fiancées as foolish, feeble, wanton, ignorant, and naïve. The newspapers deplored the presence of women in the audience and made fun of the concierges, seamstresses, prostitutes and village "gossips" who testified against Landru. As for Landru, he could scarcely be bothered with the "cackling" of these female accusers. They could not be trusted, Landru declared, precisely because they were women.

Landru preferred to address the prosecutor, the judge and the all-male jury with a single question. "Your proofs, *messieurs*, where are your proofs?" he demanded again and again, wagging his finger aloft. For *l'affaire Landru* was a murder case with no bodies, where the only forensic evidence was some charred bone debris of doubtful origin beneath a pile of leaves, and a few burnt scraps of women's apparel. Even the prosecutor "loyally confessed" that the authorities had no idea how Landru had killed his 11 known victims or how he had disposed of their remains.

***

A solution did exist to the puzzle, hidden amid 7,000 pages of case documents, only a fraction of which were ever seen by the prosecution and defence at Landru's trial. Buried in this vast depository of witness statements, interrogation transcripts and forensic reports was a more disturbing narrative.

This untold story began in the same time and place as the official version of events: a busy street near Paris's Gare de l'Est on the eve of the First World War. At this point the police and the investigating magistrate lost sight of the one clue that might have allowed them to understand how a petty Parisian conman was driven to kill more women – probably many more – than the ten missing fiancées on Landru's charge sheet.

PART ONE

THE DISAPPEARANCES
January 1915 – April 1919

Chapter 1

The Locked Chest

In the autumn of 1913, a year before the Germans swept towards Paris, a mother and her teenage son could often be seen on Sunday mornings bicycling along the Rue du Faubourg Saint-Denis. Sometimes they headed north past the Gare de l'Est and then up the long hill to Montmartre. At the top, they would pause to catch their breath and look down on the teeming, dangerous city.

She was Jeanne Cuchet, a 38-year-old seamstress whose husband had died five years earlier. Jeanne's friends all agreed later that she was pretty, a fact confirmed by a studio portrait probably taken shortly after Martin Cuchet's death. The photographer caught Jeanne's full lips, the dimple on her chin, her brown curly hair tied loosely in a bob, an air of faint bemusement playing across her face. This puzzled expression was familiar to those who knew Jeanne, for she was rather deaf, often failing to hear what people said.

Jeanne had much on her mind as she and her 16-year-old son André biked around Paris. She had tried in vain to marry again, but she was hard to please on the subject of men. A string of potential suitors had come and gone at her fifth-floor apartment on the Rue du Faubourg Saint-Denis, including a commercial traveller and a wine trader. None had lasted long.

Jeanne might have found another husband more easily if she had not been so poor. Martin Cuchet had left Jeanne nothing apart from his medical and funeral expenses, obliging her to borrow 1,000 francs (about 3,100 euros) after the funeral in order to tide her over. She cursed her "stupidity" in renting a larger apartment than she could afford, on the advice of the dress shop manager for whom she worked from home. Her savings were almost exhausted; all that remained of her nest egg were some municipal bonds, barely worth 300 francs.

Jeanne wanted to marry again for André's sake, as she told the shop manager, a well-intentioned man called Monsieur Folvary. She thought her only child needed a proper father who could help him get on in life, especially since André carried a social handicap. He was illegitimate, and probably not the son of Martin Cuchet, despite taking Cuchet's surname. From time to time, Jeanne also told Folvary that she wanted to leave France with André for a new life abroad in America. Folvary found it hard to take her seriously, since Jeanne did not speak a word of English.

André had a rather different view of his mother's situation. One day in Folvary's dress shop near the Opéra, when Jeanne was out of earshot, André told Folvary that he was not keen on her plans to find a husband. A slim, rather weedy youth, André was increasingly impatient to escape from under Jeanne's possessive wing. The prospect of a stepfather ruling the roost displeased him, for life was looking up for André that autumn.

He had just started working at a shirt factory called "Fashionable House", where he had fallen in with a gang of older lads. André's best friend, his hero really, was Max Morin, the leader of this group, who was everything André wanted to be – self-confident, at ease with girls, a real man. Privately Max thought André was a bit of a "little girl", but André did not notice his new friend's condescension. For the first time in his sheltered upbringing, André felt like a proper grown-up.

***

Autumn turned to winter. As the New Year came, no one could imagine that France would be at war with Germany in eight months' time – least of all Jeanne, as she scoured the lonely hearts adverts in the newspapers for a *monsieur* who might make a husband.

One Saturday in February, Jeanne burst into Folvary's shop with some startling news. She was engaged to a widowed industrialist from northern France called Monsieur Diard, now settled in Paris, and was handing in her notice. Folvary was astonished and asked Jeanne when they were going to marry. Jeanne hesitated before giving her reply. Unfortunately there was a minor hitch, she explained, because Diard had lost his military identity card while performing his obligatory national service in French Indo-China some years ago. He had just applied for a replacement since he would need to produce the document in order to register their marriage.

The helpful Folvary had an idea. He had a well-connected officer friend in the army who might be able to speed up the process. All Folvary required from Jeanne was Diard's full name and birth details and the dates of his

4

military service in Indo-China. Jeanne thanked Folvary and said she would pass on this information to her fiancé.

Several days later she returned to the shop and told Folvary abruptly that Diard's identity card had in fact been lost in the Philippines. Furthermore, Jeanne went on, Diard did not need any assistance from Folvary in getting a new one. With that, she hurried out of the shop before Folvary could ask any more questions.

***

Jeanne had an elder sister called Philomène, a concierge who lived and worked on the left bank of the Seine, near the Jardin du Luxembourg. Philomène, 44, was childless, having married late to a bookstore employee called Georges Friedman; both she and her rather prim husband deplored Jeanne's mildly disreputable love life. Every so often, Philomène made a point of seeing Jeanne to dispense some sisterly advice about men, to no avail. Jeanne refused to take heed and frequently she and Philomène were not on speaking terms.

This may explain why it was Georges Friedman, not Philomène, who first met Diard at Jeanne's apartment. According to Friedman, he was instantly suspicious of Jeanne's fiancé.

In his mid-forties, Diard was stocky, muscular and bald, with a luxuriant dark brown beard, flecked with grey, and deep-set, piercing eyes. He spoke with a drawling, faintly lower-class accent, yet he dressed like the respectable businessman he claimed to be, in a sober dark suit, starched white shirt and cravat. Diard was difficult to place, one moment talking knowledgeably about stocks and shares, the next performing his party trick of standing on one hand to show off his physical strength.

Friedman's doubts were aroused when Diard casually mentioned that he had done his military service in Indo-China. Friedman had also served in Indo-China, but when he remarked on this coincidence, Diard rapidly changed the subject. It seemed clear to Friedman that Diard had never been anywhere near the colony.

Friedman and Philomène could not talk Jeanne out of the relationship, although there seemed no immediate prospect of a marriage because Diard was still waiting for his new military identity card. Jeanne even told Philomène that she had made a scanty sky-blue nightdress to please her fiancé in bed. The prudish Philomène did not approve.

***

5

In April 1914, Jeanne and Diard suddenly moved from Paris to the village of La Chaussée, 50 kilometres north of the city. André stayed behind at Jeanne's apartment near the Gare de l'Est, working at "Fashionable House" and fooling around with Max and the lads. Jeanne imposed one condition on André's newly won independence: every Saturday, after work, André had to catch the train to the town of Chantilly, near La Chaussée, to spend Sunday with his mother and future stepfather.

A century ago, La Chaussée was little more than a street of houses set back from a bend in the river Oise. It was a quiet hamlet, where strangers were soon noticed.

"Monsieur and Mme Diard", as they called themselves, were spotted immediately, rattling into La Chaussée one day in a grey tradesman's delivery van or *camionnette* driven by the husband. They did not bring much – just a couple of old beds, some bed linen and a few kitchen utensils – which they installed in the ground-floor rooms Diard had rented in a house on the edge of the village. From the beginning, Diard was downright rude to his new neighbours, rarely bothering to return their greetings on the street. Jeanne was polite enough when she went shopping in the village but never got into a conversation. It was as if the two of them had something to hide.

Mme Hardy, a housewife in her late thirties, lived with her husband and children upstairs from the Diards. One Sunday, when André was visiting, Mme Hardy's curiosity got the better of her. There was a hole in her living room floor board and as she peered through it, Mme Hardy saw her new neighbours sitting down to lunch. She was struck by how frightened the boy seemed of Diard: "[he] did not dare serve himself and did not talk and it was Diard who invited him to eat."

Mme Hardy thought André looked like a son who could not wait to get away from his somewhat menacing father and catch the evening train to Paris for another week of relative independence. Jeanne's behaviour was harder to interpret. She did not say much to her surly "husband", yet nor did Jeanne appear cowed by him. Over the next few weeks, as Mme Hardy gradually managed to make small talk with Jeanne, she came across as a woman of some *sangfroid*: cool, a little distant, but quite capable of looking after herself. Jeanne seemed like a wife who might have married Diard for reasons other than love.

In early June, Diard opened a bank account in his name at the Société Générale branch in Chantilly, depositing 5,609 francs. This was roughly what Jeanne had earned in a year as a seamstress and far more than her own paltry savings. Later that month, Jeanne finally steeled herself to invite her sister to come to La Chaussée for a day in the country so Philomène could meet her future brother-in-law.

Philomène was dismayed by the shabby, barely furnished apartment and appalled by Diard. He did not speak at all during a walk in the country and was just as unpleasant over dinner at a nearby restaurant. Philomène returned by train to Paris that evening with a "strong aversion" to Jeanne's disagreeable fiancé.

Life in La Chaussée continued its settled routine in the first three weeks of July, undisturbed by anything more dramatic than the arrival of the Paris newspapers each afternoon. On Saturday, 18 July, *Le Petit Parisien* reported that the music hall starlet Suzanne Darby was in hospital after being shot in "mysterious conditions" by a boyfriend, one "Henri Z…" Less interestingly, France's president was sailing to Russia for a state visit. "Everything is fine on board" ran the headline for this dull diplomatic story.

Sometime that weekend, Mme Hardy watched Diard drive out of La Chaussée in his *camionnette*, leaving Jeanne alone at the villa. He headed firstly to Paris, where he collected his 46-year-old wife at a pre-arranged rendezvous, and then drove north-west to the port of Le Havre, one of the main crossing points to England.

On 22 July, Diard drove back to Chantilly, bypassing La Chaussée, and withdrew 2,000 francs from his bank account. He probably returned directly to Le Havre, where on Sunday, 26 July he and his wife set off in the *camionnette* to return to Paris.

At about 5.00 pm they were speeding down a hill outside the Normandy village of Gournay-en-Bray when Diard lost control of the *camionnette* and crashed into a poplar tree. Neither Diard nor his wife was hurt but the car needed repairing. Diard did a quick deal with a local farmer who had seen the accident and the couple stayed the night in the farmhouse. They carried on to Paris next morning by train, leaving the car at the farm for Diard to come back and mend.

Two days later, as Austria declared war on Serbia, Diard caught the train from Paris to Chantilly and withdrew the remaining 2,000 francs from his bank account. He still avoided Jeanne, returning directly to Paris by train.

On 29 July, a week after the crash, Diard showed up at the farm, accompanied by a young man who helped him fix the *camionnette*. Diard explained to the farmer that the situation in Paris "did not look good" and war seemed likely. He asked if it would be possible to bring his wife and children to stay on the farm for a month or so, in exchange for more money. After some negotiation, the farmer and his wife agreed.

On Saturday, 1 August, as France began to mobilise, Diard made two round trips in his *camionnette* from Paris to the farm outside Gournay. In the morning he delivered his eldest son (who had helped repair the vehicle) and his 18-year-old daughter. By late evening, Diard had returned with his wife, his 25-year-old daughter, his 14-year-old son, and the family's pet dog, which the farmer remembered as a "ratty" little animal.

All this time, Jeanne had remained in La Chaussée. It was only on the weekend of 1–2 August, as France mobilised, that Mme Hardy noticed Jeanne becoming fretful. Her anxiety was easy for a mother like Mme Hardy to grasp. Jeanne was marooned in La Chaussée, while in Paris patriotic youths like André could not wait to fight the hated "*Boches*".

On Sunday morning (2 August), Diard at last showed up at the apartment in his *camionnette*. He did not stay long. Shortly afterwards, Mme Hardy saw him drive Jeanne off to the station in Chantilly, where she caught the train alone to Paris and returned to her old apartment. After his summer of independence, André was firmly back in Jeanne's care.

Diard drove back to La Chaussée, where word was starting to spread that he might be a German spy. Several villagers remarked that he came and went in his van at all hours of the day and night; and besides, Diard never spoke to anyone, and no one had a clue what he did for a living. Mme Hardy decided to redouble her surveillance of this potentially dangerous enemy agent.

On Monday, 3 August, the day France formally declared war on Germany, Mme Hardy noticed Diard becoming increasingly agitated at Jeanne's failure to return from Paris. At last she appeared on Tuesday, without André. A day or two later, Mme Hardy observed Diard and Jeanne get into the *camionnette* and head out of the village. This time, Diard did not come back to La Chaussée, leaving Mme Hardy to suppose that he must have driven Jeanne all the way to Paris.

***

Something now happened to cause Jeanne serious alarm. Diard vanished soon after their arrival in Paris, giving no indication of where he had gone. Jeanne assumed that he was lying low in La Chaussée but in fact he had gone back to his wife and children at the farmhouse near Gournay to check that they were safe.

Jeanne faced a dilemma. She was desperate to find out if Diard was in La Chaussée but seems to have feared a confrontation. She also appears to have been nervous about leaving André on his own in Paris, given the number of patriotic teenage boys who were trying to volunteer illegally for the army by pretending they were 18, the minimum age for enlisting. Swallowing her pride, Jeanne asked Philomène's husband Georges Friedman if he would travel to La Chaussée on her behalf.

When Friedman got to La Chaussée on Sunday, 9 August, he asked Mme Hardy if she knew where Diard had gone. Mme Hardy said she did not, adding that she had heard a rumour that Diard was a German spy. Friedman told her he would "check it out". Before leaving, Friedman informed Mme Hardy that Jeanne's real surname was Cuchet, not Diard.

A week later, on Sunday, 16 August, Friedman came back to La Chaussée with Jeanne and André. Mme Hardy watched them go in and when they emerged sometime later, she saw that Jeanne had "an annoyed air". The trio left in a hurry, without saying anything to Mme Hardy.

The reason for Jeanne's annoyance lay inside a small locked chest belonging to Diard that he had left behind at the villa. When Jeanne prised it open, she discovered a cache of papers, including the identity document of one Henri Désiré Landru, born in Paris in 1869. "Raymond Diard", an industrialist from northern France, was an imposter. The same *livret de famille* showed that Landru had a wife, Marie-Catherine, born in 1868, and four children: Marie (1891), Maurice (1894), Suzanne (1896) and Charles (1900). In addition, Jeanne found a number of blank identity documents and automobile licences, the stock-in-trade of a conman.

Georges Friedman insisted on taking Jeanne and André straight back to his and Philomène's apartment in Paris, where he convened a family council of war. In front of André, Jeanne agreed that she would break off all relations with Landru, alias Diard. She was crying when she and André returned late that evening to Rue du Faubourg Saint-Denis, telling her concierge that "Monsieur Diard would never set foot in her apartment again."

Next day, Philomène made Jeanne accompany her to Landru's abandoned address in Malakoff, where they soon learned from neighbours the most shocking news of all. Landru was a convicted swindler on the run from the law, having just been tried and sentenced *in absentia* to exile for life with hard labour on the French Pacific island of New Caledonia. Following the trial, Mme Landru and her children had also vanished, leaving no contact details. Seemingly chastened, Jeanne assured Philomène that she had split for good from Landru.

Jeanne went home, finally free of Philomène, and reflected on her troubles: unemployed, almost broke, abandoned by her fiancé, with a naïvely patriotic son who seemed intent on getting himself killed by the Germans. Sometime in the next couple of days she made two decisions. First, Jeanne asked her concierge not to allow the Friedmans into the building or let them know if she was at home. Next, she wrote a letter to Mme Hardy.

Chapter 2

The Lodge at Vernouillet

Jeanne wanted to know whether "Monsieur Diard" had returned yet to the villa. Mme Hardy replied that she had no news at all.

Two days later, on the evening of 20 August, Landru arrived in the dark on a bicycle. He lost his temper when Mme Hardy showed him Jeanne's letter, stuffing it in his pocket. In the morning Mme Hardy saw him cycle off to the station at Chantilly.

Another week passed, as Jeanne sat tight in Paris. From her fifth-floor window, she could watch André set off for work after breakfast, turning south down the Rue du Faubourg Saint-Denis towards his shirt factory rather than north towards the cheering crowds on the forecourt of the Gare de l'Est. Every hour, boys barely older than André were kissing their mothers and sisters goodbye and clambering onto the troop trains that snaked out of the station towards the front.

Towards the end of August, a young woman who had briefly worked for Jeanne as an assistant seamstress passed by the apartment. She found Jeanne in some distress, complaining that her fiancé was an imposter who used false identity papers and that the villagers in La Chaussée thought he was an enemy spy. Jeanne did not reveal Landru's name or the fact that he was a criminal on the run. Instead, she claimed that he had disappeared shortly after being "mobilised" and then turned up out of the blue at her apartment while he was on "military leave". According to Jeanne, he had confessed to her that he was married with children, but was divorcing his wife, whom he did not love; meanwhile, his feelings for Jeanne were unchanged.

Jeanne's visitor left with the impression that Jeanne had refused to forgive her fiancé and had ended the relationship. It was not true. Shortly before or after this visit, Mme Hardy saw Landru and Jeanne arrive at the villa in La Chaussée on foot, having walked from the station in Chantilly. They only stayed for a day or two, and to Mme Hardy's frustration, she could not engage Jeanne in a neighbourly chat. "She was not the same as before, she appeared sad," Mme Hardy recalled.

Jeanne brought a bundle of dirty linen back to Paris, grumbling to her concierge that soldiers had created "havoc" by dossing down in the villa; for La Chaussée now lay directly in the path of troops marching towards an alarmingly fluid front. This "allied offensive", dutifully reported by the censored press, was in reality a series of murderous, mobile engagements that killed around 40,000 French soldiers in one week alone.

Sometime in early September, Landru appeared again on his bike in La Chaussée and stayed for several days. Mme Hardy resumed her surveillance, still worried that Diard was spying for the Germans. In her motherly way, Mme Hardy also fretted that André might be among the French casualties. Here, perhaps, lay the cause of Jeanne's evident sadness, Mme Hardy thought.

"He has been called up," Landru lied, when Mme Hardy dared to broach the subject of André with him.

Mme Hardy remarked that André was still "very young", unaware that at 17 he could not even volunteer.

"It is necessary that he does his military service like everyone else," Landru said curtly, sounding pleased to have got the boy off his hands.

***

One by one, the "Fashionable House" lads were going off to the war. On Saturday, 29 August, André stood on the platform at Paris's Gare de Montparnasse, waving goodbye to his best friend Max. Lucky Max, André thought: at 18, Max was just old enough to volunteer for the mounted infantry and was bound for a training camp near Bordeaux.

As the train crawled out of the station, Max's mother, standing next to André, noticed this boy's "great sorrow" through her own tears. Putting on a brave face, André now kept an eye on Mme Morin, as Max had asked him to do.

"I accompanied your mother all the way to her home," André wrote shortly afterwards to Max, "reassuring her as best I could about your destiny, and telling her that I will come and give her news about you as soon as possible." It did not occur to André that Max might also be writing to his mother.

At his training camp, Max was soon learning how to ride his first horse, much to André's envy. Meanwhile, "Fashionable House" had collapsed, because the owners of the business had been mobilised. "I'm currently unemployed, the factory closed last Thursday, you cannot even imagine how time drags," André lamented to Max in early September.

Max's gang of "Fashionable House" mates, who had let André tag along with them, had also gone off to barracks or training camps.

"Your mother has no doubt told you about the departure of Robert Ballenger to Vannes, of Marcel Huber to Saint-Nazaire," André rambled on to Max. "As you can see, almost all the lads have left."

Putting his loneliness to one side, André wanted to hear more about Max's training horse: had Max already stroked its neck? Also, "the Bordeaux girls, my good chap!" André teased Max: "Are they to your taste?"

Before he left Paris, Max had thoughtfully asked his mother to make friends with Mme Cuchet, for he knew that Jeanne constantly fretted about André trying to enlist as an underage volunteer. It soon became plain that the two women did not have a great deal in common. Mme Morin was a respectable, strait-laced housewife, ten years older than Jeanne, who shocked her new acquaintance by mentioning casually that she could not wed her fiancé because he was already married. Mme Morin could scarcely believe her ears when Jeanne added that this same *monsieur* had used a false identity.

"Her account made me freeze," Mme Morin recalled. "I felt I had to advise Mme Cuchet to break with this individual, who was not an honest man. She did not speak to me about him any more."

The two women stuck from then on to the safe subject of their respective sons. Mme Morin remembered how Jeanne was "heartbroken" that autumn at a false rumour that 17-year-olds would soon be able to volunteer for the army, without parental permission. Conversely, André was full of joy at the same unfounded news.

André had at least persuaded Jeanne to allow him to attend weekly pre-army training classes for teenage boys at a barracks near their apartment. It was great, André reported to Max at the start of October, even though he could not train for the cavalry because the barracks had run out of horses. Instead, he was going to join the infantry, and this was great too. André and his classmates had marched one day around the *quartier*, singing patriotic songs.

"We are taught in a really marvellous way," André enthused to Max. "An infantryman who was passing through the barracks showed us this week how to dismantle a machine gun. He even taught us in a summary way how to fire it if necessary."

And then Jeanne stepped in. "I have to tell you that I haven't been doing any military training for the past fortnight," André informed Max in late October. "It was becoming completely useless, given that *Maman* does not want me to sign up."

André was determined to do something for the war effort, rather than stew at home with his possessive mother who seemed to have no desire to resume her old work as a seamstress. He soon found a job as a trainee mechanic at an automobile plant in north-west Paris that was making vehicles for the army.

"My old chap, it's just like barracks life," André joked in his next letter to Max. His alarm went off at 5.30 am and after a quick breakfast with Jeanne he was on his bike, in time for the early shift.

Even now, Jeanne could not leave André alone. One day, André was working on the assembly line when Jeanne turned up unannounced with Mme Morin to see how he was getting on.

"You can just imagine how I felt!" André wrote to Max indignantly. "I had my hands full and completely filthy as I was in the middle of dismantling a car."

His new job lasted barely a month. In late November, Jeanne abruptly pulled André out of the factory without informing his employer. All of a sudden, she and André were leaving Paris for a new life in the country with Landru.

***

Mme Oudry, 60, ran a property agency in Vernouillet, a quiet little town near a loop in the Seine, about 35 kilometres north-west of Paris. Towards the end of November, a bearded man called "Monsieur Cuchet" walked into Mme Oudry's little office to enquire about an unfurnished house for rent with the curious English name "The Lodge". She showed him around and he liked the place but explained that his wife would need to see it as well in order to give her final approval.

Next day, Jeanne and André caught the train to Vernouillet with Landru to inspect The Lodge. It was a peculiar double-fronted property, standing near the bottom of a narrow street called Rue de Mantes that wound uphill to the town centre. The Lodge was really two houses in one, with a small annexe or "pavilion" on the higher side adjoining the main villa further down the hill. Confusingly, a garage formed the ground floor of the villa and provided access to the rear garden, while the first-floor front door was reached via a flight of external steps.

This is what Jeanne saw when she opened the door and stepped into a narrow hallway:

- To the left, a living room and dining room, leading onto the two-storey annexe, where there was an oven;
- To the right of the hallway, a staircase going down to the garage and up to three first-floor bedrooms and a spacious attic;
- At the end of the corridor, a kitchen with no oven, a pantry and a washroom;
- At the rear of the house, more steps leading down to the surprisingly long garden, flanked by drystone walls and incorporating a disused, tumbledown stable directly behind the annexe.

Jeanne could see that the garden lacked any real privacy, because it was overlooked by the neighbouring house on the uphill side, while the wall on the downhill side had collapsed in places. It was not ideal for her purpose but she decided The Lodge would have to do. The three of them returned to Mme Oudry's office, where Jeanne and André watched in silence as "Monsieur Cuchet" signed the short-term quarterly lease.

A couple of days later, a removal van brought all Jeanne's furniture down from Paris. Landru now decided to retrieve his *camionnette* from the farmhouse in Normandy where he had billeted his family, parking it in The Lodge's substantial garage.

Around Vernouillet, Landru and Jeanne soon aroused the same suspicion as in La Chaussée. Landru pretended to Mme Oudry that he was a designer of aircraft tailfins, prompting rumours that he might be a German spy. He also informed Mme Oudry that Mme Cuchet held a senior position with a leading Paris fashion house and had to go "constantly" to America. André, meanwhile, was rarely seen outdoors.

***

At his training camp in Bordeaux, Max was fed up with André, who had not written to him for the best part of a month. Finally, just before Christmas, André got round to replying to Max's last letter.

"What a hassle!" André declared, blaming the move from Paris for the delay. "It has been worse I'm sure than fatigue duty," André prattled on. "*Enfin*, that's how it is, we are almost settled in and I am starting to get my breath back."

André did not explain to Max why he and his mother had left Paris; nor did André mention the man masquerading as his father. Indeed, André had never referred to Landru, alias Diard, alias Cuchet, in any of his letters to Max.

Over Christmas, Jeanne received a letter from Mme Morin who – possibly prompted by Max – was worried that she had heard nothing from Mme Cuchet since her departure from Paris. It took Jeanne a week to reply, and when she did, her tone was guarded and unwelcoming.

Jeanne began by explaining implausibly that she had not written sooner because she had not wished to "disturb" Mme Morin during her mobilised husband's recent home leave. Besides, Jeanne continued, there was "the speed with which we decided [to move], in two or three days everything was rushed through." Jeanne assured Mme Morin that she planned to come to Paris soon and would not fail to call on her.

"Please believe me that I also look back fondly on the moments we spent together and I really hope that we don't lose sight of each other."

On the other hand, a visit by Mme Morin to Vernouillet might be difficult because "at the moment the place is rather muddy". Of course, Jeanne added, she would be pleased to see Mme Morin at The Lodge "as soon as the weather will allow", which might not be till the summer. Jeanne's hint to Mme Morin was obvious; for the time being, she wished to be left alone.

Sometime in January, Jeanne wrote a similar letter to the sister of her late husband, who had also expressed a desire to visit Vernouillet. Once again, Jeanne explained that the "poor weather" meant such a visit was currently impractical.

Even after a month in Vernouillet, the reclusive new tenants at The Lodge had made almost no impression on their immediate neighbours. The local butcher, who lived with his family at the bottom of Rue de Mantes, dimly recalled "Monsieur Cuchet" strolling up the hill one day with André, who was wearing mechanic's overalls. The butcher's wife thought she might have seen Jeanne and André heading off somewhere on their bicycles. On the other side, the young housewife whose property overlooked the rear garden of The Lodge could only remember later that the man might have been a secret German agent.

In early January, Jeanne allowed André to travel twice to Paris to collect the post from their old apartment. It was probably on one of these trips that André picked up some fantastic news, at least from his point of view. France had lost around 300,000 men in the first five months of the war, a staggering casualty rate that had already forced the government to bring forward the mobilisation of young men born in 1895 and 1896, the so-called "classes" of 1915 and 1916. By the second week of January, the press was reporting accurately that the government was about to announce the call-up in the summer of 1915 of André's contingent, the "class" of 1917. Suddenly, Jeanne faced the prospect of losing André to the army within a matter of months.

André could not wait to tell Max, who had just been posted to the front. "Ah! You lucky dog," André wrote enviously on 20 January, before alluding to his own good news. "I believe I too will soon be savouring the pleasures of garrison life," André continued. "Perhaps you and I will meet one day in the trenches, you as a dragoon and me as a foot-soldier, for I am sure in advance that I cannot avoid this destiny."

André was still pumped up with patriotic fervour a week later when he wrote to his mobilised uncle, the husband of Jeanne's sister-in-law. André had heard that his uncle had just been promoted from private to the lowly rank of adjutant. It was a signal honour for the family, André believed, and he felt obliged to convey his congratulations.

Then André and Jeanne fell silent, as if they had simply disappeared.

Chapter 3

The 'Carnet Noir'

Max was furious about André's failure to reply to any more letters. "He's a little fool," he told his mother that spring, when he was home on leave. Max even wondered whether to catch a train to Vernouillet to give André a piece of his mind.

At the end of March, Mme Morin sent another letter to Jeanne, expressing concern that she and Max had heard no more from their friends. A few days later, a short, bearded man, wearing a top hat and smart gloves, called at the Morins' apartment in northern Paris. Landru introduced himself as a "friend" of Mme Cuchet who, he explained, had gone to England with André. He tipped his hat and was on his way, before the startled Mme Morin could probe a little further.

She had little doubt that her caller was Jeanne's fiancé and assumed that Jeanne must have broken off their engagement. Gradually, Mme Morin and Max stopped dwelling on Jeanne and André's rude behaviour. It was clear that this strange mother and her immature son did not wish to see them, which was all a bit sad, Mme Morin reflected.

***

Landru was busy that spring – so busy that he acquired a little black moleskin diary or "*carnet*" to keep track of his hectic schedule. On 1 May 1915, *Le Journal*, a mass circulation daily, published a lonely hearts advert he had concocted, which read in French:

> *M. 45 ans, seul, s. famil., situation 4.000, ay. intér. désire*
> *épous. dame, âge situation rapport.*

Meaning:

> *Monsieur*, aged 45, single, with no family, savings of 4,000
> francs, having own home, wishes to marry a lady of a similar
> age and situation.

Landru had pitched his advert cleverly. He was neither an obvious swindler, like the *monsieur* in the same column who claimed to own a chateau, nor too poor to attract interest. A middle-aged man in his forties with savings of 4,000 francs (about 12,400 euros) sounded solidly respectable, a good catch for a woman seeking bourgeois security.

Next morning, the first replies began to arrive at the PO box attached to Landru's advert.

"Excused me having seen your announcement in the newspaper," Célestine Buisson wrote. "I am a widow with 12,000 francs I am 44 years old I have a 19 year old son in action so I am alone I would like to change my situation if my situation pleases you Accept my respectful sentiments, Buisson."

A photograph of Célestine, taken shortly before the war, showed her as she was: a hard-working domestic servant from south-west France, scarcely educated, with a warm, trusting nature and a strong desire to show the right man that she would make a good wife.

Célestine was the widow of an innkeeper in Montpellier and had moved to Paris after his death in 1912 to be closer to her two sisters, taking a job as a housekeeper. One of her sisters, Catherine, was married with young children and lived near Célestine's apartment in south-east Paris. The other, Marie, was in reality a half-sister with a different father from Célestine and Catherine. Now in her late twenties, Marie worked as a housemaid for a well-to-do family in the fashionable third *arrondissement*. Marie walked with the help of a cane because of some illness or injury to her leg, a disability that perhaps explained why she was still single.

Naturally honest, Célestine had permitted herself two little omissions in her letter to Landru. Firstly, her son Gaston was illegitimate, born sometime after Célestine's marriage. In addition, Célestine had until recently been the mistress of a gendarme who had been killed during the early months of the war. This was why she had spotted Landru's lonely hearts adverts; the term exactly described how Célestine felt.

Landru replied swiftly to Célestine, introducing himself as "Georges Frémyet", a manufacturer and bachelor from the city of Lille, close to the Belgian border. When the Germans occupied Lille in October 1914, he had abandoned his home and factory and fled to Paris, a wrenching experience. To be clear, it was not Célestine's money that interested him, Landru explained in his devious letter. No, it was the depth of the sentiments she had expressed in her response. Would it perhaps be possible to arrange a meeting?

"I agree with you a meeting is preferable," Célestine wrote straight back, "for what you tell me is really true money is all very well but if one has a wife who is loose disorganised and who does not like her home and does not have affection for her husband it is a very sad existence for one and the other as for me I believe that one will not be able to reproach me for that for if I take a husband it is to love him and cherish him as a wife who loves her husband must do."

They met at Célestine's apartment near the Gare d'Austerlitz and again the following day. At this point, Célestine decided she had better double-check the investment certificates that she kept in her wardrobe, just in case "Frémyet" proposed to her. To her horror, she realised her stocks and bonds were only worth about 10,000 francs, not 13,000 francs, as she had mistakenly told him. Célestine confessed all in her next letter to Landru, hoping he would forgive her.

"There is no doubt at all that you will find I make you a good wife," she pleaded. "You have suffered a thousand misfortunes from the Germans I will make you forget them certainly my situation is a lot more modest than yours but the affection I will give you really counts for something."

Landru felt he had got far enough with Célestine to start one of his case files. "44", he wrote in Célestine's dossier. "A son of 19 at the front… Got her loot and furniture on the death of her old man." He then considered how to classify Célestine in his filing system. "In reserve", he eventually scribbled.

***

Landru continued to work his way through the other respondents to his advert in *Le Journal*. At 8.00 pm on 18 May, he arrived at an apartment on Rue Rodier, a few blocks west of the Gare du Nord.

"I am 39 years old," Anna Collomb had written to him. "I am a widow with no children and thus have no family. I make 210 francs per month in an office and, being economical and fairly astute, I have managed to build up some savings, which, with the little I received from my husband when he died, amounts to 8,000 francs."

Anna was an attractive, dark-haired woman who worked near the Paris Bourse as a typist for an insurance company. Her letter, like her personality, was not entirely candid. Her real age was 44, and she had an illegitimate little daughter who had supposedly been placed with nuns in the Italian port of San Remo. This story may also have been untrue, for Anna's concierge later recalled seeing the infant at Rue Rodier.

Anna omitted another detail in her reply to Landru. Her elderly father, a retired salesman, and her mother lived in an apartment in eastern Paris with her much younger sister Victorine, 24, who was engaged to a soldier serving at the front. Anna was especially close to Victorine, or "Ryno" (pronounced "Reeno"), as she was known in the family. For her part, Ryno kept a fond, watchful eye on Anna, mindful of her elder sister's sorry history with men.

Anna had originally married a silk trader, living with him in the 1890s in Guatemala, childless and increasingly miserable, as he steadily went bankrupt. On their return to France, Anna's husband had cadged a job managing an uncle's farm in the French Alps, where Anna had watched him steadily drink himself to an early death. After a brief stint as a lady's companion in Marseille, the widowed Anna had moved back to Paris. Over the years her concierge at Rue Rodier had observed a string of gentleman callers going up to her apartment and often staying the night.

Landru, alias "Monsieur Frémyet", an industrialist from Lille, may have been tempted to sleep with Anna on this first visit. Certainly they got on well enough to fix another rendezvous.

***

Next morning (19 May), in showery weather, Landru dashed around Paris in his best suit and bowler hat, meeting other women who had answered his advert in *Le Journal*. His first rendezvous, jotted in his *carnet*, was at a café near the Gare de Lyon where he met "Mlle Lydie", whose accent must have given her away immediately. She was in reality a German-born widow of a Frenchman, desperate to find another French husband to avoid imprisonment as an enemy alien.

Landru did not stay long, racing off to meet Mme Heurtot near the Gare Saint-Lazare (10.30 am); Mlle Le Couturier just south of the Gare de l'Est (11.30 am); Mme Leclerc off the Place de la Concorde (2.30 pm); Mme Dupuis by the Hôtel de Ville (3.30 pm); Mme or Mlle Vailly at an unrecorded location (5.30 pm); and finally, Mme or Mlle Labrouve at another unknown address (8.00 pm).

Spoilt for choice, Landru was preying on a city denuded of young men. In these early months of the war, the hospital trains pulling into

Paris's great terminals and the crippled soldiers begging at street corners were a portent of what became known as France's "hollow years". More than a quarter of all French males born between 1891 and 1895 would die during the war, most of them killed at the front. In their wake, swarms of older men, some of them marriage swindlers, closed in on vulnerable single women.

Landru moved fast, jotting down his impressions of his latest female target in the files he kept on women at a garage he had just rented in the north-west suburb of Clichy. A 36-year-old widow was "vulgar with a grating voice". A 39-year-old woman had "intolerable sinuses". A 43-year-old widow was more promising, Landru thought. Her husband had just been killed in the trenches, she had no children, and she confessed that she could not bear the thought of being all alone. "Has money", Landru scribbled; he would see her again.

***

"Brazil", Landru wrote in his *carnet* on 27 May. She was in fact Argentinian, a 46-year-old widow called Thérèse Laborde-Line who lived on her own on a rundown street in south-east Paris. Landru climbed all the way up the stairs to Thérèse's garret apartment, pausing for breath at the top. "6th floor", he scrawled, making a mental note not to repeat the experience too often.

Thérèse had once been a striking young woman, captured in a studio portrait with her long black hair tied up in complicated tresses, a white feather boa draped glamorously around her shoulders. Gradually Thérèse's veneer of self-confidence had been chipped away, exposing her brittle, needy character. Born in Buenos Aires, Thérèse's family had emigrated to France when she was still a small child, settling in the foothills of the Pyrenees. She had married a local innkeeper, but they had soon separated and he had died in 1902, leaving her to raise their only son Vincent, the one real love of her life.

When Vincent, still unmarried, got a job in Paris as a postal clerk, Thérèse decided to follow him. Vincent soon found that sharing a tiny apartment with his difficult mother got on his nerves, especially as she refused to find employment while expecting him to pay the rent. Vincent married in early 1914 and straightaway Thérèse began bossing her daughter-in-law, who soon loathed her. That summer, Vincent was transferred by the post office to the eastern city of Nancy, taking his wife with him and leaving Thérèse in his apartment. From Nancy, Vincent wrote his mother a careful letter, pointing out that if she wanted to stay she would have to get a job, because he could not afford the rent.

"*Bien cher petit*", Thérèse replied: "I must tell you that I am making and continue to make every possible effort not to abuse you; I will not hide from you that since the day you left, I have neglected nothing to find a position."

In the spring of 1915 Vincent finally lost patience with Thérèse, who was still unemployed. He gave her three months' notice to move out, a shock that finally roused her to action. She placed a notice in *Le Journal*, advertising herself as a lady's companion, and began checking the lonely hearts adverts. By one or the other route, she came to Landru's attention.

Once again, Landru was "Georges Frémyet", an industrialist from the occupied north with a country villa near Paris. Thérèse soon paid a visit to Vernouillet, returning with a bag of cherries she had picked for her concierge in her fiancé's garden; for she and "Frémyet" were now engaged to be married. She did not know that another woman, codenamed "Crozatier" by Landru, had just got engaged to him as well.

***

Marie-Angélique Guillin, 52, was a short, plump woman who lived on Rue Crozatier, near the Gare du Lyon. Originally from a village in Normandy, she had married a peasant who had died young, leaving her no money and two little children. Sometime in the 1890s, Marie-Angélique had found a job as a housekeeper for an affluent civil engineer in the town of Melun, 50 kilometres south-east of Paris. She had placed her young daughter in a state orphanage and left the older boy to fend for himself; and then, it appears, she had probably become the engineer's mistress. When he died in 1913, he had left her 22,000 francs (about 68,000 euros), a substantial sum that she had used to set herself up in a nice apartment in Paris.

As far as Marie-Angélique was concerned, she had no family ties that needed to bother her. In 1912 her widowed railwayman son had been killed in an accident at the Gare du Lyon, leaving a baby boy whom he had entrusted in his will to a friend rather than Marie-Angélique. "He feared that the boy would be mistreated [by Marie-Angélique], as he had been from an early age," the friend later explained. Meanwhile, Marie-Angélique's married daughter now lived in a village north-east of Paris, having never forgiven her mother for abandoning her as a child.

In sum, Marie-Angélique was neither attractive nor likeable. Landru, alias "Georges Petit", an entrepreneur from Lille, sized up this uneducated woman in her absurd chestnut wig and decided to test her credulity with an utterly ludicrous tale. He confided that he was not merely a highly successful businessman but a former undercover agent working against the Germans behind enemy lines. In gratitude for his clandestine work, the foreign ministry had just appointed him as France's next Consul-General to Australia. His ship was due to depart in a matter of weeks.

There was only one minor hitch, Landru explained to Marie-Angélique. He was a single man and it was clear that as Consul-General he would need a wife with taste and elegance to accompany him to the many banquets and receptions he would be required to attend. Hence his little lonely hearts advert in *Le Journal*. Would Mme Guillin perhaps consider joining him in Australia?

At the end of June, Marie-Angélique wrote urgently to the mayor of her home village to obtain her birth and marriage certificates, which she would need in order to marry again. She also commissioned a wedding dress from her favourite *couturière* in Melun.

Briefly, Landru switched back to Thérèse, the Argentinian-born widow, intent on not having to climb her wretched staircase too many more times. On 28 June he brought Thérèse down to The Lodge, where she wrote a letter to a former boyfriend in southern France, announcing that she was going to marry an unnamed "*monsieur*". Thérèse did not put an address at the top of the letter, which was never sent. No one ever saw her again.

A fortnight later, Marie-Angélique made her first visit to Vernouillet, where Landru set her another test. He told her there was one locked bedroom that she must never enter. Curiosity got the better of Marie-Angélique, and thinking her fiancé was out of the house, she peered through the keyhole. She was startled to see women's clothes and shoes scattered everywhere. At this moment, Landru appeared silently by her side.

"You little rascal!" he exclaimed, apparently on the verge of hitting her in his fury. And then, just as swiftly, he calmed down, explaining wistfully that the clothes and shoes had belonged to his dear, late mother, whose memory was sacred to him.

In late July, Marie-Angélique's conscience made her visit her estranged daughter outside Paris to reveal her marriage plans and imminent departure for Australia. At last she was ready to go. On Saturday, 31 July, a warm, hazy day, Marie-Angélique departed early from Rue Crozatier with Landru, carrying only hand luggage and leaving all her furniture and other possessions behind. He had arranged to come back alone in a day or two to clear the apartment.

During the weekend, Marie-Angélique wrote a letter from The Lodge to her daughter and son-in-law, saying she had arrived at her fiancé's house, without giving an address. Landru added a postscript, expressing his eagerness to make the couple's acquaintance and assuring them that Marie-Angélique was "enjoying herself in the country".

Then she vanished, like Jeanne, André and Thérèse before her.

***

During the summer of 1915, Thérèse's son Vincent wrote twice to his mother from Nancy to ask for her new address and to check whether she had received a postal order to pay for her move. When Thérèse failed to reply he gave up trying to contact her, deciding his mother was angry with him for forcing her out of his apartment.

Marie-Angélique's daughter and son-in-law were also puzzled that they never heard anything more from her, following her brief letter from Vernouillet. In the end, they decided that her ship had probably been torpedoed by the Germans, somewhere between France and Australia.

Chapter 4

The Villa Tric

All that summer, a 55-year-old woman with a little dog was often seen at the Bagneux cemetery in southern Paris, tending a newly dug grave. In recent years, Berthe Héon had endured a succession of tragedies that would have destroyed a less courageous woman. Berthe's two children by her late husband had died; then her long-term partner had died; then their daughter Marcelle's fiancé had been killed at the start of the war; and finally, in the spring of 1915, Berthe's beloved Marcelle had died in childbirth. As Berthe laid flowers on Marcelle's tomb, all she had left were her memories of Marcelle and her dog Nénette, who kept her company wherever she went.

Born in Le Havre, Berthe had no money of her own, scraping a living as a bartender and cleaning woman. She could not afford a tombstone for Marcelle, but hoped one day to be able to pay a mason to give her daughter a decent last resting place. As she and Nénette made their way back to Marcelle's old apartment in central Paris, Berthe could only see one thing clearly: she had to pick herself up, find a man who would look after her, and start her life again.

When she inspected herself in the mirror, Berthe thought she looked quite presentable for a woman in her mid-fifties. She had dyed blonde hair, a nice buxom figure and despite her grief, was naturally sociable, always ready to have a good gossip. Putting Marcelle temporarily out of her mind, she began to check the lonely hearts columns.

She soon spotted one in *Le Journal* that looked just the job. It read:

> Monsieur, 47, having completed his military service, 4,000 francs plus savings, about to establish himself in a pretty, healthy colony, desires to meet with view to marriage, lady of similar age and equally modest situation, if single, who consents to accompany him, very serious proposal, agency and intermediary not involved.

Landru could scarcely disguise his fury when he got his first look at Berthe, as she opened the door of Marcelle's apartment one late June or July day. She had obviously lied about her age, claiming to be only 39 in her reply to his advert. He needed to teach her a lesson.

He was "Georges Petit", an entrepreneur from Tunis. Soon, he and Berthe were discussing his various North African business ventures and his yearning for a companion to share his colonial home. A marriage proposal was made, eagerly accepted: Berthe knew she had made the right decision, even though she would no longer be able to take care of Marcelle's grave.

Berthe had a friend called Mme Dalouin, a housekeeper in the same apartment block, who was taken aback by the speed of Berthe's engagement, so soon after Marcelle's death. "I am all on my own and my goodness, I will never find another opportunity like this one," Berthe explained to Mme Dalouin. Berthe pointed out that her *monsieur* had an excellent situation in Tunisia and had come to Paris to liquidate the estate of his sister, who had recently died. "She must have been a posh tart," Berthe thought, for on a visit to the sister's former house in Vernouillet she had seen stacks of lacy underwear.

Mme Dalouin met Berthe's fiancé soon afterwards and did not like what she saw. Landru, alias Petit, was playing man-about-the-house, helping Berthe's concierge bang some picture nails into a wall in the hallway. Berthe agreed that she and Mme Dalouin would go off to a nearby café where Landru joined them a few minutes later. Something about his manner made Mme Dalouin suspicious. In her view, it just seemed too unlikely that a man of his means and background should want to marry an almost illiterate, working-class woman like Berthe.

Without telling Berthe, Mme Dalouin went to a public library and looked up "Georges Petit" in a commercial directory for Tunisia. To her relief, a "Georges Petit" really did live at the address that Mme Dalouin had wheedled out of him at the café. She still thought Berthe's fiancé was a bit fishy but decided it was none of her business if Berthe wanted to take a chance with him.

By the start of October, Berthe was all set to marry. She had obtained her birth and marriage certificates from Le Havre, while her fiancé had kindly agreed to pay the last quarter's rent on Marcelle's apartment. Landru had also paid off the rent on Berthe's old apartment in the small town of Ermont, 22 kilometres north-west of Paris, where he had enquired with her former landlady about Berthe's "morality".

Next, Landru sold at auction all Berthe and Marcelle's shabby furniture from their two apartments, realising barely 1,000 francs. Berthe meekly agreed that he should manage this money on her behalf, while she entrusted her dog Nénette to a friend in Ermont, promising to send money for pet food before she sailed for Tunis.

At this point, an obstacle to their wedding plans arose. Landru probably explained to Berthe that he had mislaid one of his identity documents and was waiting for a replacement. The real reason for the delay was that he had nowhere to take her.

In early August he had ended his lease on The Lodge at Vernouillet and moved out, storing Jeanne Cuchet's furniture, clothes and other belongings at a garage in the western Paris suburb of Neuilly. Landru's neighbours in Vernouillet had become too curious about his activities; one of them had even complained to the local policeman about the smoke that wafted up the street whenever he lit a fire. He needed to find another country house with rather more privacy before he could finish his business with Berthe.

At the start of October, in cold, misty weather, Berthe left Marcelle's apartment for the last time, bound for a cheap travellers' hotel opposite the Gare Saint-Lazare. She stayed there for about a week, and was then transferred by Landru to some cheap rooms he had rented in western Paris. Here, Berthe survived on pocket money he parcelled out from the proceeds of her furniture sale, all noted in his *carnet* as "loans". One such "loan" of 40 francs allowed Berthe to buy a new pair of shoes.

***

That autumn Célestine Buisson, the homely, trusting housekeeper, and Anna Collomb, the insurance company typist, separately thought Landru was already in Tunisia on an extended business trip. It was too bad, Célestine remarked stoically. She would just have to hope her fiancé returned from his travels by the New Year, when he had vaguely promised they could wed. Anna was less tolerant of Landru's long absence. Her watchful concierge at Rue Rodier recalled Anna receiving at least one other gentleman caller during the autumn of 1915 who was certainly not Mme Collomb's bearded, bowler-hatted *monsieur*.

Meanwhile, Landru was house-hunting. He required more money for the kind of country retreat he had in mind, one that was well away from neighbours, preferably with a big garden and outdoor sheds for storage. Fortunately, the recently vanished Marie-Angélique Guillin still had almost 12,000 francs in bank savings, the residue of her inheritance from her former employer in Melun; and Landru had plenty of experience at fooling dozy bank clerks.

During November, as Berthe waited patiently to start her new married life in Tunisia, Landru went back and forth at the two banks where Marie-Angélique had kept her investments. He posed as her brother-in-law "Georges Petit" (here he flashed a fake identity paper), having been asked by her to withdraw her savings (here he waved a forged letter of authority). As Landru knew, the fraud worked because men routinely looked after their womenfolks' assets and a male bank official was unlikely to check his credentials, provided he acted with confidence. The obliging manager at one of the banks even insisted on delivering the cheque for "Georges Petit" once Marie-Angélique's funds had been cleared.

Flush with cash, Landru set off in search of his ideal house or "hermitage", as he liked to think of it. North or east of Paris was out of the question, because the villages directly behind the trenches were infested with busybodies, keen to report any stranger who looked like an enemy agent to the authorities. "The war would go better if there weren't so many spies," observed a character in a short story currently being serialised by *Le Petit Parisien*. "It seems that General Joffre [the French commander-in-chief] only has to order an advance at 9.00 in the morning and the Germans know all about it by 10.00."

Landru decided to look in the countryside south and west of Paris, near enough to reach in an hour or two but well away from the war. Trawling through the property adverts, he found a house that sounded promising.

At the start of December, he caught a train to the village of Garancières, 50 kilometres west of Paris, bringing his bicycle with him. From Garancières he cycled a further nine kilometres south-west, a conspicuous figure in his city clothes and black woollen cycling cap as he rode through gently rolling farmland. Approaching the village of Gambais, he saw that the road skirted dense woodland to the east, the outer fringe of a vast, ancient hunting forest. He cycled on, past a row of stables leading up to the gates of a sixteenth-century chateau, where he swung sharp right into the centre of the village.

In most respects, Gambais was no different from many other French villages after more than a year of war. It had a *mairie*, set a little back from the main street, and the usual small shops; it also had a noticeable dearth of able-bodied men. Officially, Gambais had just over 1,000 inhabitants, but the actual population was far lower, since almost all local men in their twenties and thirties had gone off to fight. Even the police had been mobilised, leaving Gambais under the fitful watch of a 70-year-old part-time constable. On the mayor's orders, this elderly officer was primed to keep an eye out for non-existent German spies rather than the thieves who came down from Paris for easy pickings. The nearest regular gendarme was stationed in the market town of Houdan, seven kilometres away.

THE VILLA TRIC

There was only one oddity about Gambais, which Landru could see as he left the village and headed north-west across open countryside towards Houdan. The village church, visible on the horizon, was almost a mile beyond Gambais, an ancient, rather ugly hulk surrounded by a graveyard.

About 250 metres before the church, Landru dismounted by a set of iron gates; here was the property he had seen advertised for rent in a newspaper. As agreed, the village cobbler who acted as janitor was waiting to show him around. Landru introduced himself as Raoul Dupont, an automobile salesman based in Paris, and the cobbler unlocked the gates.

The Villa Tric, built in 1904, was named after its owner, a local entrepreneur called Tric who had since left the area with his family. It was a boxy, two-storey red-brick building, half-hidden from the road behind a perimeter wall and with no immediate neighbours. The nearest house was the sexton's cottage by the church, further along the road to Houdan.

No tenant had lived at the villa for almost four years and damp was starting to peel away the wallpaper in the living room that led off to the left of the hallway. The ground floor "bathroom" on this side of the house was equally dispiriting, with a musty basin and toilet, but no bath. Across the hallway, a dining room at the rear and a small connecting kitchen had been stripped of all fixtures and fittings, including the oven. From the kitchen, stone steps led down to a windowless cellar and coal store. Upstairs, three drafty unfurnished bedrooms sat beneath a large attic.

The cobbler unlocked the kitchen door at the back of the house and they went out into a small enclosure. Here, Landru inspected the outdoor pantry and laundry and then passed through a wicker gate that led onto a large unkempt lawn, stretching a full 70 metres down to the end of the garden. In the far corner, facing the church, he had a good look at a large open shelter or "hangar" with two adjoining locked sheds.

He could see there were disadvantages. The house was not well protected from intruders and nosy passers-by, because the low perimeter wall on the side facing Gambais was in poor repair and only extended 20 metres back from the road. The rest of the garden was bounded by a rough fence until it reached the hangar, where another brick wall offered better concealment on the side looking towards the church.

Landru made his judgement. He informed the cobbler that he would take the house and make arrangements in the next few days to sign the rental contract with Monsieur Tric, who lived south of Paris.

**

Several days later, Landru and Berthe caught the train to Garancières. He bought a one-way ticket for her and a return ticket for himself, duly noted in his *carnet*. Berthe must have been travelling light, because Landru made her walk all the way from the station to the villa in her new shoes, a distance of more than ten kilometres.

Berthe may have realised something was wrong when she saw there was no oven in the kitchen. Although the weather was cold, Landru did not feel any great urgency to put this matter right. He finally got round to buying a little oven in Houdan on 31 December, along with some coal, having returned to Paris in the meantime. Shortly afterwards, Mme Dalouin received a postcard purportedly signed by Berthe with the solitary one-word greeting, "*Bonjour*". Mme Dalouin was perplexed; she was sure the writing was not in Berthe's rough, unschooled hand.

Several of Berthe's former neighbours in Ermont also thought it odd when they received similarly dubious postcards from her. One of them was thoroughly annoyed with Berthe, who had never sent the money she had promised for her pet Nénette's dog food. Over time, these friends and acquaintances steadily forgot all about Berthe and her unlikely fiancé. Everyone assumed the couple were now married and happily settled in Tunis.

Only one person still remembered Berthe on a regular basis. Most Sundays, a young woman made sure to visit the grave of her best friend Marcelle, Berthe's late daughter. Juliette Auger had got to know Marcelle when they had both worked together in the same shoe shop. She had promised Berthe that she would look after Marcelle's resting place while Berthe was in Tunisia.

Juliette had not liked Berthe's fiancé on the only occasion she had met him, and each time she visited Marcelle's grave, her hostility towards him increased. This wealthy entrepreneur had promised Berthe that he would pay for Marcelle to have a proper marble tombstone. And yet here Juliette was, still placing flowers on poor Marcelle's rough tomb, which only had a cheap cross to honour her memory. Juliette could not forgive Berthe's *monsieur* for his callousness. One day, Juliette thought, she would like to get her own back on him.

Chapter 5

Madame Sombrero

Landru was too busy in the first half of 1916 to keep detailed day-by-day records in his *carnet*. In late May or early June a bicyclist riding by the Villa Tric on a clear, moonlit night noticed a grey, tradesman's *camionnette* parked outside the front gates. More curiously, the cyclist saw and smelt foul white smoke churning out of the chimney and the glow of a fire in the kitchen. Later, by a pond in the forest near Gambais, the cyclist saw the *camionnette* pull up and a bearded man get out. He lugged some heavy package over to the far side of the pond where he dropped it in the water and then returned to the car. After the car had gone, the cyclist decided the man must have been a poacher concealing his catch.

Around this time, a local woman, walking in the same part of the forest, glimpsed the man from a distance, working away in a hole he appeared to have dug. The man looked up and gave her such a stare that she hurried off without seeing what he was doing.

Mme Andrieux, the butcher's wife in Gambais, knew all about the ladies who came and went at the villa. She especially remembered how one of them flounced into the shop in the spring of 1916, wearing only a pair of blue pyjamas and white buskin boots. The woman was the typist Anna Collomb, who had resumed her affair with Landru in the spring. On this shopping trip, Anna also bought a postcard of Gambais and its environs to send to her younger sister Ryno. Helpfully, Anna drew an 'X' above the Villa Tric, so Ryno could pinpoint the house where Anna was staying.

Ryno had not yet met Anna's fiancé. One day, alluding to Anna's poor track record with men, Ryno asked her sister if she was sure this "Frémyet" would make her happy. Of course, Anna replied briskly, adding that "she did not wish to be unhappy, as she had been with Monsieur Collomb." The normally taciturn Anna then mentioned something her fiancé had told her that instantly raised Ryno's doubts about his credentials. According to

Anna, the affluent Frémyet used the false name of Cuchet when claiming his means-tested refugee's allowance, so he could receive the full entitlement. Ryno was shocked, realising that Anna's fiancé must be using fake identity papers, a serious criminal offence. Full of suspicion, Ryno demanded to meet this devious man to check him out properly. Anna reluctantly agreed, but then kept making lame excuses for why she could not introduce her fiancé to Ryno.

As usual, Landru explained to Anna that he could not get married until he had obtained replacements for his "real" identity papers, which he said he had left behind in Lille when the Germans arrived. Anna was still prepared to live with him, moving in the spring of 1916 to an apartment he had rented on Rue de Châteaudun, a short walk from her old apartment on Rue Rodier.

In doing so, Anna ended her long on-off relationship with a man called Monsieur Bernard, the probable father of her little girl. There was no evidence that Anna had placed her daughter in the care of nuns in Italy, a rather unlikely tale that she told a friend in the typing pool where she worked. Only two facts were clear: the real father – in all likelihood Bernard – had disowned the girl; and Landru had given Anna the impression that he would adopt her daughter once they were married.

This prospect did not seem to make Anna any happier, despite her assurances to Ryno. It was as if she felt trapped between a fiancé she could not entirely trust and the hard truth that a woman in her mid-forties – even one as pretty as Anna – had limited choices in Paris's wartime marriage market, given the dearth of eligible men.

She was drinking that summer, buying her favourite tipple, *eau de vie*, from a woman friend who ran a wine shop near Anna's office. Landru, who did not drink, watched Anna in the evening getting quietly sozzled. At the liquor store, the manageress thought Anna lacked "her usual gaiety" when they talked about her forthcoming marriage.

A businessman friend, probably another of Anna's former lovers, was alarmed by the "great change" in her behaviour and appearance after she told him about her marriage plans. "She was less *soignée* [presentable], more reserved, and sometimes she had a strange look about her," he said. He cautioned Anna to tread carefully with a man she hardly knew, but Anna would not listen. "She told me that her marriage was decided, even as she seemed to get less enthusiastic about it."

***

MADAME SOMBRERO

From their fifth-floor apartment on Rue de Châteaudun, Anna and Landru looked down on streets awash with wounded and mutilated young soldiers. Every hour, trains pulled into the Gare du Nord and the adjacent Gare de l'Est, offloading their latest human cargo from the front onto waiting ambulances and taxis for transport to Salpêtrière, Val-de-Grâce and the city's other historic hospitals, already crammed with casualties. The glittering Grand Palais at the foot of the Champs-Élysées, dedicated "to the glory of French art", now served as a gigantic operating theatre, employing sculptors to make moulds for prosthetic limbs. In warm weather, men with bandaged stumps for arms or legs recovered from their amputations on the street outside.

Landru was at large in this city of male cripples, harvesting women. He was using his *carnet* more these days, jotting down every romantic purchase he deemed significant – flowers, hacksaws, *bonbons*, coal – and still he could not keep up. Increasingly, he resorted to what he called "mnemotechnical indications"; little codenames, numbers, phrases and hieroglyphics that only he could decipher.

As he trawled the city, homely, faithful Célestine Buisson was also back in his sights. Célestine was thrilled that summer when he began calling again at her apartment. One Sunday, she invited her younger housemaid sister Marie to stay a little longer in order to meet the charming "Monsieur Frémyet". Marie did not say so, but she found Célestine's "very friendly, very obliging" fiancé just a little too unctuous. In Marie's view, it did not quite add up that this cultured man, with his fancy manners and vocabulary, had fallen for Célestine, who had never read a book in her life.

A few weeks after this visit by Marie, Célestine's 20-year-old son Gaston came to stay with his mother. Gaston had just been discharged from the army because of poor eyesight, possibly due to a mustard gas attack. His misfortune had not deterred Landru, alias Frémyet, from expressing his displeasure at Gaston's presence. Célestine panicked, writing her fiancé a letter as soon as he had gone.

"*Mon Cherie,*" Célestine began, getting her genders mixed up: "I am not calm for I am afraid that you are annoyed about the subject of my son. … I will tell you frankly that I would prefer to be with you and cherish you always. I love him very much but you surpass him for I know he will not stay always with me so I prefer not to have him at all since my sister can take him."

This was not true, as Célestine knew. Neither Marie, a lowly servant, nor her other sister Catherine, a mother with a husband at the front, was in a position to look after Gaston. Under Landru's sway, even Célestine was becoming a dissembler.

Still more meetings with lonely women piled up in Landru's *carnet*. One day, Landru made a rendezvous by the Medici fountain in the Jardin du Luxembourg to check out a 43-year-old nurse.

"You don't interest me at all," Landru snapped, eyeing her up and down. "You don't even have the advantage of being pretty."

He hurried off, disgusted at how she had wasted his precious time.

He needed more women, as many as he could find, to sift and select, file and discard. On 13 September 1916, he placed another lonely hearts advert in *La Presse*, a popular Paris evening paper.

***

Sometime that evening, Anne-Marie Pascal, known to her family as Annette, paid 50 centimes for a copy of *La Presse* and turned as usual to the lonely hearts adverts at the foot of page two. She read:

> Monsieur, 47, savings of 4,000 francs, desires marriage with person with simple tastes, similar age and situation. Apply to Forest, bureau 61, Paris.

In her reply to Landru, Annette described herself as a 36-year-old widow. Somewhat scatterbrained, Annette had accidentally added a year to her age and then she had lied. Annette was not a widow but an impoverished divorcée, who lived with her white angora cat Minette in a tiny attic apartment on a street confusingly called Villa Stendhal, a block east of the Père-Lachaise cemetery. She worked from home as a dressmaker on contract for a small Paris fashion house.

When she stepped outdoors, Annette looked what she longed to be: an elegant lady who lunched, svelte and dark-haired, sweeping around the *quartier* in one of her slinky home-made dresses and her favourite wide-brimmed hat. "Mme Sombrero", as her neighbours called Annette, was a skilfully coutured illusion, for what she wanted more than anything else was a "*vieux monsieur*" (sugar daddy), loaded with money, who could keep her in this style.

Some locals thought Annette might be a prostitute, given her unashamed promiscuity. Among her various lovers were "*petit Marcel*", a teenage ticket collector on the Paris metro, "*grand Marcel*", a commercial salesman serving at the front, and a fellow she nicknamed "Hayose", also in uniform. One neighbour disapproved so strongly of Annette's affair with "*petit Marcel*" that he or she took to sending her crude, threatening postcards. "So you old snub-nosed whore," the anonymous correspondent scrawled, "you're always out and about with your handsome young man, you old camel, you old cow."

Annette's much older sister Louise, 48, was the only person who knew the full, sad story of Annette's chaotic life to date. Both Annette's parents had died soon after her birth in Toulouse and Louise, whom Annette called "*maman*", had brought her up. Louise had married and settled in the Mediterranean port of Toulon, bringing Annette with her, and then Annette had lost her way.

Annette's own marriage in 1903 had gradually disintegrated following the death of her baby boy in infancy. Abandoned by her husband, Annette may have turned to part-time prostitution to make ends meet, because in 1912 she was fined in Toulon for a minor offence, possibly soliciting. This police record in a naval port seething with prostitutes may also explain why Annette moved to Paris several months later, hoping to kick over her traces. After a series of short-term lets, she eventually rented her attic apartment on Villa Stendhal and set up shop as a *couturière*.

Such was the complicated background of the woman who stood outside her local metro station a few days after spotting Landru's advert in *La Presse*, dressed as agreed in a blue jacket and grey, wide-brimmed hat. Unknown to Landru, alias Forest, Annette also put in her handbag the little emergency note that her "*maman*" Louise insisted she must carry with her at all times. It read:

> In case of accident, alert my family, my sister, Mme Fauchet,
> 10 rue de la Fraternité, Toulon, Var.

"Lucien Forest" suggested they should go for a promenade in order to get to know each other better. He was a bachelor, he explained, the owner of a factory in the small town of Rocroi, next to the Belgian border, now sadly occupied by the Germans. After fleeing Rocroi, he had opened another factory involved in war work just north of Paris, whose location and purpose he was not permitted by the government to divulge. It was all very top secret, as was his home address, which he could not under any circumstances give to Mlle Pascal. Instead, she should send all correspondence to "Monsieur Berzieux", care of the Iris matrimonial agency.

At the end of their little walk, Landru fixed another rendezvous with Annette and once he was out of sight, wrote an *aide memoire* in his *carnet*:

> Pascal Anne, 36, widow for the past five years, no children, young appearance, tailored, sombrero hat.

He took a fortnight to make his move. On the morning of 4 October, a cloudy day, Landru bought a bunch of flowers and rang Annette's doorbell at Villa Stendhal. After his visit, Annette wrote him a letter.

"*Mon cher ami*," Annette began with curious formality, thanking him for his "great attentiveness" towards her:

> All my desires that you asked of me as much as to dictate you I will not be able any less to formulate them, now that the act is accomplished, for I have lost your respect and the great respect that you address to me each day. I consider myself in your eyes as no more than a vulgar mistress, too bad for me, I have only to suffer the yoke and I no longer believe I have the right to love you as such.

After this contorted preamble, Annette got to the point. She was about to travel to Toulon on one of her regular visits to see her sister Louise and was transparently desperate not to lose touch with "Monsieur Forest" while she was away. Annette begged him to write to her *chez* Mme Fauchet, 10 rue de la Fraternité, Toulon.

Landru did write, saying how much he missed her. In reply, Annette failed to tell him that she planned to return to Paris with a female companion.

Louise's 20-year-old daughter Marie-Jeanne, pretty, worldly and self-assured, had two good reasons for leaving Toulon to live for a while with Annette. Marie-Jeanne's boyfriend was serving in the navy and rarely visited Toulon on shore leave. In addition, there were few wartime jobs in Toulon for a clever working-class girl like Marie-Jeanne, short of joining the prostitutes who swarmed around the docks. All things considered, Marie-Jeanne was quite content to spend some time in Paris, helping Annette make dresses while keeping a quiet eye on her scatty, wayward aunt.

Marie-Jeanne got her first inkling that Annette's *monsieur* might not be reliable when their train from Toulon pulled into the Gare de Lyon. Annette had written ahead, asking "Lucien" to meet her and Marie-Jeanne off the train "so I can have the pleasure of giving you a little kiss". She and Marie-Jeanne struggled onto the platform with their heavy suitcases, searching in vain for him among the crowds milling around the station. Finally they gave up and made their own way to Villa Stendhal, wondering what had happened to him.

Landru was furious when he heard by letter from Annette that she had brought Marie-Jeanne to stay with her. He wrote straight back to explain that he would not in future be visiting Annette *chez elle*, if her niece was also at home. Instead, he proposed a plan. On agreed dates, at agreed times, Annette should despatch Marie-Jeanne for a long walk – preferably a *very* long walk. Annette would then stand at her window and look out for him, giving a secret sign to show it was safe to come up.

Even this subterfuge failed to reassure Landru. At the end of October, Annette wrote to complain that she had not heard from him for more than a week. He replied that he had just returned from another business trip. Annette wrote immediately by *pneumatique*, the express postal service that shot mail around Paris through a network of pressurised underground air tubes. She would be waiting for him next day at 3.00 pm outside the Bourse metro station, just in case he had time to see her. If not, she would be delighted to see him next morning at Villa Stendhal.

Landru failed to make either rendezvous. Annette wrote again, fearful that Marie-Jeanne's arrival had "cast a shadow" over their relationship.

"*Mon chéri*," she went on, "I have however a great need for affection and yours would make me so happy. You know that I will always be at your disposition on the day and the hour that you want to see me again."

Annette did not say that she desired a bit more than affection from her *vieux monsieur*. She was "enchanted by his kind attention in bringing her little cakes", a woman friend recalled, but would have preferred him to give her some money.

***

Across Paris, Célestine Buisson had not seen or heard for weeks from her fiancé, who was supposedly away on another of his important business trips. She would just have to be patient, Célestine told her younger sister Marie, who was increasingly suspicious of this oily, evasive *monsieur*. On one of her weekly visits to see Célestine, Marie tried to express her reservations. It was hopeless; Célestine simply refused to listen to such nonsense.

Landru's main goal during the autumn of 1916 was to fleece the typist Anna Collomb, even as he bustled around Paris looking for other women to snare. Step by step, he was getting his hands on all Anna's precious savings: 500 francs here, 800 francs there, and then a big one on 10 November, 2,000 francs, all noted in his *carnet*. The normally secretive Anna told her younger sister Ryno about these "loans" and Ryno then told their mother. Pressed by both of them, Anna said that while her fiancé had lots of money he was sometimes short of cash. Besides, he always promised to pay her back soon.

In late November, Anna handed in her notice at the insurance company's typing pool. She and her fiancé would soon marry and move to his country house, Anna explained to a work friend; best of all, her little daughter would at last be able to live with her. It was not clear whether Anna had ever dared tell anyone in her family about her illegitimate girl. Ryno probably knew; her parents probably did not; and later, none of them was keen to talk about the subject in public.

As Christmas 1916 approached, Ryno sensed that Anna's attempt to rebuild her life with a new husband had gone badly wrong. In front of their mother, Ryno insisted to Anna that the family had to meet her fiancé. Cornered by Ryno, Anna explained tearfully that she, too, wanted to introduce him to the family but unfortunately he disliked the idea.

"Here was her great sorrow," Ryno remembered Anna saying. "She hoped, however, to encourage him to have better feelings towards her family."

Finally, Anna persuaded Landru, alias Frémyet, to have Ryno over for dinner at their apartment on Rue de Châteaudun on Sunday, 17 December. At the last minute he went out on "urgent business", leaving Anna to dine alone with her sister. Ryno would not be put off. The following Sunday, Christmas Eve, she turned up again, having been assured by Anna that "Frémyet" would definitely be there.

This time he opened the door, bowed elaborately to Ryno and ushered her into an apartment decked out with bouquets and garlands of flowers; not for Mme Collomb, he explained, but in honour of her delightful sister.

Over dinner, Ryno observed this peculiar man with his over-polished manners and "cold inquisitorial stare" and decided she did not like him. To Ryno's surprise, he escorted her back across Paris to her parents' apartment, leaving Anna behind. On the metro, he chatted away about the factory he planned to build in the south of France, where he would live with Anna after their marriage. But not to worry, Landru went on; he would personally drive all the way to Paris to collect Ryno and her parents for regular visits to see Anna, the soon-to-be Mme Frémyet. His fulsome performance seemed even more dubious to Ryno when he insisted on delivering her all the way to her parents' apartment door.

Next morning, Christmas Day, Anna arrived at the family's apartment on Boulevard Voltaire without her fiancé, who had also been invited. He was "busy", she said vaguely. Over lunch, Anna blurted out what she had already told Ryno: that her fiancé used the false name "Cuchet" when claiming his refugee's allowance. Anna's mother was appalled and demanded that Anna reveal her fiancé's financial situation. Anna started to cry. He had almost cleaned her out, she confessed, having "borrowed" nearly all her nest egg of 8,000 francs.

Anna left the apartment at about 6.00 pm, explaining that she and "Frémyet" would be visiting his country villa on Boxing Day, returning on 27 December. The family could not talk Anna out of this trip, so they made her promise to see them again as soon as she returned to Paris. Their plan was to disentangle Anna from this obvious swindler and somehow get her money back.

At dawn on 26 December, Landru and Anna took a taxi from Rue de Châteaudun to the Gare des Invalides, carrying only hand luggage. Landru purchased a return ticket for himself and a one-way ticket for Anna to Garancières, one of the stations for Gambais.

On 27 December, he bought two beef steaks from the butcher in Gambais, noted in his *carnet*. Sometime later, Landru wrote "4h" (4.00 pm) beneath the date on the page. His business done, he caught the evening train to Paris on his return ticket, travelling alone.

Chapter 6

Lulu

A few days later, Annette Pascal's sharp-eyed niece Marie-Jeanne spotted the man she had sarcastically dubbed "Monsieur Mystère" as she looked out of Annette's sixth-floor window. There he was, pacing up and down the street below, waiting for Annette to give him her "secret signal". It was too late; Annette had forgotten to make Marie-Jeanne go on one of her boring, enforced walks.

Marie-Jeanne skipped downstairs, opened the door and had the pleasure of registering Landru's shock. Then she introduced herself with a smile.

"Cheeky," Landru said, wagging his finger at Marie-Jeanne.

For the time being, he put up with this impertinent young woman. During January and February 1917 he visited Annette regularly, bringing her and Marie-Jeanne little presents of brioches, biscuits and fruit. Then he would take Annette off to a cheap hotel for a few hours, leaving Marie-Jeanne to mind the little dressmaking workshop.

***

In early March, Landru cast around for another outlet for one of his lonely hearts adverts. He selected *L'Echo de Paris*, a conservative Catholic newspaper that saw the soldiers dying in the mud and squalor of the trenches as necessary martyrs for the nation's sins.

"Nothing is more beautiful and more mysterious than these children, now frozen, who gave to a France in flames the virtues needed to save it," the nationalist writer and politician Maurice Barrès declared in a front-page essay on 9 March. Further inside, Landru's notice appeared:

> Man, 50, widowed for a long time, no children, educated, savings of 20,000 francs and good situation to marry lady in similar situation.

Louise Jaume, a 38-year-old dress shop assistant, was ardently patriotic and devout, just like *L'Echo de Paris*, her regular newspaper. Louise was also lonely, despite at least four men in her life. There was Joe, who would soon be killed by a German shell; Paul, somewhere in the trenches in northern France; Raphael, an art teacher bunkered down near Verdun; and Léon, a former priest turned military ambulance orderly. Joe, Paul, Raphael and Léon were Louise's pen pals and honorary godsons, for she was one of thousands of French women who were so-called "war godmothers" ("*marraines de guerre*"), writing morale-boosting letters to homesick soldiers at the front.

A fifth man wanted nothing to do with Louise ever again. Paul Jaume, Louise's estranged husband, lived in Italy, and was the reason why the childless Louise had replied to Landru's intriguing advert. Risking God's wrath, Louise had recently written to Paul to announce that she was suing him for divorce.

A miserable pilgrimage had brought Louise to this crisis for her soul. Her widowed and remarried father, a retired businessman in Toulouse, had long since washed his hands of Louise, as had her sister, married to a doctor in Montpellier. Both were convinced that Paul Jaume had fleeced Louise of her dowry, before bolting to Italy in 1914. In their view, Louise must now suffer the consequences. Almost broke, Louise wrote begging letters from time to time to her only sympathetic relative, an uncle who ran a grocery in Toulouse. He sent her small sums, on condition that she did not tell his wife, who also disapproved of Louise.

Paul Jaume later suggested that he had left Louise because she was frigid and hysterical. He had found her "rather cold" and "reserved", while also being prone to sudden bursts of laughter or weeping, for no apparent reason. Louise's intense Catholic faith "verged at times on mysticism", her husband complained. All in all, he found her tiresome.

Louise had made two attempts to rescue her marriage. The first time, in the summer of 1915, she had gone initially to a village near Montpellier for the funeral of her grandmother, hoping to repair relations with her family. Louise's sister told her she would most definitely *not* be welcome to spend some time at the sister's home; nor was Louise's father interested in seeing her. She continued on her way, stuffing her travel money into the folds of her dress to guard against bandits when she crossed the Italian border.

Louise made it safely to the farm in Tuscany that Paul Jaume managed for a business friend. He agreed to take her to see Rome but refused to share his bed with her. Finally she gave up and returned to Paris. She then had second thoughts, showing up again at the farmhouse a few months later. Her husband once more insisted on what he called "brother/sister" sleeping arrangements until Louise despaired of him.

It took her another 18 months before she summoned the courage to write to Paul and announce she was seeking a divorce. Louise now set out to find another husband who she hoped would treat her a little more kindly.

***

Landru introduced himself to Louise as "Lucien Guillet", an engineer from the occupied Ardennes region in north-eastern France. They met outside the same metro station where he had made his first rendezvous with Annette Pascal the previous year, because Louise's little apartment on Rue des Lyanes was only five minutes' walk from Villa Stendhal. Perhaps mindful of Annette's proximity, Landru suggested that he and Louise should take the metro to western Paris for a promenade in the Bois de Boulogne.

As they strolled through the woods, Landru impressed Louise with his seemingly sincere religious faith; he may even have told her, truthfully, that he had once been a church sub-deacon. She was charmed as well by his courtesy. He delivered her all the way back to her apartment on Rue des Lyanes, where he presented her with a bouquet of poppies, a keepsake until their next meeting.

When he left Louise, Landru recorded the street number in his *carnet*, wrote "possible" against her entry, and caught another metro, heading north, still on the prowl; for the one thing he had not managed to do with Louise was the thing that, right now, he wanted most of all.

***

As usual, 19-year-old Andrée Babelay had just spent Sunday visiting her mother and two younger sisters in the northern suburbs. Now she was travelling back on the metro to her latest job as a nanny for a fortune teller in north-east Paris.

During the past seven years, Andrée's remarried mother Mme Colin had found her flighty daughter positions as a florist's assistant, a dairy maid, a factory girl and a chamber maid. None of these jobs had lasted long, with Andrée either failing to turn up for work or walking out in a huff. Once, Mme Colin had spent five frantic days hunting for Andrée, eventually finding her sleeping rough at an employment agency. Andrée was a loving daughter but "a little indisciplined", Mme Colin later admitted.

On this Sunday evening, sitting alone on the metro, Andrée may have been looking for the sort of proposition she had probably accepted before. She was a plump, jolly girl, not averse to being chatted up by older men with a bit of money and then spending the night with them.

Landru looked at Andrée and closed in. He took her to a room he rented near the Gare du Nord, bluffing to the concierge that Andrée was his niece.

Two days later, Mme Colin became aware of Andrée's latest escapade when her daughter did not make a rendezvous for an afternoon's shopping together in central Paris.

Feeling apprehensive, Mme Colin headed to the home of the fortune teller, who explained that Andrée had dropped by the previous day to quit her job and collect her belongings. Andrée had announced grandly that she had met an older *monsieur* with a car and a place in the country. Mme Colin was used to Andrée's tall stories, but this one seemed to have some basis in fact. The fortune teller had seen a bearded gentleman at the wheel of his *camionnette* on the street outside, while Andrée was fetching her suitcase.

When Mme Colin finally got home that night, she found a brief letter from Andrée waiting for her. Andrée said that she had got a temporary job in the suburbs and would be in touch again in a few days' time; she gave no address. Mme Colin began rummaging through Andrée's handbag, which Andrée had accidentally left behind after her last visit. Inside the bag, Andrée had stuffed two letters from her current boyfriend, a young soldier in the trenches. The boyfriend was evidently in a panic, because Andrée had just told him she might be pregnant. This news, Mme Colin decided, was probably why Andrée had gone to ground.

All this time, Andrée was enjoying herself with "Lucien" or "Lulu", as she had decided to call her pretend uncle. "Dinner with Andrée, 2 francs", Landru noted on 14 March; and then, two days later, "a dinner with Andrée, a purchase of *bonbons* for Andrée, an evening with Andrée at the Petit Casino music theatre".

On 23 March they caught the train to Houdan, the nearest station for Gambais. Landru travelled on a return ticket, Andrée on a single, carrying only a soft holdall bag. Over the next fortnight, Landru made three return trips to Paris, leaving Andrée on each occasion at the villa. She passed the time learning to ride a bicycle, well enough for Landru to suggest one day that they cycle all the way to one of his favourite haunts, a pond set deep in the forest on the other side of Gambais.

On 10 April, Landru gave Andrée 5 francs pocket money to spend in the village, writing two question marks in his *carnet* after her name. This was the last time he mentioned her. On 12 April, he wrote "4 o'clock, evening" beneath the date on the page. He had almost left it too late, because there was no cab service at this time of day. Walking briskly, he just managed to catch the train that left Houdan for Paris at 5.23 pm, the next note in his *carnet*.

***

Landru returned to a city transfixed by the military fantasies of General Robert Nivelle, the new French commander-in-chief. Self-assured and persuasive, Nivelle planned to deploy overwhelming force to smash through a supposed weak point in German defences north of the Aisne. In Nivelle's abstract strategic mind, a projected 10,000 French casualties during the first day of the offensive on 16 April 1917 seemed an acceptable level of losses.

Throughout that week, Landru read the newspapers with concern as they prematurely heralded "the victorious Franco-British offensive". Lille, Rocroi, the Ardennes – all seemed within the Allies' sights. If the censored military bulletins were accurate, Landru's cover stories set in German-occupied northern France would soon be blasted away.

In Paris, Célestine Buisson was oblivious to the sound and fury of this latest "big push". She was busy homemaking, her favourite *métier*, at the little apartment near the Porte de Clignancourt in northern Paris where Landru had just moved her. Célestine applied her woman's touch to their new home, bringing plenty of sheets and towels from her old apartment, all with her embroidered initials, as well as her prized porcelain tea service for entertaining guests.

Landru had rented the apartment in Célestine's name, explaining that he was still waiting for replacement identity papers for the ones he had left behind in Lille. It was all too frustrating for Célestine who was sure – as her fiancé was sure – that this obstacle to their impending marriage would soon be sorted out.

Célestine's younger sister Marie came to inspect the apartment and also, discreetly, to get a better sense of whether Célestine had fallen into the hands of a swindler. Marie could not make any headway with Célestine, who proudly showed off the gold earrings with inlaid pearls that her *monsieur* had just given her. Unknown to Célestine, Landru had stolen them from an earlier fiancée.

Landru regularly told Célestine that he could not spend the night with her because of one of his mysterious "work trips". She had no idea that he was seeing other women. On 27 April, for example, he visited Annette and her niece Marie-Jeanne at Villa Stendhal, splashing out on a bottle of fortified Malaga wine and biscuits for the two of them. He came again the following day and then his visits to Annette abruptly ceased as a fresh distraction came into view.

Towards the end of April, Landru was riding a tram when he spotted a slightly built young woman with a frizz of curly blonde hair. Fernande Segret, 24, lived near the Gare du Nord with her widowed mother, an usher at a vaudeville theatre. Fernande worked by day as an assistant in a fur shop, but described herself as an "*artiste lyrique*", a cabaret performer of songs and sketches. In truth, Fernande's dreams of stardom were almost as far-fetched as Nivelle's fast-disintegrating plan to smash the *Boches* with a knockout blow.

Landru made his approach and next day he and Fernande went boating in the Bois de Boulogne. According to Fernande, she and "Lucien Guillet" discussed literature and other subjects of mutual interest as they paddled around an ornamental pond. In between spouting snatches of romantic poetry, Landru measured up this dippy shopgirl. He decided she would make a more agreeable, less needy mistress than the much older Annette, whose inquisitive niece was starting to get on his nerves.

***

"*Mon cher ami*," Annette wrote to Landru on 16 May. "The hours, the days seem like interminable months passing by, alone with my thoughts and suffering at your continual absence. Do you believe I have no worries, ah yes, life is very tough for me sometimes and, you see, at the end of this month, I have a bill to pay for 200 francs, and that gives me a lot of trouble."

Preoccupied with Fernande, Landru dashed off a soothing note.

"How happy I am to know that, despite your absence, I am always in your thoughts," Annette replied by return of post. "Please believe that it is the same on my side and what happiness there will be for me when you come to look for this lovely little kiss that I so look forward to giving you."

Landru had no time for Annette's promised treat. All through the summer of 1917, he was busy entertaining Fernande, Célestine and at least one other guest at the house outside Gambais, which he had privately rechristened "The Hermitage".

***

Louise Jaume, the devout shop assistant, came down to Gambais for the day, reporting back to her concierge's daughter that while her fiancé's country villa was nice enough, his behaviour had been "a little bizarre". Instead of attending to *her*, Louise complained, he had spent much of the time sweeping up dead leaves in the back garden to add to the pile in his shed.

Louise was not entirely friendless as Landru drew her into his orbit. At the dress shop where she worked, a short walk from her apartment, three women kept an attentive eye on their highly strung assistant. Louise's employer, Mme Lhérault, a middle-aged widow, ran the shop with her two grown-up daughters. Louise was keen to get the Lhéraults' approval for her new fiancé and one day she invited the daughters to join her at her next rendezvous, near the Gare du Nord.

It was a fleeting encounter, but Mme Lhérault's daughters saw enough of Landru to be a little unsure whether this smarmy gentleman was the right husband for Louise. She had no such doubts, while insisting to "Lucien" that she could not sleep with him till her divorce came through and they were married.

"*Enfin*, I hope that better times will come for both of us." Louise wrote to him that summer. "I want to have the strength of character to wait patiently for the happiness I desire."

***

In July, as Célestine fussed about her wedding dress, her married sister Catherine suffered a miscarriage and fell gravely ill. Célestine and her younger sister Marie swept into action, taking care of Catherine's young children, whose mobilised father was away at the front. Landru, alias

Frémyet, was also kindness itself, bringing fruit and flowers most days to Catherine's hospital bedside, where he could see for himself that she was dying.

Catherine's husband wrote in despair to Célestine from the trenches, explaining that he could not get compassionate leave and fretting that he might not be able to afford his wife's funeral costs. Tactfully, Landru suggested that as a man who understood stocks and bonds he could perhaps check the current market value of Catherine's investments. Célestine could not thank him enough, whisking him off to Catherine's apartment. Marie came too, for she had reached a point with Célestine's questionable fiancé where she wanted to keep an eye on his every move. Landru did not let Marie get anywhere close to him. He insisted that she and Célestine made themselves comfortable in one room while he inspected Catherine's investment titles in the other. After some time, he reappeared with the news that Catherine's portfolio was in "less critical" shape than he had feared. *Bien*, he said briskly, it was time for all of them to get back to the hospital.

When Célestine returned to the apartment to put away the title deeds, she was surprised to discover that one of them seemed to be missing. Perhaps Catherine had cashed it in, Célestine wondered. By now, Catherine was too ill to give a clear answer about anything, so Célestine did not mention the matter. Marie was much more alarmed, increasingly sure that Célestine's fiancé was some kind of crook. What Marie lacked was any firm proof to show her foolish sister.

Catherine died in late July, releasing Landru from his hospital duties. One sunny Saturday, he and his new love Fernande, the aspiring *artiste lyrique*, went for a bike ride in the Bois de Boulogne. He hired a changing hut and after Fernande had put on a loose-fitting cycling costume, they rode off to find a nice secluded spot in the trees. Fernande unbuttoned her costume and in her own words, "became his mistress".

The following weekend they sampled the forest of Saint-Germain-en-Laye, further west of Paris. Afterwards, Landru found time to send identical postcards to Louise and Célestine, each with a cursory greeting. Célestine, accustomed to her fiancé's "work trips", was delighted he had even bothered to write. Louise was most unhappy. "I was waiting impatiently for a word from you," she wrote back tetchily. "A little letter would have given me pleasure, much more than two words on a card."

In the middle of August, Célestine's sister Marie was due her annual week's leave from her housemaid's job. To her surprise, Célestine's fiancé invited Marie to join them at his country retreat in Gambais. Marie accepted;

it would be a chance to have a good, hard look at this *monsieur* and decide if he really was a swindler.

***

His setup at Gambais disturbed Marie, beginning with the fact that the house was hardly furnished. She and Célestine had to share a cot bed in one room, beneath a cheap print of the wolf in sheep's clothing from Aesop's fable, while Landru, alias Frémyet, slept across the corridor. Looking around the villa, Marie doubted that he had much money, despite his air of being a man of means. This impression was reinforced when he spent several days wallpapering two of the downstairs rooms, both dripping with damp, in order (so he said) to sublet the property.

In between decorating, Landru made two trips to Paris, leaving Marie and Célestine alone at the villa. Marie nosed around, eventually coming to a locked shed at the bottom of the garden. Squinting through the keyhole, she could just make out what looked like bundles or packages, but in the gloom it was impossible to tell what they were. She returned to the house without investigating a pile of dead leaves in the adjoining hangar, an unusual sight in August.

Landru came back from his second trip to Paris with a "gift" of about 50 francs for Célestine, promising to give her more on their wedding day. The money was part of the latest sum that Landru had withdrawn with Célestine's permission from her bank account in order to manage it better. Hoping to soften up Marie, he gave her a ring from his horde of stolen women's jewellery.

Marie was not so easily led. As soon as she could have a private word with Célestine, Marie demanded to know how much money Célestine had handed over to her fiancé from her original nest egg of about 10,000 francs. Reluctantly, Célestine said that her *monsieur* had taken about 3,000 francs. Marie was incensed, telling Célestine she was an idiot to trust her money to this man. Célestine was just as furious, refusing to hear any further unkind remarks from her meddling younger sister about "Monsieur Frémyet".

At the end of the week Landru and his guests took the train to Paris, with Marie and Célestine barely on speaking terms. On their arrival, Landru left for another vague appointment, while the sisters went off to lay flowers on Catherine's grave. Then Célestine and Marie parted company, glad to see the back of each other.

Next morning, Célestine and Landru caught a train to Houdan, the main station for Gambais, with Célestine travelling on a one-way ticket. On 24 August, Landru made a round trip to Paris to sell some bonds belonging to Célestine for 1,880 francs.

Something now disrupted the smooth progress of his thefts from Célestine. So far, Landru had retained almost all the proceeds from his steady liquidation of Célestine's portfolio, only permitting her a little pocket money. Perhaps Célestine had finally heeded Marie's warning, because when Landru returned to the villa, she made him give her 1,000 francs. Furthermore, Célestine demanded that Landru repay her a small debt of 30 francs. Both transactions were carefully recorded by Landru in his *carnet*.

Landru's repeated visits to Célestine's bank in Paris now ceased. Over the next week, he visited the village shops each day to buy enough food and drink for two people: two pork chops, two steaks, and so on. Finally, on 1 September, he reached for his *carnet* and noted the time, 10.15 am. Shortly after, he set off alone for Paris, as gunfire echoed across the fields and woods around Gambais. It was *"le moment de la chasse"*, the start of the annual hunting season, when the local farmers blasted away at any wild bird or animal they could eat.

Chapter 7

Sacré Coeur

On Sunday, 30 September 1917, Landru and Louise caught the early train to Houdan in time to celebrate morning mass in the village church across the fields from the villa. Landru popped ten centimes in the collection box and then they walked up the road to the house. Sometime that afternoon Louise felt obliged to tell Landru that she was not prepared to go to bed with him, and would he please take her back to the station. She did not, however, break off their engagement.

***

A few days later a letter arrived at the *mairie* in Gambais from the typist Anna Collomb's younger sister Ryno.

It was now nine months since Anna's disappearance, immediately after her traumatic Christmas lunch with the family at their apartment on Boulevard Voltaire. During this period, Ryno had lost all patience with a series of men who had failed to establish what had happened to Anna. Ryno feared the worst, based on her enquiries so far.

In January, a basket of flowers left outside her parents' apartment had instantly made Ryno suspicious. The flowers had purportedly been sent by Anna from southern France with her calling card slipped inside. It looked to Ryno like a crude attempt by Anna's fiancé to deceive the family about her whereabouts, following her failure to come back from her last visit to Gambais.

Ryno's elderly father, prodded by her, had enlisted one of Anna's gentlemen friends, known to the family, to make enquiries about her disappearance. This man – who had been shocked by Anna's dishevelled appearance when he had last seen her – had checked with Anna's former concierge and passed on the family's concerns to the police. His duty done, he had given up looking for Anna, as had Ryno's father. The police had not even registered Anna as a missing person.

Enraged by all this male incompetence, Ryno had launched her own one-woman investigation. She had gone first to the Paris office of the exiled municipal government of occupied Lille. Using all her charm, Ryno had persuaded an official to check whether the Lille authorities had any record of a man called "Georges Frémyet", Landru's alias. The official had drawn a blank. He had also confirmed that no one called "Cuchet" had ever claimed a refugee's allowance, as Landru had pretended to Anna.

Ryno next wrote to the mayor of Gambais, asking if a man called Cuchet or Frémyet lived in the village with a woman matching Anna's description. She identified Landru's villa precisely, using the postcard that Anna had sent her from Gambais two years earlier with an 'X' above the house. The mayor had failed to reply, so on 1 October Ryno wrote again; still, no one replied.

On 24 October, Ryno wrote a third letter, concealing her fury beneath icily formal prose:

"*Monsieur*", she began, "Permit me to confirm that I sent you an earlier letter on the subject of a disappearance and am surprised not to have received any response."

At last the mayor of Gambais, a 58-year-old local businessman called Alexandre Tirlet, instructed the village schoolmaster François Bournérias to reply. Bournérias explained that unfortunately the *mairie* had no record of anyone called Frémyet or Cuchet renting a house in the village.

Ryno wrote back on 4 November on behalf of the whole family:

"It is one more surprise for us all to learn that there is no house rented at Gambais under one of the two names that I indicated," she observed incredulously. Once again, Ryno gave full particulars about the man and the location of the house. She added:

"My sister adored my mother, and for me she was like a second *maman*, and precisely because of the affection and *entente* between us, it is inconceivable that she does not wish to see us voluntarily anymore or to write to us."

On Tirlet's orders, Bournérias did not reply.

Bournérias had told Ryno an extremely compressed version of the truth, for he and Tirlet knew perfectly well which man and house she had identified. Like many other people in Gambais, they had noticed this bowler-hatted *monsieur* around the neighbourhood with a series of women, ever since he had first rented the Villa Tric two years ago. The mayor and the schoolmaster had also seen him driving his *camionnette* through the village and assumed that since he said he was an automobile trader, he had a wartime licence to drive the vehicle.

However, the man called himself Dupont, not Frémyet or Cuchet. As far as the mayor was concerned, that was enough to invalidate Ryno's enquiry. A man's private life, after all, was his own business – a point that the *monsieur* in question would later make repeatedly.

The mayor and the schoolteacher had managed to throw Ryno off the scent. Reluctantly, she now started to suspect that Anna and her imposter fiancé must have eloped after all, who knew where.

***

That autumn, while Ryno got nowhere with the *mairie*, Landru was struggling to allay the suspicions of Célestine's younger sister Marie about Célestine's disappearance. He tried to fool Marie with his postcard trick, sending several from Gambais to the house in Paris where Marie worked as a maid. Each card carried a one-line greeting from "Célestine", but Marie saw instantly that the handwriting was forged.

Crucially for Landru, Marie did not yet believe that he had killed Célestine. Marie still imagined he was a run-of-the-mill marriage swindler and that Célestine, having ignored Marie's advice, deserved to suffer the consequences.

What stirred Marie into action was a letter she received in October 1917 from Célestine's war-wounded son Gaston, now blind and living with an uncle near Biarritz. Gaston needed money to pay for a hospital operation and had written to his mother in Paris for help, but she had not replied. Could Aunt Marie please try to track her down?

Marie wrote to Célestine at her sister's old apartment near the Porte de Clignancourt, where Landru collected her letter on one of his regular visits to pick up Célestine's correspondence. Realising the danger, he turned up unannounced at Marie's employer's house in central Paris and when she answered the front door, abruptly handed her 250 francs for Gaston's operation. Landru explained to the sceptical Marie that "Mme Buisson" was "very distracted" because they were about to depart on a trip to the provinces; this was why she had failed to reply to Gaston or deliver the money herself.

By now, Marie's friend and fellow maid Laure Bonheure had joined her on the doorstep, curious to get a look at this suspicious caller. After Landru doffed his bowler hat and hurried off down the street, Laure agreed with Marie that he was obviously up to no good.

Landru was still worried about Marie. A fortnight later, he showed up again at the house, ostensibly to enquire on Célestine's behalf about Gaston. With Laure looking on, Marie asked why Célestine could not write to Gaston herself and indeed, why she had failed to reply to any of Marie's letters. Landru remarked flippantly that Mme Buisson had become "very lazy" about correspondence since hiring her own secretary.

Landru could see from Marie's reaction that his answer was not good enough. Somehow he had to deal once and for all with this wretched maid. In late October he came up with a plan. He wrote to Marie with the news that he and Célestine would be spending a few days in Paris at the apartment near Porte de Clignancourt. Would Mlle Lacoste care to join them for dinner? Marie was unaware that the apartment had been empty since Célestine's last journey to Gambais in August, other than for one overnight stay by Fernande. She did not therefore sense a trap. For several days Marie pondered the invitation and then decided to say no. *Enfin*, Marie reasoned, it was up to Célestine to make peace directly, rather than use "Frémyet" as her messenger.

A few days later, Landru appeared yet again at the house where Marie worked. Could Mlle Lacoste, after all, be persuaded to join him and Mme Buisson for dinner that evening? No, she could not, Marie replied, as her friend Laure glared at Landru. He returned next morning; surely she would come to dinner tonight?

"I asked him why he was not with my sister," Marie recalled. "He assured me she was working and could not come."

Marie had had enough. She told Landru to wait while she collected her coat and then ordered him to take a walk with her round the block. As soon as she was away from the house, Marie handed him the 250 francs that Landru had given her for Gaston's operation. It was up to Célestine to help Gaston, Marie said. Then she sent Landru on his way, with the parting shot that Célestine knew exactly where to find her if she wanted to get in touch.

***

At the start of November, Louise Jaume gave in her notice at the dress shop where she worked. Louise explained to her motherly employer, Mme Lhérault, that her wedding would take place immediately after the divorce from Paul Jaume, which was imminent. She and "Monsieur Guillet" would then divide their time between his house in the country, whose precise location Louise did not reveal, and his Paris apartment near the Gare du Nord, whose address she gave Mme Lhérault.

This was not the apartment Landru had shared with Anna Collomb, which he had given up, or the nearby room where he had taken the teenage Andrée Babelay, which he continued to rent. In September, Landru had begun renting a cramped first-floor bedsit at 76 Rue de Rochechouart, several blocks west of the Gare du Nord, which would increasingly become his main Paris base.

He had one last piece of unsettled business with Louise before he moved her out of her apartment on Rue des Lyanes, where she had also given notice. On 19 November he stayed the night there for the first time, noting this landmark in his *carnet*. He slept with Louise again on the following three nights, all recorded; and then on Saturday, 24 November, finally satisfied, he arrived with a blond-haired youth he called his "apprentice" to remove her furniture. The boy took Louise's belongings to a commercial storage depot while she and Landru, alias Guillet, proceeded to Rue de Rochechouart, carrying only light luggage.

Next morning, Sunday, 25 November, the nervous Louise kept to her usual habit when she was going on a journey, secreting just over 274 francs in the folds of her dress in case of an emergency. The weather was grey and drizzly as she and Landru walked up the hill to Montmartre to attend morning mass at the Basilica of Sacré-Coeur. Louise prayed for forgiveness, Landru put 15 centimes in the collection box and then they were off, catching the afternoon train to Tacoignières, eight kilometres north of Gambais.

Louise travelled on a one-way ticket, bought for her by Landru. He made her walk with him in the rain, all the way to the villa, where he decided to spend one last night with her.

On Monday, 26 November, he wrote "5.00 pm" beneath the date in his *carnet*. Next, he wrote "*Récuperation Lyanes*: 274 francs 60". Two hours later, he caught the evening train to Paris, using his return ticket.

***

During December, Louise's former employer Mme Lhérault and her two daughters became increasingly concerned at Louise's failure to collect her post, which she had arranged to be forwarded from Rue des Lyanes to the dress shop. Two letters in particular looked like they might concern Louise's divorce petition. Shortly before Christmas, Mme Lhérault's elder daughter wrote to Louise's *monsieur* at 76 Rue de Rochechouart, asking him to tell Louise to come to the shop as soon as possible. She did not receive a reply.

A few days after Christmas, Mme Lhérault's younger daughter went to Rue de Rochechouart to deliver the two letters. "Monsieur Guillet [Landru] was at home and made me wait a little," she remembered. "Before opening the door, I heard whispering in the apartment and in the end I was received by him on the landing itself."

Landru took the correspondence and told his unwelcome visitor that Louise was in the country. He added that she would return to Paris in a few days' time, when he was sure she would visit her friends at the dress shop. Still uneasy, Mme Lhérault's daughter left with the firm suspicion that Louise had been hiding in the apartment and that for some reason, her fiancé had made her stay out of sight.

Thoroughly alarmed, the Lhéraults decided to write to Louise directly, inviting her to come to see them. On 3 January 1918, Mme Lhérault's younger daughter returned to Rue de Rochechouart, where the concierge explained that "Guillet" was not at home and that she knew nothing about a woman called Mme Jaume. The daughter left the letter with the concierge, hoping that it might still reach Louise.

On 8 January, Landru passed by Rue de Rochechouart and collected the letter from the concierge. Now it was his turn to be worried. He dashed off a note to the dress shop, announcing that he would be in Paris next morning and if convenient, would be pleased to call on the Lhéraults at 10.00 am. He arrived on the dot, bringing a box of chocolates, which he said was a New Year's present for the Lhéraults from Louise. Mme Jaume, Landru continued smoothly, had just sailed for the United States to take up a position as a governess at a girls' boarding school.

The Lhéraults did not believe him and told him so. As they explained, Louise spoke no English and besides, her divorce had finally been approved – a fact they knew for certain, because they had started opening Louise's forwarded correspondence. Why, then, would she abandon her fiancé, Monsieur Guillet, for a country where she knew no one?

Landru blustered that Louise had not been able to call on the Lhéraults before her departure because she had been busy obtaining a passport. As for the divorce, she had decided that her religious scruples would not allow it. Their engagement was consequently over. He bid them *adieu* and darted out of the shop, leaving the Lhéraults to wonder what on earth they could do to rescue Louise from this almost comically incompetent liar; the problem being, that he seemed to have committed no crime.

***

Annette Pascal's niece Marie-Jeanne had known for some time that "*Monsieur Mystère*" was trying to get rid of her, all the way back to her family in Toulon. In October, Landru, alias Forest, had reappeared at Annette's apartment to resume their affair after an interval of five months. He had immediately told Annette that Marie-Jeanne's continuing presence displeased him. Desperate not to lose him again, Annette had written a placatory letter. He only had to "say the word", Annette said, and Marie-Jeanne would be on the train home.

At the start of 1918 Annette buckled – or at least, she was keen to give Landru that impression. She wrote him another letter, promising that Marie-Jeanne would leave for Toulon by the end of January provided he married her in February. To be sure he read the letter, Annette despatched Marie-Jeanne to deliver it to Rue de Rochechouart, where Annette had recently spent the night. Annette had forgotten the street number, but Marie-Jeanne managed to find the right door from her aunt's description of the building.

Marie-Jeanne knew several things as she hovered on the first-floor landing outside the apartment, clutching Annette's letter. First, Annette was not at all sure that she trusted her fiancé enough to marry him; what Annette wanted was his money. Second, Marie-Jeanne had just discovered that "Lucien Forest" was an imposter, because the concierge downstairs had informed her that his name was "Lucien Guillet". Lastly, Marie-Jeanne knew Forest/Guillet was at home, because she could see beneath the door that the light was on in the apartment.

Some defensive instinct stopped the normally assertive Marie-Jeanne knocking on the door, perhaps from fear of what else she might learn about this man who no longer seemed funny; in particular, Marie-Jeanne could not rule out the possibility that Forest/Guillet had another girlfriend inside. She slipped Annette's letter under the door and crept downstairs, before anyone picked it up.

Marie-Jeanne's discovery about Annette's fiancé made Annette even more nervous about him. As always, Annette turned for advice to her big sister and "*maman*" Louise, Marie-Jeanne's mother:

"Since he was so secretive and not being able to know what he wanted to do with me…we have made him believe that she [Marie-Jeanne] would be going at the end of the month," Annette wrote to Louise on 14 January. "So today he has come here to check the date when she was leaving and he has insisted on knowing the date, you say that we do not know how to respond, given that this was not our intention. But now he has said that since she was leaving our marriage would take place in February."

Landru's decision threw Annette into agonies over what to do about "*Grand Marcel*", her middle-aged lover at the front, "*Petit Marcel*", her teenage boyfriend who worked on the metro, and "Hayose", her other lover in the trenches.

In Toulon, Louise Fauchet despaired of Annette and her endless entanglements; in Louise's mind, this Forest/Guillet fellow sounded like all the other disastrous men who had passed through Annette's bed. Louise told Annette to send Marie-Jeanne home by the end of January, leaving Annette to sort out the two Marcels, Hayose, Forest/Guillet and whoever else was currently competing for her affection.

Landru was delighted when he heard this news, even giving Marie-Jeanne a little cash to help pay for her train ticket. He also invited Annette and Marie-Jeanne to a farewell dinner at Rue de Rochechouart on the eve of her departure.

After dinner, Landru got a reminder of why he was so pleased to see the back of Annette's astute niece. When Annette and Marie-Jeanne offered to do the washing-up, Landru handed them two women's kitchen aprons.

"Why have you got these?" Marie-Jeanne enquired. "I thought you were a bachelor."

Landru looked at her and realised his mistake.

"You are too curious," he ticked her off half-jokingly.

***

A couple of days later, Annette wrote to "*Grand Marcel*" to announce that she was marrying another man.

"He was not happy," Annette told Louise in her next letter. "He implored me not to make a decision before seeing him. I wrote back to him that given the danger there is in Paris, I am leaving Paris to put myself somewhere safe, for I have to tell you that every day he is writing to me very anxious to hear if anything has happened to me and in these letters he is always making beautiful promises but you understand that time is short and one can't live on promises."

German bombs, not men, had just crashed into Annette's little world. On 30 January, German "*Gotha*" bomber planes killed 49 civilians in Paris and the surrounding suburbs, the start of a week of terrifying air raids.

"We passed a terrible night," Annette wrote frantically to Louise on 3 February, "and how many times can I repeat that I am so happy that Marie-Jeanne has left, for we tremble every night before going to bed."

The "we" referred to Landru, whom she was seeing every day, now that Marie-Jeanne had gone. "He is more and more kind, yesterday evening he was here, as ever, he has seen this letter and asks me to send you his greetings and he is going to write to you one of these days."

Landru's non-existent factory north of Paris had just been bombed, he lied to Annette, shortly before he went down with a fictitious dose of flu.

He sent her a cursory sick note; Annette wrote straight back. "Why, *petit ami*, if you are so ill, as you tell me, why haven't you asked me to be with you, not to know where you are or how you are suffering, not even to let me come and see you?" she implored:

> All of this makes me suppose that I can't have your confidence, for reasons of which I am unaware and which you are afraid to let me know. Believe me, I am currently living in a state of uncertainty which is making me ill and is breaking my heart. The feelings which you seem to show me and all your fine projects which you only let me glimpse make me doubt your sincerity.

***

Fernande Segret, the 24-year-old shop girl and would-be cabaret artist, was the cause of Landru's "flu". For several months Landru had been trying to juggle Fernande, who had started to spend the odd night at Rue de Rochechouart, with Annette, now all alone at Villa Stendhal with only her cat Minette for company. Increasingly, he preferred to spend time with Fernande, who was younger and less inquisitive than Annette.

Sometime in February, Landru asked Fernande's widowed mother for permission to marry her beautiful daughter. Mme Segret, who was only a theatre usher, warned Landru when giving her consent that Fernande would bring no dowry. No matter, Landru said grandly: he had large sums invested in various highly successful manufacturing and automobile businesses, and other promising ventures in Brazil. It was agreed that the wedding would take place by Easter 1918.

Landru now made a mistake by inviting Fernande and her mother down to Gambais for the day. Mme Segret took one look at the villa's lack of furniture and damp, mouldy walls and began to have second thoughts about her prospective son-in-law. She rather doubted he was even half as rich as he claimed and in this regard, could not help commenting on his rusty little oven, better suited to a peasant than a man of substance.

"Don't worry," Landru said cheerily, chucking some old meat and vegetable scraps into the base of the oven. "Everything burns in here."

As if to prove his point, the oven was soon ablaze, providing some welcome warmth.

***

The dreaded *Gothas* returned to Paris on the night of 9 March, killing seven civilians. In the morning, Annette scribbled an urgent note to "Lucien", complaining that he had abandoned her just when she needed his protection from the bombs. He did not reply. Several days later, another air raid killed dozens more Parisians, directly from the bombs or indirectly as they were crushed to death in the stampedes to reach the safety of underground metro stations.

Fernande's mother was in fear for her life, to the point where she was even willing to endure the bleakness of the Villa Tric, if that meant being out of range of the *Gothas*. Mme Segret asked Fernande to approach "Lucien" to see if she could stay at the villa while the raids continued. Landru regretted that he could not oblige his future mother-in-law. Mme Segret would find the property most "inconvenient", he told Fernande, given the need to hunt far and wide for fuel to light the oven.

Landru was temporarily tired of Fernande and her irritating mother. In mid-March, two days after rebuffing Mme Segret's request, he sent a message to Annette.

"As he is afraid of the *Gothas*, like everybody he wants to flee Paris," Annette reported to her "*maman*" Louise. "He has suggested that I should leave with him for Haute-Marne, near Dijon. We are still living through terrifying hours…if you knew the terror that we have known and the shaking and tremors all around me, you speak of fear and we have rushed down to the cellar for we did not know what it was."

Just as abruptly, Landru cancelled his proposed flight to Haute-Marne, informing Annette that he still needed to put his affairs in order. Annette and her beloved cat Minette were left to cower every night with the other residents in the cellar at Villa Stendhal.

At 7.20 am on Saturday, 23 March, Annette heard two tremendous explosions reverberating from the Place de la République, less than a mile away. It took French military intelligence several hours to establish that the shells now raining down all over Paris were being fired from a monstrous German artillery cannon 120 kilometres north-east of the city. By nightfall, 16 civilians had been killed at random.

Annette could bear it no more. "You must know the state in which I find myself, no rest, nothing to eat, everything is shut, burrowed down in the cellars," she wrote next day to Louise. "If this continues I will die of hunger, don't worry, I'll keep you updated about everything." Mercifully, she was writing from Rue de Rochechouart, where dear "Lucien" was finally letting her stay.

Landru had a fresh plan to put to Annette. The two of them could stay at his rural villa to get away from the bombs and shells. He then made an odd condition: Annette would need to make an initial inspection of the house before moving in properly. Annette accepted, keeping her misgivings from Landru. She confessed in her next letter to Louise how she, a city girl, really felt about moving to the country with her unpredictable fiancé.

"I am so unhappy, crying that I cannot embrace you as I would like to," she wrote. "Above all, don't think worse of me, for I would be even unhappier."

On Tuesday, 26 March, she and Landru took the train to Houdan, both travelling on return tickets. At the villa, Annette saw the barren little kitchen with its gimcrack oven, the rough cot beds, the picture of the wolf in sheep's clothing, the peeling wallpaper, and the shed with its pile of dead leaves. She returned to Paris on the evening of 27 March, almost certainly alone, Landru having decided to stay on in Gambais. When she got back to Villa Stendhal, shortly before midnight, "she looked sad and worn out, like someone who had been ill," her concierge recalled.

Annette went straight upstairs and wrote another letter to Louise.

"Everything is beautiful, more than beautiful," Annette lied, hoping to reassure her sister. "It's truly a palace, I could scarcely believe my eyes," everything was in "luxurious, modern taste". After dashing off her letter, Annette scooped up Minette and went straight down to the cellar to shelter from the *Gothas*.

"Quick two words in haste to calm you on the terrible night we have just passed," she scribbled to Louise a few hours later. "*Ma chère maman*, it's horrible what they did last night, one still doesn't know the details, but it's terrible what we have experienced I am dying of fear today."

On Good Friday, 29 March, the German field gun scored a direct hit on a church in the central Marais district, killing 88 worshippers attending Easter Mass. That weekend, tens of thousands of Parisians fled the city, just as Landru headed back to Paris from his unexplained business in Gambais, with a special gift for Annette.

"For Easter he gave me a beautiful gold watch that belonged to his mother," Annette told Louise. "Little by little he will give me all of his mother's jewellery, he is truly kind, every day, more and more, and he gives me all the money I need."

Finally, Annette felt able to banish all her doubts regarding "Lucien" and his grim villa; he, and it, would have to do, until she could think of a better option.

On Wednesday, 3 April, he arrived at Villa Stendhal with his silent, blond "apprentice" to clear Annette's apartment for storage, prior to the transfer of her belongings to Gambais. When they were gone, Annette gave Louise a quick update. "Lucien asked me to send you his best wishes, for he has said that he would like to make your acquaintance soon," Annette wrote. Meanwhile, "he sends a lovely kiss to Marie-Jeanne."

Before leaving Paris, Annette went to find "*Petit Marcel*", the teenage metro conductor who had dreamed of marrying her. "After many tears", he accepted that Annette was irrevocably engaged to another man. "We have parted good friends and also with his parents," she told Louise.

***

Rain was falling when Annette and Landru reached Houdan, late on Thursday afternoon. Annette looked out of place on the station forecourt, dressed smartly in a black satin dress, black velvet hat, and green overcoat with fur trimming. Somewhere in this get-up she had concealed her trusted

SOS note: "In case of accident, alert my family, my sister, Mme Fauchet, 10 rue de la Fraternité, Toulon, Var."

She was not carrying much luggage – just a mustard yellow suitcase in one hand and a wicker basket in the other, for she had brought Minette to keep her company. They caught the local horse-and-cab service between Houdan and Gambais which passed the Villa Tric. On their arrival, they ate a quick dinner of meat and bread, purchased before they left Paris. Then they went upstairs to bed with Minette, who spent the night frozen with fear beneath the eiderdown.

In the morning the weather was still grey and chilly. Annette stayed indoors, writing at least two letters to confirm her safe arrival, while neglecting to provide a proper address.

"Here I am in my new home, with my *petit Lucien*, who is all kindness," she told Louise. "I am so happy to be with him, although this will be a big change from the active, busy life one leads in Paris."

Annette also wrote to Mme Carbonnel, an older woman friend and fellow seamstress who had seen her and Minette off the day before at the Gare de Montparnasse. Annette confided that she found it "a little strange here, it is so quiet". Still, she added cheerily, she was enjoying the fresh air.

Not long after finishing these letters, something happened to alarm Annette. She now wrote a second, one-line note to Louise, slipped in the same envelope:

"If I don't send you any news, be worried and hurry to find out what has happened to me."

The note, unlike the letter, was never sent.

At 5.15 pm, Landru recorded the time in his *carnet*. He then grabbed Minette, strangled the miserable animal and took the corpse out to the garden for burial.

Chapter 8

The Fatal List

Landru was not a smoker but he bought a packet of cigarettes for Fernande on his way to Rue de Rochechouart to spend the night with her. His little apartment was becoming a real home from home for him and Fernande. He had his bust of Beethoven, his Japanese-style lamp, his volumes of Balzac and Victor Hugo and a nice big table where he could spend his evenings sketching his plans for a new automobile radiator. It was going to make him a fortune, he told Fernande.

She was happy enough, despite "Lucien" breaking his promise to marry her by Easter. Perhaps in recompense, he had begun to pay her an allowance, and she had given up her job as a fur shop assistant. Fernande could now spend long hours dreaming about how she would resume her theatrical career as soon as the war was over.

Landru had no trouble fooling Fernande about his frequent "business trips" out of Paris. One such journey in April or May, probably to Gambais, purportedly concerned a service contract with US forces based to the east of the city.

"Four long days without seeing you!" he wrote to Fernande. "… How much time has it been since we were apart for so long! But is it really a separation, since all my thoughts are close to you."

Fernande's mother was more of a problem. Mme Segret was still smarting from his refusal to let her stay at his villa during the bombardment of Paris. She began to suspect he was an imposter when Easter came and went while he continued to trot out his familiar excuse about lost identity papers. Shortly after Easter, Mme Segret dragged Fernande along to the Paris office of the exiled *mairie* of Rocroi, the little town on the Belgian border where Landru, alias Guillet, claimed to own a factory. A quick check of the municipal files found no record of anyone called Lucien Guillet.

Mme Segret was emphatic: the relationship with this conman had to end, she told Fernande. "Guillet" was summoned to Mme Segret's apartment but he merely shrugged when she confronted him with her discovery.

Obviously the *mairie* had been unable to evacuate all its files when the Germans invaded, he told her matter-of-factly. The same evening, he took Fernande out to the Opéra-Comique to make up for the needless distress her mother had caused her.

***

During the spring and early summer of 1918, the Germans attempted to blast their way through the British and French lines north of Paris. At times, the front came alarmingly close to the city but on 11 June the French counter-attacked near Compiègne, halting the German advance. Soon the road would be open, not to Paris, but to the occupied cities and towns of northern France, blowing Landru's cover.

Mme Segret chose this moment to take Fernande to stay with relatives in Burgundy, well away from Landru. He went in search of company to share his bed at Rue de Rochechouart, patrolling the metro or hanging around factory gates to pick up girls. "Mlle L." (her full name was never revealed) noticed him stalking her one evening as she went home after her shift:

"He finally approached me and asked where I worked and whether he could wait for me at the end of the day by the exit to my factory."

Keen to land this "*vieux monsieur*", she agreed to "clean" his apartment at Rue de Rochechouart one morning. The arrangement did not work out as she expected. He did not take her to bed, but locked the door on her and went out, supposedly to his office. Landru returned at midday, took her to lunch at a nearby restaurant and then sent her on her way with some money for the cleaning. For the next appointment, he locked her all day in the apartment, with enough food for lunch and supper. In the evening, he took her to a music hall and then back to Rue de Rochechouart, where she at last spent the night with him.

Mlle L. now pushed her luck too far. She confided to him that her family was hard-up, bringing an abrupt end to the cleaning job and the nights at Rue de Rochechouart. Landru had also made an error in underestimating this worldly working girl. She knew exactly where to find him and would not be shaken off so easily.

***

On 8 August, around 120,000 British, French and Dominion troops, supported by several hundred tanks, forced a 15-mile gap in the German lines south of Amiens. The Germans were finally on the run and so was Landru: for as summer turned to autumn, he moved into unfamiliar territory, besieged by a series of women who held the upper hand.

In early September, Fernande returned to Paris and moved back in at Rue de Rochechouart. Mme Segret's plan to separate the couple had failed. One day, when Landru was out, Fernande answered the door to a young woman who refused to introduce herself. She came again when Landru was in and he went onto the landing to talk to her, shutting the apartment door so Fernande could not hear them.

His caller was Mlle L., his former "cleaning woman", who claimed she was now pregnant with his baby. What, she asked, was Monsieur Guillet going to do about her, the baby, and the three of them generally? Her ruse worked. Landru agreed to give her an allowance and started spending the odd night with her, possibly at another room he rented near Rue de Rochechouart.

Like Fernande, Mlle L. had no idea that Landru was almost broke by the autumn of 1918, ruined by his extensive liabilities. He was paying several "allowances" to different women, and also had to find cash for the rent on at least three apartments, the house at Gambais, the garage space in Clichy, and a network of storage depots around Paris.

Squeezed from all directions, Landru turned to Mme Jeanne Falque, twice divorced, still only 42, well off, and minded to marry again. Once again, he miscalculated.

Mme Falque, whom he met via a matrimonial agency, had substantial savings and lived in a comfortable apartment only a short walk from Rue de Rochechouart. Landru, alias Guillet, took tea with her in late September. Soon Mme Falque was travelling down to Gambais with her new fiancé to admire his country estate.

The visit did not go well. Mme Falque shivered in the back garden while they ate an open-air picnic, unimpressed by everything. She broke off their engagement as soon as they got back to Paris.

***

Early on 11 November, a detachment of Italian soldiers "liberated" Lucien Guillet's purported home town of Rocroi, which in reality had already been abandoned by the Germans. The Italians were only just in time to claim their victory, because at 11.00 am the armistice came into force. At Rue de Rochechouart Landru grumbled to Fernande that the war had finished too soon. Seeing the startled look on her face, he rambled on that "the cessation of hostilities" would create numerous difficulties for various military contracts he had negotiated.

Having failed with Mme Falque, Landru was scrambling for cash. On 14 December, President Woodrow Wilson's train pulled into Paris at the start of a triumphal tour of Europe, the prelude to the peace conference due to begin in Paris a month later. As Wilson and his entourage checked into the Hotel Crillon, Landru hurried over to his garage in Clichy to cadge 40 francs off a man who also rented space there.

This hand-to-mouth existence could not last. In the run-up to Christmas, Landru somehow managed to persuade Mme Falque to see him again. Once the ice was broken, he tried to con her into letting him "invest" her savings. She told him to get lost. Landru next asked if she could advance him a loan. Mme Falque said she would consider the matter. After a week, she came back with a proposal apparently designed to pay him back for the lies he had told her about his country estate: she would lend him 900 francs for a month, at a punitive interest rate of 26 per cent. "Monsieur Guillet" could take it or leave it, Mme Falque said. He took it.

***

At this crisis in his financial affairs, Landru's eye alighted irrationally on a debt-ridden prostitute.

Every day, 37-year-old Marie-Thérèse Marchadier walked her two little Belgian griffon dogs along the Rue Saint-Jacques, joking to passers-by that she much preferred dogs to men. Originally from Bordeaux, Marie-Thérèse also kept a pet canary, which matched the flamboyant green and yellow dresses and hats she liked to wear. The rest of her story depended on whom to believe.

Her best friend Yvonne Le Gallo, another prostitute, said she had lent Marie-Thérèse several thousand francs to lease other rooms in Marie-Thérèse's apartment block during the war. Marie-Thérèse's idea was to sublet the rooms, but her venture had flopped, leaving her heavily in debt to Yvonne, with no means to pay.

A "broker" and possible pimp called Moret, who later claimed to know Landru as a second-hand furniture dealer, said he had first introduced Landru to Marie-Thérèse in October 1918. According to Moret, the financially stretched prostitute had stuck a note on her apartment door, announcing the sale of her furniture.

The truth about how Landru met Marie-Thérèse may have been simpler. She had spent time during the war in Le Havre, a port that Landru knew well, and more recently in the town of Beauvais, 90 kilometres north of Paris, where Landru had also stayed on at least one occasion. It is therefore possible that when Landru went to Marie-Thérèse's apartment on Christmas Day he knew her already and wanted sex. What he lacked was money to pay her. A deal needed to be struck between two people who were short of cash.

Events moved fast. On 27 December, Marie-Thérèse told her concierge that she was engaged to a man who had "the hots" for her; she would soon be leaving for his house in the country. She also told her friend Yvonne, who later said casually that Marie-Thérèse had "a mania for marriage", implying that she was a veteran of previous "engagements" with other *messieurs*.

On New Year's Eve, Landru passed by Mme Falque's apartment: Could he perhaps borrow an additional 3,000 francs from her, just to tide him over? He did not tell Mme Falque that this sum would allow him to "buy" some of Marie-Thérèse's furniture.

According to Mme Falque, she insisted that Landru first had to show her his garage in Clichy, so she could see for herself what kind of business he was running. Once there, she grudgingly agreed to lend him the money at the same extortionate interest rate, provided he could produce his identity papers. Landru, alias Guillet, went off to fetch his papers, only to return half an hour later empty-handed. He had just made a phone call, Landru told Mme Falque, and realised that he could borrow the cash from someone else.

***

New Year's Day dawned, cloudy and mild. At 9.30 am, France's Prime Minister Georges Clemenceau arrived at the Elysée Palace with the rest of his cabinet to present their greetings for 1919 to President Raymond Poincaré (whom Clemenceau loathed). Landru had a similar New Year's duty, or so he told Fernande. He put on his best dark suit and bowler hat, informing her that he was off to wish his boss at Paris police headquarters a happy New Year. Pressed by Fernande, Landru revealed that he was, in reality, an undercover detective.

While he was out, a letter arrived from Marie-Thérèse, who told him that she asked "for nothing better than to live in the countryside". On 2 January, Landru made a note to "bring to Hermitage [Villa Tric]: Petrol, lighting fuel, coal, small tongs, iron grate". On 7 January, Marie-Thérèse went down to Gambais for the day, telling another prostitute friend on her return to Paris about her future country home. Landru remained in Gambais for a few days, so short of money that he had to borrow the price of his return train fare to Paris from the village cobbler who acted as the villa's janitor. Meanwhile, Marie-Thérèse sold some of her furniture and paid a few bills, leaving her with 1,800 francs in cash.

In this dizzying round of transactions, Landru next cleared all the furniture out of Marie-Thérèse's apartment and her sublet rooms, assisted by his silent teenage "apprentice" and his fellow tenant at the garage in Clichy.

On 13 January, Landru and Marie-Thérèse left for the Gare Saint-Lazare, in time to catch the afternoon train to one of the stations serving Gambais. She stood on the platform, resplendent in a bright green hat, yellow suitcase in one hand, bird cage in the other, as her pet canary twittered in terror. Beside her, Landru held three yapping griffon dogs on a lead; the third dog, called Auguste, had been lent by Marie-Thérèse's friend Yvonne to give Marie-Thérèse a little more animal company in this gentleman's desolate house. Marie-Thérèse was also carrying more than 1,000 francs in cash, the residue from her furniture sale.

Landru had to buy two single tickets, lacking the money for his usual return fare or the price of the cab at Houdan. Instead, they got off the train at either Garancières or Tacoignières, walking in damp, misty weather across country to the villa. Next morning, Marie-Thérèse was seen walking her adored griffons in the village, indifferent to the stares she attracted. Then she was gone.

***

Landru's memory was becoming more and more "rebellious", as he put it a few months later:

> I have reached a point where I am obliged to write down everything that I need to recall, even the smallest things. At certain moments, my life flows before me like a dream without it being possible for me to say if it really happened to me or another person. At other times the details come back to me

with a clarity and precision which make me suppose that the facts have just happened or, having lived another existence at another time in other places, I had died, and, coming back to life as another person, I had kept the memory.

Shortly after dealing with Marie-Thérèse, he found a blank page in his *carnet*. In his neatest handwriting, he drew up a list, trying to make his "rebellious" memory obey him. It read:

Cuchet, J. Idem
Brésil
Crozatier
Havre
Collomb
Babelay
Buisson
Jaume
Pascal
Marchadier

He left it there, since no one else came to mind.

***

Célestine Buisson's housemaid sister Marie Lacoste was back on Landru's trail. For more than a year, Marie had tried hard to put Célestine's disappearance out of her mind. In Marie's thinking, Célestine had gone off in a sulk, offended by Marie's correct assessment that her sister's fiancé was a fraudster. So be it, Marie told herself, as she made the beds and washed the dishes at her employer's house near the Rue du Rivoli.

In December 1918, Célestine's blind son Gaston dictated another letter to Marie from his home in Biarritz. Gaston explained that he had suffered a serious accident and needed to contact his mother, who had not replied when he had once again written to her. Could Aunt Marie try one last time to see if she could track down Célestine?

Marie went to the apartment near the Porte de Clignancourt where she supposed that Célestine was still living, either with or without her so-called fiancé. She was dismayed to learn from the concierge that Célestine had left in the summer of 1917 and never been seen since. The concierge added that not long after Célestine's departure, a younger woman (Fernande) had spent the night at the apartment with Mme Buisson's *monsieur*. He had then returned in October 1917 to hand in Mme Buisson's notice and clear her furniture.

Marie sensed that "Frémyet" might be worse than a swindler, perhaps even a murderer. She was so alarmed that she painstakingly prepared a dossier, containing all the information she knew about Célestine's relationship with "Frémyet". Despite her lack of education, Marie was a born sleuth. She described Landru's appearance, his sinister house at Gambais, his fleecing of Célestine, and his efforts to persuade Marie that her sister was still alive – in sum, everything the police might need to pursue and arrest this man.

On 11 January 1919, Marie took her dossier to a nearby police station, bringing along her fellow maid Laure Bonhoure, who remembered "Frémyet" very well. In Laure's considered opinion, the man looked downright fishy.

The officer who saw Marie and Laure said he could not help at all. He explained that Mlle Lacoste would need to direct her enquiry to the authorities in Gambais, where Mme Buisson had last been seen. It was not a matter for the Paris police.

Suppressing her fury, Marie dutifully wrote to the mayor of Gambais, Alexandre Tirlet, who repeated his obstructive performance of eighteen months earlier when Anna Collomb's sister Ryno had made an almost identical enquiry. With regret, Tirlet's secretary, the village schoolteacher François Bournérias, informed Marie that no man called "Frémyet" was known in the village.

At this moment, Tirlet had his little *crise de conscience* and ordered Bournérias to add Ryno's name and address, in case Marie wanted to compare notes with her.

***

Marie and Ryno were not natural comrades in arms; one, a lowly, unmarried *domestique* from southern France, the other a beautiful, recently married *Parisienne*. When the two women met in late January at Ryno's parents' apartment on Boulevard Voltaire, it took a while for Marie to feel at ease with this *bourgeois* family. What drew Marie and Ryno together was the similarity between their two sisters' disappearances and the brush-off they had both received from police and village officials.

Tellingly, Ryno did not put her name on the formal complaint about Anna's disappearance that her elderly father filed at the start of February in Mantes, the capital of Seine-et-Oise, where Gambais was located. Monsieur Moreau had played almost no part in Ryno's quest to find Anna. However, he had the priceless advantage of being a man and was therefore more likely to be taken seriously by the authorities than Ryno. Following up next day, Marie sent her own, handwritten complaint, copying much of the language from Moreau's lawsuit.

Ryno's use of her father as a frontman worked. The public prosecutor in Mantes opened two case files on Anna and Célestine and after a week, sent the dossiers to a police officer in Versailles who was charged with tracing missing persons. This detective then put the two complaints to one side until he had time to pursue them properly.

***

In Paris "Mlle L.", the factory girl who had faked her pregnancy, was pestering Landru again. She had just lost her job and kept calling at Rue de Rochechouart, demanding an increase in her allowance. If he was out, she took care not to reveal her identity to Fernande. When he was in, she would not budge from the landing until he slipped her some money to go away. He tried another tack, proposing that she come down to his country retreat for a nice, relaxing time. She declined his invitation. "He told me the house was isolated and I didn't like the sound of this adventure," she recalled tartly.

Mme Falque also kept appearing at Rue de Rochechouart, demanding that he repay her overdue loan, with full interest. On one occasion, Fernande answered the door when Landru was out and Mme Falque introduced herself by name, without explaining the nature of her business. On his return, Landru told the disbelieving Fernande that Mme Falque was his boss at police headquarters, come to discuss his latest top secret assignment.

He finally paid back Mme Falque in the middle of March, using some of his profit from his dealings with Marie-Thérèse Marchadier. Meanwhile in Houdan, the Collomb and Buisson case files had at last landed on the desk of Jules Hebbé, a mounted gendarme whose beat included Gambais.

On 14 March, Hebbé saddled his horse and set off along the road to Gambais to investigate the Collomb and Buisson cases. Hebbé's route took him straight past the Villa Tric but he did not stop, because he had no arrest warrant for the man known as "Dupont". Besides, Hebbé could see that the shuttered house was empty.

In Gambais, Hebbé interviewed the 73-year-old village constable, who did not realise that he had once seen Célestine at the villa, when he paid a call in the summer of 1917 to remind Dupont about a local tax he had not paid. Hebbé also interviewed the cobbler who was the part-time janitor at the villa; he said he barely knew Dupont. It was a similar story with the mayor, the schoolmaster and the grocer's wife. There seemed a general consensus in the village that the man was dodgy, often seen with women, and therefore might well be a spy.

All things considered, Hebbé thought the man sounded like a suspicious customer. "I could not tell you what happened in this house but there is something strange going on," he wrote in his report to the prosecutor in Mantes, 30 kilometres north of Gambais. Hebbé noted that he had ordered the constable in the village to alert the authorities the next time he saw Dupont.

Hebbé's report contained one detail whose significance he failed to recognise. In August 1917, when the constable had visited the Villa Tric to enquire about unpaid taxes, Landru had given the address of Célestine's apartment near the Porte de Clignancourt as his permanent residence. The prosecutor in Mantes noticed the same address in Marie's carefully assembled dossier and decided to refer the two cases back to Paris. They landed on the desk of Inspector Jules Belin of the Paris flying squad (*brigade mobile*).

***

At the age of 34, the unmarried Belin ate, drank and smoked the life of a full-time detective. Belin was a fan of Sherlock Holmes, whose adventures he had read in translation, and fancied himself as a similarly cerebral investigator. Where Holmes wore a deerstalker and puffed on a pipe, Belin favoured a crumpled Homburg hat and half-smoked cigarette, perched perilously on his lower lip. Yet unlike his fictional hero, Belin had a carefree relationship with facts.

Belin claimed in an internal police report that he visited Gambais and interviewed villagers about the dubious tenant at the Villa Tric. All the facts gleaned from these "interviews" came from Hebbé's report, while the "multiple and difficult researches" Belin said he had conducted in Paris were lifted almost entirely from Ryno and especially Marie's research.

On 4 April, while Belin pursued his desultory enquiry, the constable in Gambais failed to notice the arrival by car of Landru, Fernande and Landru's blond-haired "apprentice" turned chauffeur. They stayed one night, and then drove back to Paris.

By the afternoon of Friday, 11 April, Belin was obliged to concede that the trail had run cold. He did not know that Marie's friend and fellow maid Laure Bonhoure was about to crack open the case.

Laure had gone shopping that afternoon and was in a crockery shop on Rue de Rivoli when she spotted the man she knew as Frémyet at the counter, accompanied by a young woman. Quickly, Laure hid behind a display stand and watched the *monsieur* as he purchased a tea set, left his business card for home delivery, and walked out of the shop with his girlfriend. Laure followed the couple a few blocks west along the Rue de Rivoli to the Place du Châtelet, where the *monsieur* and his companion got onto a bus heading north towards Montmartre.

At the last moment Laure hopped on board, only to jump off again when Landru caught her eye. Convinced he had recognised her, Laure ran east along the Rue de Rivoli, past the Hôtel de Ville, and then north until she made it to Rue du Plâtre, gasping for breath, and relayed her news to Marie.

Marie had no confidence in Belin, who had interviewed her the previous week and made a poor impression. She did, however, have his phone number. Marie now called Belin, who went to the crockery shop, where the sales assistant retrieved the man's business card. It read: "Lucien Guillet, 76 Rue de Rochechouart". When Belin arrived at this address, the concierge confirmed that Guillet rented an apartment on the first floor.

Much later, Belin gave various explanations for why he did not proceed upstairs and arrest Landru on the spot. In one version, Belin said he learned from the concierge that "Guillet" and Mlle Segret had departed for their country villa. According to Belin, he had to wait three weeks to make the arrest. In reality, Belin needed an arrest warrant, which he collected next morning. Belin had not considered the possibility that Landru might leave the apartment before the detective returned to Rue de Rochechouart with two fellow officers as back-up. Yet this is exactly what happened.

At about 10.15 am on Saturday, 12 April 1919, 35-year-old Adrienne Deschamps was travelling on the metro between the Réamur and Opéra stations when she was accosted by a bearded man who introduced himself as Lucien Guillet. Adrienne was interested in Guillet's proposal but did not wish to continue their discussion in front of the other passengers. The two of them got off at Opéra where they carried on chatting for some time on the platform.

They fixed a rendezvous for the following Wednesday, outside Denfert-Rochereau metro station in southern Paris. Landru also gave Adrienne his fake name card, with the address of a room he rented near the Gare du Nord – the same lodging where he had taken the teenage nanny Andrée Babelay in the spring of 1917. His business done, Landru returned to Fernande at Rue de Rochechouart.

Belin subsequently gave two different times for Landru's arrest: 10.00 am and 11.00 am. However, if Adrienne's testimony was accurate, Landru could not have returned to the apartment before about 11.30 am. In all likelihood, Belin and his fellow detectives did not show up until almost midday, suggesting a distinct lack of urgency on their part. As far as Belin was concerned, he had come to arrest a run-of-the-mill marriage swindler, not a serial killer.

Eventually, Landru unlocked the door and the police officers barged in. Landru refused to answer any questions and demanded a lawyer. He also declined to produce any identity papers. Years later, Belin put out a story that Fernande chose this moment to collapse "stark naked on the floor". However, Belin did not mention this probably invented melodrama in his internal police report.

What is certain is that Landru and Fernande were brought back to Belin's police station on Rue Greffulhe, a quiet side street just south of Boulevard Haussmann. Here, Belin's commanding officer immediately took charge.

Commissioner Amédée Dautel sized up the silent suspect, dressed in a bowler hat and dull yellow tunic, and ordered him to empty his pockets.

PART TWO

THE
INVESTIGATION
April 1919 – November 1921

Chapter 9

The Enigma of Gambais

Item by item, Landru dumped his bits and pieces on the table: here a fake driver's licence in the name of "Chapelle"; there a blank identity document, waiting to be completed; here a couple of letters from women answering lonely hearts adverts. Dautel, 39, had seen plenty of marriage swindlers and this surly individual looked like another. Then Dautel came to a little black moleskin *carnet*.

He flicked through the notebook, trying to make sense of the jottings, until he reached the list of 11 names that Landru had written neatly on a clean page, seemingly in one sitting: "Cuchet, J. Idem, Brésil, Crozatier, Havre, Collomb, Babelay, Buisson, Jaume, Pascal, Marchadier".

Dautel deduced from "Collomb" and "Buisson" that the rest of the list referred to other women. He tried to get the silent suspect to explain the list but Landru calmly demanded a lawyer before he would speak, refusing even to confirm his name, which the officers still thought was Guillet.

Getting nowhere, Dautel decided to go back to Rue de Rochechouart with Belin to search the apartment more thoroughly, leaving Landru behind at the police station. In his own mind, Dautel mitigated this breach of the arrested man's rights by calling the search a "summary visit" and bringing the weeping Fernande along as a witness.

At the apartment, the detectives found a letter from Marie-Thérèse Marchadier, plus a patent application for an automobile radiator made out in the name of "Henri Landru". Back at Rue Greffulhe, a phone call to Paris police headquarters rapidly established that Landru had a string of convictions for fraud and should have been deported to New Caledonia.

It was now late afternoon. Landru was still mute, at times pretending to sleep, so Dautel switched his attention to Fernande. He could not stop her talking: on and on she rambled, about broken marriage vows, gifts of jewellery, the doubts of her mother, "mysterious meetings" with other women, and the day when "Lucien" administered ricin oil after she fell ill with food poisoning. Fernande gave Dautel plenty of sinister leads, but nothing to indicate that Landru was more than a petty crook. Even the ricin oil, lethal in large doses, was a commonly used laxative.

Dautel released Fernande without charge late on Saturday evening, when she was collected by her equally distressed mother. With Fernande off his hands, Dautel then made a reckless decision.

The few surviving photographs of Amédée Dautel show a thin man with a toothbrush moustache and worry lines on his forehead. He looks anxious and out of his depth and that is how he now behaved. Dautel sensed that he was circling a serial killer, easily the biggest case of his rather humdrum career to date. He also knew that time was running out to make a breakthrough, especially given Landru's obdurate silence. By noon on Sunday, 13 April, 24 hours after Landru's arrest, Dautel had to deliver the suspect to the public prosecutor's office in the town of Mantes, where Anna Collomb's father and Célestine Buisson's sister Marie had filed their complaints.

Without consulting his superiors, Dautel decided to transport Landru to Mantes via Gambais, in order to conduct a brief inspection of the Villa Tric. Dautel had no time to recruit any forensic experts for what he was careful to call a preliminary "survey" of the property, rather than an official "search". In reality, Dautel and Belin wanted a pretext that would allow them to find the bodies of Anna Collomb, Célestine Buisson and perhaps the other names on Landru's list, before the department of Seine-et-Oise took control of the case.

***

They began the "survey" just after 9.30 am on 13 April, watched by a trail of curious locals who had seen the small police convoy as it passed through Gambais and followed the cars up to the villa. Dautel had brought only half a dozen officers down from Paris and chose not to assign one of them to guard the front gates. As a result, the villagers were able to walk straight into the garden and even into the house.

Upstairs, Dautel told the handcuffed Landru to stand in one corner while he and Belin rummaged through the sparsely furnished bedrooms. They found nothing of interest. Downstairs, the two detectives spotted what they thought might be a tiny bloodstain on the kitchen wall above the oven. They peered inside the oven but saw nothing suspicious. Next, they descended to the cellar, where they identified another possible speck of dried blood on a wall.

Moving outside, Dautel ordered a rapid search of the enclosed kitchen garden at the rear of the villa. According to Dautel's subsequent report, Landru suddenly started to become agitated as the officers approached a patch of disturbed soil near the washhouse adjoining the kitchen. Dautel instructed some local men he had hired as diggers to get to work with their spades and they soon unearthed the strangled corpses of Marie-Thérèse Marchadier's three little griffon dogs.

At first, Landru pretended that the dogs had belonged to him. One of the diggers interrupted, saying he had seen a woman walking the dogs in the village only a few months before.

"Is this true?" Dautel asked Landru.

"The dogs belonged to a lady friend whose name I have to withhold," Landru replied primly. "She authorised me to put them to death."

In any case, it was no big deal, Landru continued nonchalantly, for he had also strangled a vicious stray cat he had found in the garden. Helpfully, he pointed at the spot where two years before he had buried Annette Pascal's pet angora Minette.

Dautel had no time to investigate this second grave or search the hangar and the locked sheds at the bottom of the main garden beyond the enclosure. Mantes lay 30 kilometres north of Gambais along poor country roads and Dautel was already cutting it fine to get to the prosecutor's office by noon. The police briefly inspected the garage by the villa, where they found Célestine's battered old trunk, with more of her initialled linen. Dautel then called off his "survey", reasoning that he could always come back and do a more thorough job once Landru had been formally charged.

Dautel was in such a hurry that he did not bother to attach official police seals to the property, as the law required. Instead he told Landru's guard to bundle the suspect back into one of the waiting cars, which sped off down the road to Mantes, leaving the onlookers to wonder what other macabre secrets might yet be discovered at the villa.

***

After the handover in Mantes, Dautel and Belin drove straight to the garage in the north-west Paris suburb of Clichy where Landru rented space.

They arrived at about 2.30 pm and finding the garage open, began searching through what initially looked like a pile of junk behind a dismantled automobile.

The two detectives soon uncovered an astounding trove of incriminating material, including identity documents matching several of the names on the list in Landru's *carnet*. Delving further, Dautel and Belin pulled out photographs of various women, cheap jewellery, dusty old petticoats, bloomers and chemises, a chestnut wig, a solitary denture, all stuffed together with dressing tables, chairs and various knick-knacks, as if for a jumble sale. Most sinister of all, they came across a length of knotted cord, perfect for strangling victims.

There were scores of letters from women replying to Landru's lonely hearts adverts, sorted according to his level of interest into different categories: "suspicion of fortune", "no money", "don't follow up", and so on. The detectives also found draft replies by Landru to his correspondents.

"Madame," one template began, "I have received your letter of XXX and thank you for the information that you have given me. Rest assured, whatever befalls these projects, of my absolute discretion..."

"Madame," Landru wrote, if the woman had sent her photograph, "There is indeed always a little curiosity on the part of a man, being able to appreciate the culture and education of *une personne amiable*, to become acquainted with her physical charms. Do I need to tell you that, in your case, they are all to your advantage and have only increased my desire to merit your esteem."

"Madame," he wrote, if a woman complained about not hearing from him, "Your little note of XXX has covered me in confusion in making me understand that I have been impolite in not responding immediately. Must I confess the truth? It would nonetheless give me pleasure; there was something about you that spoke to me of a gracious correspondent whose image I cannot forget."

As Dautel and Belin sifted through this correspondence, a slim youth with blond hair strolled into the garage. He saw the policemen and tried to bolt, but they grabbed him and asked for his name.

"Charles Frémyet", the young man stuttered, explaining that he worked as an apprentice for "Monsieur Frémyet". It did not take long for Dautel and Belin to get "Charles Frémyet" to change his story. He admitted to being Landru's youngest son Charles, aged 19, living with the rest of his father's family a few blocks away.

Charles's mother, "Mme Frémyet", was at home when her son arrived with Dautel and Belin. She was a dumpy woman in her early fifties with brown hair scraped back in a tight bun, the beginnings of a double chin and an air of being defeated by life. Seeing the detectives, she acknowledged that she was in reality Mme Marie-Catherine Landru, while insisting she had not seen her husband since before the war. Her 27-year-old daughter Marie, a laundress like Mme Landru, similarly disclaimed any knowledge of his activities, as did Marie's 22-year-old sister Suzanne, who lived with her fiancé on another floor in the same nondescript apartment block. Only 24-year-old Maurice, Charles's elder brother and a convicted swindler, was not at home because he was still waiting to be demobilised.

Disconcertingly for the detectives, it was common knowledge among the family's neighbours that "Monsieur Frémyet" was in trouble with the law. Furthermore, he had been seen visiting the family at irregular intervals, contrary to what Landru's wife had just said. Nobody in the *quartier* had felt the need to alert the authorities.

***

While Dautel tried to fathom this family of imposters, Landru was giving the authorities in Mantes the runaround. On Monday morning (14 April) he was brought from the town jail to the public prosecutor's office for his first formal interrogation. Under French law, criminal enquiries were led by an investigating magistrate (*"juge d'instruction"*), who weighed the evidence against a suspect to determine whether there was a case that would stand up in court.

One *juge d'instruction* immediately withdrew from the case, pleading illness. His replacement, a provincial magistrate called Rossignol, struggled to make any headway with Landru.

"Is it true that you have three or four country houses?" Rossignol asked inaccurately.

"I adore the countryside," Landru replied.

"A cheque book has been found showing that you deposited money in a bank near Chantilly. Why?"

"It's a business requirement."

"For what motive do you go by the name of Dupont in Gambais?"

"But I have many other names."

"What was the purpose of this piece of cord, carefully knotted, which was found in your garage at Clichy?"

"*Mais monsieur le juge,* one perhaps could find one of those at your house. It's simply a piece of twine."

"This jewellery, which belonged to women who were your mistresses, why was it in your possession?"

"Because I lent them money! The jewels were security."

"*Enfin,*" said Rossignol, "what has become of these women who have been sought for months?"

"*Ah! monsieur!*" Landru exclaimed, "does one ever know where women go after they leave you?"

A local lawyer had been temporarily assigned to represent Landru at this interrogation. Landru, however, had someone better in mind to act as his permanent defence counsel. Shortly after his interview with Rossignol, Landru wrote an urgent note, addressed to "Maître de Moro Giafferri, barrister at the Court, Paris." He scribbled:

> I will be obliged to you where appropriate to let me know if
> you will accept to take over my defence, before all jurisdictions
> where my current case may lead.
> Please accept, *monsieur*, my respectful assurances.

Landru did not include an address, but there was no need. He had just requested the services of the most famous lawyer in France.

Chapter 10

Why Would I Have Killed Them?

When he was seven or eight, Vincent de Moro Giafferri's parents took him one morning from their village on the northern tip of Corsica to watch his barrister uncle defending a client in court.

"My whole life has been illuminated by this spectacle," Moro recalled at the end of his illustrious career. "I saw the majesty of Justice, the reaction of the gallery, the unfurling of the witnesses, the pursuit of the truth... Above all, I saw the poor trapped devil whom everyone seemed to be trying to tear to pieces: in front of him, a black robe, protecting him, the symbol of humanity and pity: the robe that my uncle wore. My vocation was born on that day."

Moro (as everyone knew him) grew up to be a staggeringly precocious defence lawyer, called to the Paris Bar in 1898 at the age of only 20. He posed soon afterwards for a studio portrait, a slim, boyish figure with black curly hair and a troubadour's moustache, his clever eyes twinkling at the camera. Moro could have been a mere salon wit, straight out of the pages of Proust, especially after he married a beautiful Corsican heiress and developed a taste for fighting duels. What rescued Moro from absurdity was the moral passion he brought to his cases. He sought out the "wretches" who swarmed across *belle époque* Paris – pickpockets, swindlers, drunks, pimps, and thugs – convinced that justice had no meaning if it did not apply impartially to everyone.

Fellow barristers came to watch Moro defend these "indefensibles", marvelling at his ability to envelop even open-and-shut prosecution cases in clouds of doubt. To that end, Moro could be in turn eloquent, humorous, solemn, forensic, magisterial, chilly and warm, as he transfixed the twelve jurors sitting in judgement on his miserable clients. He almost always won. At the Palais de Justice in Paris, rival lawyers joked that Moro was on a one-man mission to make trial by jury pointless.

Moro's great cause was the abolition of the death penalty, which he regarded as an outrage against his abstract ideal of justice. "Let us decapitate the guillotine," Moro demanded in 1902, arguing that it was impossible to reverse the fall of the blade if the condemned criminal was subsequently found to be innocent.

Moro's hatred of capital punishment was crystallised by the case of Eugène Dieudonné, a peaceable young house decorator he defended in 1913 against a charge of attempting to murder a Paris bank messenger. Dieudonné was an anarchist, rounded up with a gang of bank robbers, some of whom professed anarchist tendencies. The gang swore that Dieudonné had nothing to do with them, and a friend of Dieudonné confirmed that they had met for a drink in the eastern city of Nancy on the day of the shooting near Paris's Gare du Nord. However, the investigating magistrate maintained that Dieudonné could have shot the bank courier at 9.00 am and then caught a train to Nancy in time to bump into his friend by chance on the street at 2.30 pm.

Dieudonné's wife Louise mounted a one-woman campaign to prove his innocence, even though the couple had been estranged because of his anarchist views about free love. "I love him even more now that he is overwhelmed by misfortune," she informed the press defiantly. Still the authorities persisted in charging Dieudonné.

"In pleading for Dieudonné, Maître de Moro Giafferri made tears flow," *Le Figaro* reported at the end of the trial. Despite Moro's eloquence, Dieudonné was sentenced to death, obliging Moro to appeal in person for clemency to the President of France, Raymond Poincaré. A former barrister, Poincaré was persuaded by Moro's arguments. Hours before Dieudonné's scheduled execution, Poincaré commuted the sentence to life imprisonment with hard labour in the French Caribbean colony of Guyane.

Before leaving France, Dieudonné insisted on divorcing Louise. He did not want the rest of her life to be ruined by his shadow, he told her; she needed to be free of him.

***

Moro certainly knew all about Landru by the time Landru's handwritten note arrived at the barrister's *cabinet* on Boulevard Saint-Germain. Within days of his arrest, Landru was all over the front pages, labelled the "Bluebeard of Gambais" after the mythical medieval French nobleman who had tricked and slaughtered his wives. One evening newspaper, *Bonsoir*, even suggested half-seriously that *l'affaire Landru* had been cooked up by the government to distract the public from its feeble performance at the Paris Peace Conference:

WHY WOULD I HAVE KILLED THEM?

Why the devil worry about war and peace, our admirable government insinuates. Occupy yourself with Landru, an astonishing, prodigious man.

Landru was in a sense Moro's dream client – the ultimate wretch, condemned by the press, requiring all Moro's formidable array of courtroom skills to escape the guillotine. Moro made it known to the press that he would defend Landru *pro bono*, but he then failed in his duty to Landru.

In April and early May 1919, Moro was fully engaged as defence counsel for Charles Humbert, an immensely rich businessman and politician who was accused by the army of taking "German" money during the war to fund his acquisition of the mass circulation daily *Le Journal*. Denied access to newspapers, Landru did not learn that Moro had agreed to represent him until the end of April, more than two weeks after his arrest. While Landru remained literally defenceless, the police and the judiciary raced to assemble a case that not even Moro could demolish.

***

On the morning of Tuesday, 15 April, three days after Landru's arrest, Gabriel Bonin, 40, stood in the back garden of The Lodge at Vernouillet and surveyed the site he was about to search. Plump and bald, with a sallow, unhealthy complexion, Bonin was a senior *juge d'instruction* in Paris, his investigative energies fuelled by the hand-rolled cigarettes that he chain-smoked all day.

The weather was blustery, with rain forecast later. Bonin decided nonetheless to start in the house, hoping it would remain dry for any excavation work outside. Dautel, Belin and a detachment of police officers were on hand, as was Dr Charles Paul, head of the Paris police laboratory, who had brought a team of forensic experts. Bonin noticed irritably that a clutch of reporters and photographers were also on the premises, tipped off about the search by police contacts and hoping to get their first sight of Landru. They were disappointed to hear that Bonin had decided to leave Landru at the town jail in Mantes – in strict law, a further breach of the suspect's rights.

Bonin and Paul rapidly realised that the chances of finding any usable forensic evidence at The Lodge were slim. It was more than four and a half years since Landru had lived at The Lodge and in the intervening period, a series of short-term tenants had tramped all over the property. The Lodge's latest tenant, a chirpy young widow called Mme Calendini, was enthralled by the thought of a mass murderer at large in her home, alerting Bonin to a particularly suspicious "subsidence" in the cellar. Yet as the morning continued, it gradually became clear even to Mme Calendini that the investigators had drawn a blank.

For form's sake, Paul took away a few charred scraps of rags from the ashes of an ancient bonfire at the end of the garden. Under the microscope at the Paris police laboratory, the material yielded nothing of interest. Bonin could have ordered the whole garden dug up, but his impatient eye saw nothing except overgrown grass and weeds.

After the search, Dautel went off to interview the neighbours, accompanied by the press. Monsieur Vallet, the local butcher, who lived at the foot of Rue de Mantes, had never seen or smelt nauseous smoke coming from a bonfire lit by Landru in the garden. Even so, Vallet continued, his wife and maid had assured him the stench was "frightful". Mme Vallet had nothing to add to her husband's observations.

Mme Picque, who lived on the uphill side of The Lodge, dimly recalled a man who looked like Landru living there in 1915 or 1916 with a woman and a youth. She remembered seeing another woman in the garden sometime later. As for the smoke, Mme Picque's memory failed her. "Everything was mysterious about this man and one supposed he must have been a spy," she remarked darkly.

Émile Mercier, 58, the local constable, remembered going to The Lodge after receiving complaints about the smoke. It would have been sometime in 1915 or 1916, Mercier said vaguely. He was only sure of one fact about this incident: It was a woman, not a man, who had popped her head out of an upstairs window and told him to buzz off; which he had, Mercier explained, seeing no reason to enquire further.

***

While Dautel was struggling to extract anything useful from the locals in Vernouillet, two far more promising witnesses had just surfaced in Paris. Jeanne Cuchet's sister Philomène and brother-in-law Georges Friedman had known Landru's identity since August 1914, when Jeanne and Georges had discovered his personal papers at the villa in La Chaussée. The Friedmans had also known that Landru was a convicted criminal, on the run from the law, following Philomène and Jeanne's visit to Landru's abandoned garage in the southern suburb of Malakoff. It seemed odd, therefore, that the Friedmans had stayed quiet throughout the war, rather than take their information about Landru to the police.

The Friedmans probably felt ashamed that Jeanne had eloped with a crook and fearful that she was now in serious legal trouble. But this was not the story Georges Friedman gave to the press on 15 April, the same day as the search in Vernouillet, when he and Philomène emerged from giving witness statements at Paris police headquarters. Friedman merely said that he and his wife had come forward after recognising Landru's photograph in that morning's edition of *Le Journal*.

The reporter from *Le Journal* wondered all the same why the Friedmans had not alerted the police in 1915 about the disappearance of Mme Cuchet and her son.

"I was mobilised and I have only just come back," Friedman replied. "My wife and I supposed that Mme Cuchet had become Mme Diard so we were not particularly worried."

Friedman blustered that he and Philomène were aware that Mme Cuchet had been "worth" about 100,000 francs (roughly 310,000 euros) and was therefore never going to be in need. Friedman's steer to the reporter was plain: Jeanne had been duped and then killed by a lethal marriage swindler.

***

Over the next week, other relatives and friends of the ten missing women on Landru's list approached the authorities with their stories. In Toulon, Annette Pascal's elder sister Louise Fauchet, her surrogate "*maman*", wrote directly to Bonin:

"I am in the most dreadful despair," Louise announced, "having already the agony of knowing her [Annette's] name is inscribed on the famous list of victims, I was more than a sister for her, I was a mother."

In Paris, Mme Colin, whose 19-year-old daughter Andrée Babelay had disappeared at Gambais two years before, was just as desperate for news. "My daughter Andrée had good morality and was full of respectful sentiments," Mme Colin told the police loyally, while conceding that her wayward teenager "was also a fantasist who loved change."

Day by day, the authorites were gathering more evidence of Landru's thefts from his fiancées, as police gradually located his network of garages and storage depots around Paris. He seemed more a human magpie than a systematic thief, stashing at random furniture, identity papers, wigs, hair clips, shoes and even André Cuchet's treasured propeller pen, a gift from his Aunt Philomène.

Bonin, meanwhile, was exasperated by a legal tug of war over Landru. The prosecutor in Mantes maintained that the department of Seine-et-Oise should take charge of the case because all the missing women had disappeared in its jurisdiction. It was obvious, though, that the local police and judiciary were out of their depth with Landru, who had just seen off a second investigating magistrate. Rossignol, the poorly briefed *juge d'instruction* in Mantes, had resigned immediately after his futile interrogation of Landru, pleading pressure of work.

On 24 April, the justice ministry formally appointed Bonin as *juge d'instruction* for the whole case, on the specious grounds that all the missing women had lived in Paris when Landru first met them. Bonin was appalled by Dautel and Belin's sloppy "survey" of the Villa Tric and failure to secure the property with official police seals, an error he immediately rectified. He now lobbied successfully for Brigadier Louis Riboulet of Paris's *police judiciare* to take charge of the enquiry in the French capital, leaving the smaller *brigade mobile*, led by Dautel and Belin, to focus on Vernouillet and Gambais.

It looked on paper like a neat geographical division of labour. Yet it soon became clear that Riboulet, Dautel and Belin had no intention of steering clear of each other's territory.

***

On Sunday, 27 April, in cloudy, cool weather, Riboulet drove down to Mantes with Belin and two other officers to collect Landru from the local prison and bring him back to Paris. Riboulet, 42, shared Belin's taste for Homburg hats and trench coats but was more of a dandy, with a waxed, twirly moustache and a penchant for tailored suits. Like Belin, Riboulet was also prone to fanciful deductions that were not always supported by facts.

Riboulet suggested they should offer Landru cigarettes on the return journey to put him at ease and encourage him to talk.

"Useless, he doesn't smoke," Belin retorted, putting Riboulet in his place.

Instead, they stopped on the way to buy a large box of chocolates, which both officers were confident would loosen Landru's tongue. First they had to extract Landru from the jail without the prisoner being lynched.

WHY WOULD I HAVE KILLED THEM?

All morning, the police in Mantes had tried in vain to clear a mob outside the prison gates, as news percolated down from Paris that Landru was about to be transferred. When Riboulet and Belin emerged with Landru – instantly recognisable in his bowler hat and grubby yellow tunic – the crowd surged forward past the police cordon. Landru ducked into the waiting police car, followed by his escort, and the driver hurtled off down the street, narrowly avoiding a hail of stones and rotten food.

Sitting in the back, Landru worked his way through the box of chocolates, with no evident change to his surly mood. He was not happy about his transfer, he grumbled; indeed, he would have been perfectly content to stay in Mantes until the police had rectified their obvious "error" in arresting him. That was all he had to say about his case. He spent the rest of the journey to Paris munching chocolates and gazing out of the window.

At 3.00 pm the car pulled up in front of the headquarters of the Paris police, an imposing three-storey edifice on the Île de la Cité. Landru got out and saw the photographers gathered on the forecourt.

"He walked hesitantly," *Le Journal* reported, "panicked by the flashing cameras aimed at him. He turned his head, raised his hand, shielded his eyes; he ended up by using a large red-check handkerchief to cover his face, which allowed one to see that he had a strong hand with a long, very splayed thumb, the criminal thumb observed by Lombroso [an Italian criminologist]."

***

Bonin and the police had carefully scripted the next few hours, determined to take advantage of Landru's lack of a defence counsel to provoke or trick him into a confession or at least some incriminating remark.

First, the desk sergeant informed Landru that he was being charged with the murders of all the missing women so far identified. This was a lie, because Bonin still had to establish whether Landru had a murder case to answer. Landru was outraged, demanding to make a formal statement. "Why would I have killed them?" Landru asked, since all the women had been his friends: "it seems certain that they have disappeared, but I am sure that you will find them."

Landru continued to harangue his opening interrogators, senior police commissioners Mouton of the *brigade mobile* and Tanguy of the *police judiciare*. "If I killed the women, one would find their corpses," Landru protested. "The fact of looking for these persons and not finding them does not indicate that they are dead."

In his fury, Landru got carried away. He explained that he had "invited" Jeanne and André Cuchet to Vernouillet in December 1914 in order to "rest". Jeanne had wanted to get a job in England, Landru said, while André had expressed a desire to enlist in the British army. Indeed, Landru went on, Jeanne had given him a British *poste restante* address.

Mouton pounced: "What was the address?"

Landru shrugged, realising his mistake. He could not remember, he said. All he knew was that he had written to Jeanne, who had never replied.

Tanguy and Mouton went through all the other nine names on the telltale list in Landru's *carnet*. Again and again, Landru refused to answer their questions, clearly aware of his right to remain silent. At 6.00 pm, the commissioners gave up. Now it was Bonin's turn to try to break Landru.

Bonin's bureau was situated in the adjacent Palais de Justice, at the other end of a maze of internal corridors. When Landru arrived, escorted by Riboulet and Belin, Bonin was sitting at his desk surrounded by fake Rodin sculptures, the booty from another enquiry into a counterfeit art scam. Bonin waved Landru to a seat and laboriously took down his name, age and most recent address, a piece of theatre designed to put the suspect on edge. Finally Bonin looked up.

"I don't want to interrogate you today," he announced briskly. "Have you chosen a defence lawyer?"

Landru said that he had written to "Maître de Moro Giafferri" but had not yet received a reply. No matter, Bonin said: today he and Landru were only going to have an informal "chat". Caught off guard, Landru relaxed enough to protest his innocence again to Bonin. He was especially offended by Tanguy and Mouton's "disgusting" slur that he might have sold the missing women into prostitution.

"I have never been engaged in that ignoble trade," Landru declared loftily.

He said nothing more for the best part of an hour, pretending to admire the fake Rodins as Bonin peppered him with questions. At about 7.00 pm, Bonin abandoned his attempt to coax an indiscretion out of Landru and tried another ploy. Riboulet and Belin took Landru to the police headquarters canteen, where he ate a hearty dinner while declining the offer of a carafe of wine. Landru told the officers that he rarely, if ever, drank alcohol, alive to this familiar police trick to loosen his tongue.

Next, Landru was escorted to a cell to digest his meal and invited to get some rest. For two hours he stayed rigidly awake, staring disdainfully at his guards.

WHY WOULD I HAVE KILLED THEM?

At 10.30 pm, he was abruptly summoned for a second interview with Tanguy, who got nothing more out of Landru. Shortly before midnight, Tanguy threw in the towel, ordering Belin and Riboulet to take Landru to the Santé, the city's main jail for prisoners on remand. So far, the full resources of the Paris police and judiciary had got no further with Landru than the prosecutor's office in Mantes.

***

Moro knew he had to get on Landru's case as soon as he heard about Bonin's "chat" with his client. He was fully occupied with the trial of Charles Humbert, the newspaper tycoon accused of treason, so on Tuesday, 29 April Moro despatched another lawyer in his *cabinet* to the Santé for an initial interview with Landru.

Auguste Navières du Treuil, 38, was a spruce, tidy man with a trim moustache that accurately expressed his punctilious character. Navières had spent most of the war in a German prisoner-of-war camp, an experience that had wrecked his health, and on this chilly spring morning, he was wearing his army greatcoat for extra warmth. When Landru was brought into the Santé's interview room, Navières felt the full force of his client's contemptuous glare. Landru was appalled; he had been expecting "*le grand Moro*", not this shivering milksop.

Navières decided to put Landru in his place: "I ended up by telling him that having commanded a company of soldiers under fire, I could withstand such staring perfectly well." Landru instantly softened, noting that he too had once been a *sous-officier*, so they were really comrades in arms.

"We parted on the best of terms," Navières recalled of this introductory meeting. "He offered to help me on with my coat and handed me my sword and cap. I left after giving him a military salute."

***

Unknown to Moro, Navières or Landru, Bonin had a few hours earlier begun a full-scale police and forensic investigation of the Villa Tric. Once again, Landru's legal right to witness a search of his property had been violated. In the absence of Landru or his defence counsel, the mayor of Gambais was in attendance, supposedly to "guarantee" Landru's rights. Other officials who deemed their presence essential included the two police commissioners Mouton and Tanguy, three senior Paris prosecutors and the prosecutor in Mantes, representing the department of Seine-et-Oise. Dautel and Belin were also on hand, largely to verify their cursory "survey" of the villa a fortnight before.

Bonin knew that if the searchers found evidence of murder, perhaps even corpses, there was only one member of the party whose opinion counted. Born in Boulogne, Dr Charles Paul, 40, was one of a new breed of forensic pathologists who exuded an aura of scientific infallibility in court. Paul's closest peer was his British contemporary Bernard Spilsbury, another masterful expert witness; but where Spilsbury was a lean ascetic loner, the bullishly built Paul was a team player, willing to share out the work at the Paris police laboratory he headed.

At Vernouillet, Paul had hung around with little to do. Now, like Bonin and the watching press, Paul was eager for the search to begin, because the Villa Tric was potentially a critical crime scene. Landru had rented the house for more than four years and had made his last visit less than a month before. Furthermore, even the hapless Dautel and Belin had found three strangled dogs – perhaps a sinister portent of human remains elsewhere on the property.

Inside the house, the journalists noted Landru's cheap, tattered print of the wolf and the lamb ("a symbol", *Le Figaro* thought), his makeshift kitchen table, his tin cutlery, his grimy blue apron, and his rickety little oven – the domestic *appareil* of a cheapskate. Dautel and Belin showed Dr Paul the tiny "blood stains" they had spotted on the kitchen and cellar walls. Paul ordered samples of these stains to be removed for closer inspection in the police laboratory, as well as scrapings of soot from the wall of the oven.

Outside in the kitchen enclosure, light rain drifted down as the diggers excavated the remains of Annette Pascal's cat Minette, whose grave had been identified a fortnight before by Landru. The search team moved on to the expansive, unkempt lawn beyond the enclosure, creeping methodically towards the open hangar and adjacent sheds at the far corner of the garden.

Inside the hangar, "in an angle at the back, a dark corner, there was a little pile of ashes and cinders mixed up with dead leaves," *Le Journal* reported:

> Everything was passed through a sieve and this is what was found: Debris from small calcified bone fragments, one of them appearing to be the phalanx of a toe; molten glass, hair

clips and pins; the remains of a whale-bone from a corset. All
of this was charred. Finally, there was a human tooth, a molar,
as proved by the four roots.

Dr Paul pronounced that the bone fragments were definitely of human
origin. Bonin had made his breakthrough, or so it appeared.

A few minutes later, Bonin called off the search for the day. It was
raining steadily, and having found the charred bone debris and women's
accessories, Bonin wanted to comb the whole property without journalists
and high-ups disrupting the operation.

Out of curiosity, rather than any serious suspicion, Bonin and Paul went
off to check the church and adjacent cemetery, a five-minute walk along the
road to Houdan. Here, the sexton "verified and affirmed" that Landru could
not possibly have buried any of his victims in the graveyard. "I know my
own digging style," the sexton stated authoritatively.

Bonin was sure the searchers would find more human remains in the villa's
garden when they returned next morning. He even remarked confidently on
the way back to the house that he expected to wrap up the whole case "in
less than three days". Yet over the next week, while the police found many
animal bone fragments scattered around the property, no further human
debris was uncovered. As *Le Figaro* observed drily, one toe bone did not
seem much to brag about in a murder case that officially numbered "eleven
entire corpses".

There was another conundrum that Bonin had hardly begun to address:
Was Landru a lone serial killer or did he have accomplices? And might
those accomplices be his wife and four children?

Chapter 11

I Will Tell You Something Horrible

"So," Mme Landru declared, "people want me to give my defence. It appears they accuse me… It's a confession, then, that I'm going to give you," she told the reporter from *Le Journal*.

It was 20 May 1919, a fortnight after her first police interrogation, and Marie-Catherine Landru was ready to set the record straight at the family's apartment in Clichy.

"Landru's wife, the great culprit, is going to tell you the story of her life. People can judge for themselves."

Her story was true in parts. It was also incomplete and broke off just at the point where she risked incriminating herself and her four children.

She was born in 1868 near Strasbourg, the eldest daughter of a working-class couple who moved to Paris in 1871 at the end of the Franco-Prussian War. The Rémys settled on the Île Saint-Louis in central Paris, worshipping *en famille* at the local parish church.

One Sunday morning, when she was 19, Marie-Catherine's eye wandered during Mass. It fell on a young sub-deacon with a "fine bearing and discreet demeanour… We got talking as we were leaving church and so my love story began."

Henri Désiré Landru, born in 1869, grew up on the adjacent Île de la Cité, opposite the Cathedral of Notre-Dame. His mother took in laundry while his father was a furnace stoker at a tool factory, a skilled industrial job. Landru had one elder sister, Florentine, born in 1862.

Like the Rémys, the Landrus were ardent Catholics and when their son was five they sent him to the nearby church school on the Île Saint-Louis. He soon became an altar boy, graduating in his late teens to sub-deacon, a secular post where he helped the priest on with his vestments, lit candles and performed other tasks around the church.

In 1887, when Marie-Catherine first met Landru, he had just started work as an architect's clerk, drafting letters and sometimes copying designs for clients. Two years later, he got her pregnant with their first, illegitimate daughter Marie, a mildly embarrassing detail that Marie-Catherine did not reveal to *Le Journal*. A few months after Marie's birth, Landru left Paris to perform his obligatory military service in the northern town of Saint-Quentin, close to the Belgian border. Still unmarried, Marie-Catherine remained with the baby at her parents' home in Paris, making ends meet as a laundress while seeing Landru from time to time when he came back on military leave.

In his 1889 novel *Sous-Offs* (slang for *sous-officiers*), the author Lucien Desclaves described the brutal all-male culture of barracks life, based on his own experience of military service in Le Havre. The hero, a Parisian bank clerk, is robbed on his first night in the conscripts' dormitory by another soldier, the prelude to a procession of crooks, blackmailers and sadistic sergeants who prey on the new recruits.

Landru thrived in this criminalised environment during his three years in Saint-Quentin. He was promoted twice, from private to adjutant (*sous-officier*) and then to deputy-quartermaster, a position that taught him basic accounting and bookkeeping. He was so well-liked by his superiors that he even gained an early discharge in the autumn of 1893, on the specious medical grounds that he was suffering from sunburn. The real reason, not mentioned by Marie-Catherine to *Le Journal*, was that he needed to marry her quickly, because she was pregnant with their second child.

Maurice was born in May 1894, seven months after the wedding, followed by Suzanne in 1896 and Charles in 1900. For the benefit of *Le Journal*, Marie-Catherine described Landru during these years as a "model husband" and father, "gentle and caring", a reliable breadwinner. Yet in her police interview, she had complained sourly that Landru was always "a skirt chaser", from the very start of the marriage.

"Mme Landru collected her memories for a moment," *Le Journal*'s man observed. "She resumed in a shaky, nervous voice."

Landru's character gradually altered, she said. "He invented machines, he didn't sleep anymore," as he poured their savings into fantastic projects that he promised would make them rich. "He invented a motorbike and exhibited it and registered a patent, but others stole his idea." Next, mechanical dolls; once again he was ripped off "by people who deceived him".

She slid past the fact that it was Landru, not his alleged "deceivers", who was acquiring a police record. In 1898 he designed and exhibited a primitive motorbike, called "La Landru", at a machinery show in the Tuileries gardens. He then duped a group of gullible investors into advancing him funds to build a factory to manufacture the motorcycle. Having pocketed the money, Landru vanished.

"Soon the police called at my home," Marie-Catherine carried on. "They were looking for my husband; he had stolen, pulled off a swindle! I thought I was going mad; I couldn't believe it."

Between 1900 and 1904 Landru was constantly on the run from the police, spending a year in Le Havre when it got too hot for him in Paris. His luck ran out in early 1904 when he fell in the street while fleeing a bank in central Paris he had just tried to defraud. He was charged with multiple offences, dating back to the motorbike scam, and remanded in custody at the Santé.

So far, Landru seemed an oddity; a reasonably well-educated, inventive man from a decent working-class family who had chosen to become an incompetent petty crook. His strange downhill journey now took him into darker territory.

Shortly after Landru's arrival at the Santé, a guard entered his cell and found him standing on a chair, apparently poised to slip his head through a noose made from his sheet. Landru meekly handed the noose to the guard and stepped off the chair. It looked like a fake suicide attempt, staged by Landru to secure his release on medical grounds. As Landru probably intended, the prison authorities summoned a psychiatrist to assess his mental state.

Dr Charles Vallon, director of the nearby Sainte-Anne asylum, made an ambivalent diagnosis. Vallon observed that at times Landru behaved like a typical swindler, rueing the "misunderstandings" that had led to his arrest. On other occasions, Landru exhibited signs of depression and was not entirely rational. Hedging his opinion, Vallon concluded that Landru was "on the frontiers of madness, but had not yet crossed them".

Vallon's tentative report failed to satisfy the court, which wanted clearer guidance about whether Landru was mentally fit to stand trial. Two other eminent psychiatrists, Dr Joseph Rogues de Fursac and Dr Jacques Roubinovitch, examined Landru and concurred with Vallon. They decided that Landru was on the threshold of insanity, with diminished responsibility; like Vallon, they thought Landru should be treated leniently by the court.

At the trial that followed, Landru's lawyer argued that his client was gripped by an irrational "mania for invention" and had lost "all sense of responsibility for his actions", as he tried to raise funds by any means for his projects. He was obviously a bit unhinged, Landru's counsel argued. The judge preferred to see Landru as just another lowlife, sentencing him to two years in jail at a prison near Paris.

Something about Landru troubled Dr Vallon. After the trial, he wrote to Marie-Catherine, asking her to come to see him at his asylum. Vallon warned her that while he thought Landru was still sane, he could not answer for her husband's actions in future.

"Thus was I threatened with a husband who was a madman," Marie-Catherine told *Le Journal*. "What was I to do? Should I abandon this unhappy man completely? He was the father of my children."

According to Marie-Catherine, she spent the next miserable decade working as a laundress and wine shop manager, living with her children in a series of cheap lodgings in and around Paris. "I had to provide for my four poor little ones," she said, because Landru was in and out of jail for yet more frauds and thefts. On his rare visits home he scrounged off his family, "eating up" the 3,000 francs that Marie-Catherine had saved.

She did not tell *Le Journal* about the worst episode of all. At 9.00 am on 23 April 1912, a passer-by stumbled across an old man hanging from a tree branch on the eastern edge of the Bois de Boulogne. He was Landru's widowed father, Julien Landru, who had killed himself in despair at his son's criminality; or so Marie-Catherine told the police. Landru missed the funeral, because he was in the middle of a three-year prison sentence for a failed marriage swindle in Lille.

In the autumn of 1912 Landru was released from jail and returned home. He soon got his hands on the substantial legacy of around 12,000 francs that his father had pointedly left to Marie-Catherine and her children, not him.

At this moment, as her narrative approached the outbreak of war, Marie-Catherine broke down. She knew nothing of Landru's activities after 1914, she sobbed, absolutely nothing:

"The unhappy woman rose tragically to her feet, panting for breath, and cried out: 'I am going to tell you something horrible. I have suffered too much. My children are in so much pain. It can't go on, it can't go on!'

"And the poor haggard creature collapsed on a chair, murmuring: 'God, will he not have pity?'"

***

I WILL TELL YOU SOMETHING HORRIBLE

Over the next few months, the investigation would establish the following facts:

- July 1914: Marie-Catherine spent a week in Le Havre with Landru, thereby ensuring she could not appear as a witness at his trial in Paris for swindling.

- August 1914 – spring 1915: Landru billeted his family in a village in Normandy and then in the town of Ézy-sur-Eure, west of Paris. They lived for some of this period under a false name.

- Winter 1914–15: Landru summoned his youngest son Charles to Vernouillet to assist with unspecified "gardening work" at The Lodge.

- Spring 1915: The family moved to Paris and then Clichy. Marie-Catherine and all her children apart from Maurice lived for the rest of the war under the false name "Frémyet".

- October 1915: Maurice Landru, mobilised under his real name, was sentenced by court martial to three years in jail for various swindles and thefts. The police found Maurice in possession of jewellery and valuables that had belonged to Jeanne Cuchet, the seamstress who had vanished with her son André.

- January 1917: Following his early release from jail, Maurice assisted Landru in concocting a cover story to explain the recent disappearance of the typist Anna Collomb. Maurice repaid a small debt Anna owed to a friend who ran a wine shop in Paris. He said he had met Anna by chance with a bearded man at a hotel south of Lyon.

- January 1917: On his father's instructions, Charles Landru placed a basket of flowers with Anna Collomb's *carte de visite* outside her family's apartment on Boulevard Voltaire. The present was designed to fool Anna's family into believing that she was in southern France.

- August 1917: Landru's eldest daughter Marie bid anonymously on his behalf at a property auction in Gambais for a house located deep in the forest near the village. Marie left the auction when the bidding exceeded Landru's maximum price.

- September 1917: Posing as the widowed housekeeper Célestine Buisson, Marie-Catherine visited Célestine's bank in central Paris with Landru. She forged Célestine's signature, allowing Landru to withdraw Célestine's savings.

- November 1917: Posing as the dress shop assistant Louise Jaume, Marie-Catherine visited another bank in Paris with Landru. In the event, Landru was able to withdraw Louise's money without Marie-Catherine needing to forge Louise's signature.

- 1915–19: Posing as Landru's "apprentice", Charles Landru assisted his father in removing and storing the furniture and possessions of Jeanne Cuchet, Thérèse Laborde-Line, Marie-Angélique Guillin, Anna Collomb, Louise Jaume, Annette Pascal and Marie-Thérèse Marchadier.

***

Bonin only had some of this information when Marie-Cathérine gave her interview to *Le Journal* in May 1919. Rather than haul her in again, Bonin chose to let Landru's wife stew for a while, as he focused on her husband. By the third week of May, Bonin was ready to interrogate Landru. Landru, on the other hand, was not yet ready to be interrogated.

He was off his food, Landru told the prison doctor at the Santé, and generally out of sorts: moody, tired, irritable, that kind of thing. The doctor thought Landru might be depressed. Bonin despatched Dr Paul, a forensic pathologist, to the Santé to offer a second opinion. Paul returned from the prison with the answer Bonin required: in Paul's view, Landru was mentally fit to face his first formal interrogation by Bonin.

Landru rose early on Tuesday, 27 May, feeling buoyant. He had banished the blues and was looking forward to his appointment after lunch with "Maître Bonin", he told his guard. The main point was to look smart for the occasion. He chose his best grey suit and black woollen bicycling cap, a large pink handkerchief, and a white cotton chemise in place of his coarse prison shirt. To Landru's annoyance, his prison escort made him remove his shoelaces to stop him running away.

Landru crumpled as soon as he arrived at the Palais de Justice and saw the photographers gathered in the courtyard, ready to snap him. He covered his face with his handkerchief and shuffled into the building, pursued by a scrum of reporters, all the way up the stairs and along the corridor to Bonin's door. Navières was waiting for him, but Moro was delayed. Worse for Landru, Bonin deliberately made Landru and Navières sit outside his office for several minutes while the press crowded around the "Bluebeard of Gambais".

"Landru made himself small, as he submitted to an assault by camera lenses and magnesium smoke," *Le Journal* reported. "Soon the magnesium fumes made it almost impossible to breathe in the corridor. Landru began to cough uncontrollably and his eyes filled with tears."

At last, Bonin summoned Landru and Navières into his *cabinet*. Bonin began by slowly reading out the eleven suspected murder cases, in order:

At Vernouillet:
Jeanne and André Cuchet (January/February 1915)
Thérèse Laborde-Line (June 1915)
Marie-Angélique Guillin (July 1915)

At Gambais:
Berthe Héon (December 1915)
Anna Collomb (December 1916)
Andrée Babelay (April 1917)
Célestine Buisson (September 1917)
Louise Jaume (November 1917)
Annette Pascal (April 1918)
Marie-Thérèse Marchadier (January 1919).

"What do you have to say in reply?" Bonin asked Landru.

"But nothing, absolutely nothing, *monsieur*," Landru answered serenely. "It's for you to prove the deeds of which I'm accused. I am innocent of all the charges."

Bonin tried to unsettle Landru by starting with Marie-Thérèse Marchadier, the last of his presumed victims. He asked Landru about his killing of her dogs, his clearance of her apartment, his reason for bringing her to Gambais. Each time, Landru replied "*oui*" or "*non*" or refused to answer at all.

Bonin turned to the charred bone debris beneath the pile of leaves in the hangar at the Villa Tric.

"I have not killed anyone," Landru observed irrelevantly. "What do you want me to say?"

"You won't give me a proper reply because you can't."

"I have nothing to say to that."

Bonin was in a weaker position on the bone debris than he cared to reveal, because Dr Paul had yet to find any pelvic fragments, the only way to confirm whether the original skeletons had been female. Unhelpfully, Paul calculated that about two-thirds of the debris, measured by weight, was of animal origin.

At this moment, Moro swept into Bonin's *cabinet*, apologising profusely to Bonin, Navières and Landru for his late arrival. Moro kept quiet while Bonin asked a couple more questions and then Landru's star counsel made his first intervention in the case.

The defence had "grave reservations" about Dautel's search of the Villa Tric on 13 April, before the property had been sealed, Moro declared. Furthermore, as a matter of urgency, the defence required casts of each individual bone fragment found in the hangar, with a view to allowing "certain experiments". Bonin and Moro both knew that most of the fragments were far too small to be set in a mould. That was Moro's point; in the defence's considered view, the debris was worthless as forensic evidence.

Bonin ended his interrogation before Moro could disrupt it any further with more time-consuming requests. Moro, however, was not finished.

As Landru shuffled away down the corridor in his unlaced shoes, handcuffed to a prison guard, Moro suddenly raised his arm. *"Pardon!"* he barked at the press: Moro wished to share an important observation with them. He could not reveal what Landru had told Bonin and yet here was something remarkable, Moro said. Normally, a person displayed their emotions by blinking or fluttering their eyelids:

"Now, Landru's eyelids did not move at all. He looked straight in front of him, his eyes wide open, or if he lowered his head, he did not lower his eyes. This immobility of the eyelids, this *insensibilité*, is significant."

Moro would take no questions on the matter; client confidentiality prevented him. He and Navières proceeded down the corridor, leaving the journalists to ponder – as Moro intended – whether Landru was mentally fit for anything other than a lunatic asylum.

***

One reason Bonin did not begin his interrogation of Landru with Jeanne Cuchet, the first fiancée to disappear, was because her case was proving so problematic. It was clear that Jeanne's brother-in-law Georges Friedman was either lying or ignorant when he claimed she had been "worth" about 100,000 francs. Even Friedman's wife Philomène declined to corroborate this figure.

Instead, Philomène said she knew little about her sister's finances but supposed that Jeanne must have possessed "*une aisance*" (literally "an affluence").

Jeanne's other brother-in-law, Louis Germain, married to her late husband's sister, ventured that Jeanne had been worth between 40,000 and 50,000 francs, once all her furniture and linen was included. However, Germain said he could not "certify" this information because Jeanne did not keep him informed about her affairs.

By contrast, two well-placed witnesses confirmed that Jeanne had been almost broke by the time she met Landru. When Jeanne's husband Martin died in 1909, her friend and probable lover Pierre Capdevieille, a shirtmaker by trade, had found her the job making *lingerie fine* for a dress shop and had fixed André's apprenticeship at the "Fashionable House" shirt factory. Capdevielle knew that Martin Cuchet had left Jeanne nothing because he was one of the administrators of Cuchet's will. Three years later, Capdevieille had liquidated Jeanne's last investment apart from a few municipal bonds so she could pay the rent on her apartment on Rue du Faubourg Saint-Denis. Jeanne's finances had been "far from brilliant", Capdevieille told the police laconically.

Jeanne's friend Mme Louise Bazire was able to corroborate Capdevieille's testimony because her husband had also been an administrator of Martin Cuchet's will. Mme Bazire remembered how Jeanne had been so poor after Cuchet's death that she had been forced to borrow 1,000 francs.

In addition, Jeanne's former employer, the dress shop manager Monsieur Folvary, confirmed on less authority that Jeanne had "very few savings".

Bonin's theory that Landru had killed Jeanne once he had stolen her assets collided with another inconvenient fact. In the spring of 1914, when Landru left Paris with Jeanne for the village of La Chaussée, he was loaded with cash. In total, Landru had reaped 35,600 francs from his latest swindle, easily the most successful fraud of his career. On top of this loot, Landru still had most of the 12,000 francs that his father had wanted to leave to Marie-Catherine and her children. He was rich, while Jeanne was poor.

The difficulties got worse for Bonin, because as Landru's first alleged victim, Jeanne was supposed to serve as the template for all the "identical" murders that followed. Yet in the most literal sense, Jeanne's case did not add up.

***

All through the summer of 1919, Bonin hammered away at his maddeningly uncooperative suspect, who shuttled back and forth between his cell at the Santé and the Palais de Justice. Moro initially attended these grinding interrogations, "but little by little he realised that our client's system of defence was invariable," recalled Navières, who acted as Landru's minder.

One day in late July, Bonin concealed Jeanne Cuchet's sister Philomène and Philomène's husband Georges Friedman in a neighbouring cubicle where they could hear his questioning of Landru. Bonin tried to lure Landru into telling a lie about the Friedmans, which they would then be able to refute, after bursting out of their hiding place like characters in a Feydeau farce.

"I have nothing to reply and I will not reply, because I do not want to reply," Landru stated, retreating into his customary silence. The Friedmans stayed put in their hidey-hole.

At another session, Bonin tried to terrify Landru into admitting his guilt.

"Landru, if you carry on with such a system of defence you will be sentenced to death and guillotined," Bonin warned. "Do you hear me – guillotined!"

"*Monsieur le juge d'instruction*, let us be serious," Landru said calmly. "You say I will be sentenced to death, but you are also condemned to death, the clerk is condemned to death, the guard who keeps watch on me is condemned to death, Maître Navières is condemned to death, as well as poor old Landru, *monsieur le juge*."

Landru's 25-year-old son Maurice, suave and slim, with a wispy blond moustache, provided further torment for Bonin and the police. Maurice was at ease with the undeniable truth that he had sold some of Jeanne Cuchet's jewellery in the autumn of 1915. He had had no idea of their origin when his father gave Jeanne's valuables to him, Maurice said nonchalantly. Indeed, now that he thought about it, he had never heard of Mme Cuchet until his father's arrest. On balance, Maurice had assumed the jewellery must be some kind of family heirloom, handed down to his father.

Maurice found it harder to explain why, in January 1917, he had paid off Anna Collomb's small debt to her friend who ran a liquor store, after claiming that he had met Anna by chance in southern France. At first Maurice pretended he could not remember this transaction. His interrogator, Commissioner Tanguy, asked the question again with sufficient verbal or physical force that Maurice suddenly got his memory back.

"He [Landru] gave me a package and a 20 franc note, telling me to take the package to a nearby wine shop which he pointed out to me. He explained that there was a sum to pay for a woman whom I should say I had met in Valence."

Why had Maurice lied for his father?

Maurice regretted that he could not recall anything more about the incident.

**

By the end of July, Bonin was desperate to get away with his wife and children for his annual summer vacation in Corrèze, the small rural department in southern France where he had been born. This year, Bonin had particular reason to spend time in Corrèze because he was a candidate in the parliamentary elections scheduled for the autumn. Landru would not let him go, blocking all Bonin's efforts to get to the bottom of *l'affaire Cuchet* and move on to the other nine missing fiancées.

On 6 August, Bonin accused Landru of stealing Jeanne Cuchet's identity documents.

"All of that is of no interest to me," Landru said loftily. "I am innocent, it's for you to produce the proof of my crimes."

A week later, a hot, sticky day, Bonin summoned Landru's wife for further questioning.

"The poor woman acknowledged – it had been her birthday! – that one day her husband had given her some jewellery," *Le Journal* reported. "She has since learnt that the jewels belonged to Mme Cuchet. She was unaware of their provenance, she is sorry."

Bonin dismissed Marie-Catherine and called for Landru, who did not know that his wife had just been interviewed.

"*Bonjour, monsieur le juge*, you can see I'm quite overwhelmed by this heat," Landru said cheerily. "It feels like I've got a ring of lead squeezing my head; really, I'm amazed you want to question me in this weather."

Landru was not in the mood to discuss the Cuchets; he was sorry, but given the weather, he just did not feel like it. Bonin turned to Thérèse Laborde-Line, the next woman on Landru's list.

"Why did you give her the codename '*Brésil*'?"

"I have nothing to say."

"How did you make her acquaintance?"

"I don't know."

"Was it through a lonely hearts advert?"

"It's possible."

Bonin picked up Landru's *carnet* and flicked through the pages, noting half a dozen occasions in the spring and early summer of 1915 when Landru had visited "*Brésil*" at her sixth-floor apartment on Rue de Patay.

"She lived much too high up!" Landru exclaimed. "Can you believe what it was like to go up those stairs? *Moi*, I had a horror of it. Just put down that I went there four times and leave it there," he instructed Bonin.

Another week passed. Still trapped with Landru in his stifling *cabinet*, Bonin could bear it no more.

"I'm sick of you!" Bonin yelled at Landru, his voice echoing down the empty corridors of the Palais de Justice. "You constantly interrupt me and when I ask questions you just say 'yes' or 'no' or refuse to answer at all. You're making a fool of me."

"Try not to get so cross," Landru advised Bonin.

***

From all directions, complaints landed on Bonin's desk about the slow progress of his enquiry.

"*Monsieur*," Annette Pascal's elder sister Louise Fauchet wrote from Toulon, "very astonished to have received nothing about my deposition on the subject of *l'affaire Landru*, my sister Mme Pascal being one of the victims; would it be indiscreet on my part to ask you for some information about the case and what was the result of my deposition I believe myself to have the right to know for it was me who raised my sister and I was a mother to her."

Louise's daughter Marie-Jeanne realised better than her mother that Bonin urgently needed hard evidence of Landru's murders. Unfortunately, Marie-Jeanne had never visited the Villa Tric, where Annette had disappeared. All Marie-Jeanne could offer, following a request from Bonin, was a detailed inventory of Annette's possessions:

> A Passos brand sewing machine carrying the name of the sales agent, Chastel... a size 42 tailor's dummy, very worn, lent to her by the *maison* for which she made fashion items... an old mirror, medium size... lingerie *fantaisiste*... a *chemise de jour*... a garnet-red satin-covered armchair embroidered with baskets of flowers... some lovely new bathroom towels...

"If anything else comes to mind, I will make haste to let you know," Marie-Jeanne signed off helpfully.

Other letters in Bonin's postbag were a reminder of the agony *l'affaire Landru* was causing an untold number of women across France.

The recently married Mme Zeegers wrote from the Paris suburb of Villemomble to explain why it was not necessary for Bonin to interview her. The discovery of her name in Landru's files was misleading, she said:

"Six years ago, I believe, one of my friends asked me if I would be willing to receive her correspondence concerning certain matrimonial projects and to forward it to her… On one occasion I received a letter which I believed was for her, but which was personally addressed to me, in a very poetic, sentimental style and with a certain elevation in the thoughts and feelings expressed."

Mme Zeegers admitted that she had replied to Landru's letter, "but it was the only one I ever sent him… As you can see, *monsieur le juge*, I have nothing, absolutely nothing, to communicate to you that could possibly be useful to the case."

Mlle Dutru, a 41-year-old spinster, wrote to Bonin from her home village near Fontainebleau, south of Paris. She had also been asked to testify about her correspondence with Landru.

"Please do not give my name or my deposition to the press," Mlle Dutru pleaded. "I have committed no crime, it is very common these days for women to seek a home by this means [lonely hearts adverts]… I have always lived so discreetly and quietly that I dread this kind of publicity for all the hurt it can create for me in future and for my elderly parents (80 years old) who live so peacefully and in such esteem in a little village in Burgundy, as well as my sister, a war widow and mother of five children who is completely unaware of this affair…"

Mme Benoist, an elderly widow, wrote to Bonin from Marseille to enquire about her daughter, who had gone missing some years ago. The old lady had never given up hope that she would find her daughter again, and "perhaps this time I will have more luck." Finally, Mme Benoist steeled herself to ask the terrible question: "I am desperate, my poor daughter, has she been identified?"

From Ecrouves, a small town in eastern France, Mme Romelot wrote to the prosecutor in Versailles, who forwarded her letter to Bonin. "The Landru case has interested me to a high degree for a certain time," Mme Romelot began circuitously. She explained that in April 1916, a man describing himself as an engineer in the army had "captivated" her daughter

Marie-Louise. The man had asked Mme Romelot for permission to marry Marie-Louise, but she had refused. "One day, the 10th August, *exactement*, my daughter disappeared and I never saw this famous engineer again."

Mme Romelot finally got to the point. She had seen a picture of Landru in a newspaper and was struck by his similarity with the engineer. "I would be very happy if some light was shed on my unhappy anxiety," she said. Mme Romelot attached a photograph of Marie-Louise before she was led astray: a plump young woman in a dark bonnet and buckled raincoat, handbag clutched tightly to her waist, staring dolefully at the camera.

Chapter 12

Conscience Recoils Before Such a Monster

Mme Romelot's nightmare went on display in the summer of 1919 at the Musée Grevin, a waxwork gallery on Boulevard Montmartre. In the Chamber of Horrors, the Bluebeard of Gambais stood next to the nineteenth-century serial killers Joseph Vacher, known as "the French Ripper", and Jean-Baptiste Troppmann, who had slaughtered eight members of the same family. Unlike Vacher and Troppmann, Landru had been judged but not yet tried.

The real Landru passed his days at the Santé reading popular novels, discussing his case with Navières and fretting about real or imagined ailments. At the end of August Landru wrote to Bonin to remind him about Dr Vallon's conclusion in 1904 that he stood on "the frontiers of madness" and to request another psychiatric examination.

Bonin could see where this was heading: on Moro's advice, Landru wanted to escape justice by getting himself committed to an asylum. In response, Bonin commissioned the three original psychiatrists who had seen Landru in 1904, Vallon, Roubinovitch and Rogues de Fursac, to examine him again.

At the psychiatrists' request, Landru wrote a lengthy "autobiographical note", which was mostly a catalogue of his many illnesses and injuries. As a little boy, he had smashed his head against the angle of a chimney breast and though the wound had healed, it still periodically gave him "quite a lot of pain". At the age of 20, during his military service, Landru had been knocked unconscious by a bad fall on a route march.

A few years later, he had suffered an attack of paralysis down the left side of his body, a case of such interest to the doctors at the hospital that they had made "numerous studies, observations and charts" and prepared "a special report". Finally in 1913, "I was on my back beneath a car I was repairing – the wheel had been removed – when following on from this fact the prop gave way and the car fell onto my head." Fortunately, Landru wrote, the impact had been partly reduced by other parts of the car hitting the ground first.

Landru then mused about his increasingly "rebellious" memory and the way his past life flowed before him "like a dream", as if it had been lived by a completely different person. He may have written more, but at this juncture the psychiatrists cut the text they eventually published.

Vallon, Roubinovitch and Rogues de Fursac showed no urgency in drafting their report, which would determine whether Landru was mentally fit to stand trial. Nor is there any surviving record of Bonin pressing the psychiatrists to rule whether Landru was insane. It was as if Bonin hoped the issue would go away of its own accord.

***

At the start of November, Bonin interrogated Landru's youngest son Charles, still only 19. Bonin wanted to know why, shortly after Anna Collomb's disappearance in December 1916, Charles had delivered a basket of flowers, purportedly sent by Anna, to the door of her parents' apartment.

Unlike his self-assured elder brother Maurice, Charles betrayed his nerves whenever the police or Bonin questioned him. He stuttered to Bonin that he barely remembered the package, which he only had in his hands "for a few moments". According to Charles, he had no idea about the purpose of his assignment.

Bonin brought in Landru, who was being held in an adjacent room. Why had he used Charles to help make Anna's family think she was in southern France?

"I had reasons which I do not wish to make known," Landru stated.

***

It was seven months since Bonin had forecast he would "wrap up" the case in days and he was now a national object of ridicule. At the parliamentary election in late November, around 4,000 voters across France put "Landru" as their candidate on the ballot paper, including several hundred in Corrèze, where Bonin failed to win a seat. His humiliation was completed by Moro winning a seat as a centre-left deputy for Corsica (a position that would take second place to Moro's principal career at the Bar).

Bonin slogged on with Landru and his family. On 12 December, Bonin summoned Marie-Catherine for another interrogation. No, she knew nothing about the origin of the jewellery that Landru had given her; no, she had sold nothing on his behalf, apart from a small amount of linen; no, she had no idea about his activities; yes, she had received money from him, but only rarely. Bonin sent her away to reflect on whether it might be in her interest to come up with more convincing answers.

On 16 December, a grey, misty day, Bonin confronted Landru with Célestine Buisson's housemaid sister Marie Lacoste, whose detective work had led to Landru's arrest. As Marie watched him silently, Landru donned his glasses and read her detailed witness statement about his long on-off relationship with Célestine.

"What do you have to say regarding Mlle Lacoste's testimony?" Bonin asked when Landru had finished reading.

"I have absolutely nothing to say," Landru replied placidly, "although there are inaccuracies in the witness's declaration."

"What inaccuracies?"

"Mme Buisson never said in my presence to the witness that we were engaged."

Marie could not be bothered to correct Landru. In her view, it was up to Bonin to decide which of them was lying.

On 18 December, Bonin ordered the arrest of Marie-Catherine on suspicion of complicity in Landru's thefts and frauds. The most damning evidence was the bank documents she had signed as "Célestine Buisson", as confirmed by a handwriting expert.

"I demand a lawyer, I did not sign any of the documents you are showing me," Marie-Catherine yelled at Bonin when she was brought to his office by the police. Bonin despatched her to the Prison Saint-Lazare, a women's jail near the Gare du Nord, to consider whether she was digging herself further into a very deep hole.

The same day, the police also arrested Maurice Landru for complicity in his father's thefts and frauds. Maurice kept his cool, denying all knowledge of anything generally. Bonin slung him in the Santé, where he was given a cell well away from his father.

At the family's apartment in Clichy, Landru's eldest daughter Marie was a picture of bewilderment when the press called. "My brother

[Charles] and I do not understand these arrests," Marie declared. "What are they guilty of and why?"

Marie Landru's turn with Bonin came next. Bonin wanted to know why she had travelled to Gambais in August 1917, while Célestine Buisson and her sister were staying at the Villa Tric. The explanation was simple, Marie said. Her father had asked her to bid on his behalf at an auction in Gambais for a house in the woods near the village. When the bidding had gone above Landru's limit, Marie had walked all the way back to Houdan station and returned to Paris.

No, she had not been aware that her father rented the Villa Tric, and no, she had not seen him after the auction. That was all she could say.

On 10 January 1920, Bonin tested whether a fortnight in jail might have persuaded Landru's wife to admit that she had forged Célestine Buisson's signature on bank documents.

"Landru's *carnet* shows you caught a bus with him on 15 September 1917 to the Banque Alleaume. Is that correct?"

"*Non!*"

"Did you sign letters as Mme Buisson at the Banque Alleaume and also at a credit agent?"

"I don't remember."

"You committed a fraud, didn't you?"

"I remember nothing about it."

Bonin called for Landru to be brought into the magistrate's office. As his wife looked on, he was shown the same evidence of her forgery. Landru refused to speak, except to demand a pen and paper. He wrote:

"I have received from Mme Buisson, for motives and usage that I cannot make known, diverse items with complete propriety."

Unfortunately, Landru continued, Mme Buisson had been "indisposed" in the provinces when he needed to obtain her bank securities, so he had asked Mme Landru to sign for her. "If this act was unlawful, I am solely responsible for it, for my wife acted by order. She is an unconscious instrument."

In February, Marie-Catherine Landru finally confessed on the advice of her lawyer to faking Célestine's signature. She said her memory of the episode was "very imprecise" and she had never touched a *sou*. All she had done was obey her husband.

Having nailed Marie-Catherine, Bonin returned to Maurice and the question of how he had come to be selling Jeanne Cuchet's jewellery in the autumn of 1915.

Why had Maurice told a military tribunal that the jewels had belonged to his grandmother?

"My father was being sought," Maurice replied, "so I wasn't able to say it was him who had given them to me."

In April, Bonin assured the press that Marie-Catherine and Maurice would be "implicated" in Landru's trial. In reality, they were slipping from his grasp. Bonin's failure to pin down Marie-Catherine was summed up by one session with her in early June. Marie-Catherine acknowledged that she and two of her children, Charles and Suzanne, had visited the Villa Tric in 1917 "at the time of the hunting season" (*"au moment de la chasse"*). By one interpretation, Marie-Catherine could have meant the start of the annual hunting season on 1 September, the same day or the day after Célestine Buisson had vanished at the villa. Marie-Catherine recalled that the family had scarcely arrived when Landru left to catch the train to Paris, a detail that tallied with Landru's *carnet* entry for 1 September 1917. Bonin overlooked this coincidence, seemingly content with Marie-Catherine's story that she and her children had spent their two-day visit going for "walks" and had noticed "nothing in particular" at the property.

Bonin's problem was trying to fit this evasive family into the story he wanted to tell. There was no question that Marie-Catherine and three of her children (Marie, Maurice and Charles) were guilty of complicity in Landru's thefts. Yet the thought that they might also have been complicit in Landru's murders was almost too awful to contemplate, even if the authorities had possessed proof of their involvement. Bonin's prime concern was constructing a straightforward narrative about a lone killer that would persuade a jury to send Landru to the guillotine.

At some point in June, Bonin reached the embarrassing conclusion that he would have to drop the family from the case. His chance came in early July, when Marie-Catherine started complaining that she was suffering from terrible back pain. Bonin sent Dr Charles Paul to the Prison Saint-Lazare, where the forensic pathologist took one look at Marie-Catherine and diagnosed a severe attack of sciatica. Bonin promptly released Marie-Catherine on health grounds and closed her file. He also released Maurice Landru from the Santé, telling the press vaguely that he had let him go "because of the state of the investigation".

"How I have suffered morally and physically in jail, how I have shed tears – I, who never knew what my husband was doing," Marie-Catherine babbled to the press when she got home to Clichy. "In my misery, I was consoled many times by the guards in the notorious Saint-Lazare prison." Maurice turned up a few minutes later, apparently untroubled by seven months in the Santé. "The only hassle," he said, "was a prisoner directly above my cell who played the drums with his shoes all day and night."

***

Shortly after Dr Paul's helpful sciatica diagnosis, a far longer submission from the forensic pathologist landed on Bonin's desk. This was Dr Paul's 142-page report on the bone debris found at the Villa Tric, written with two other forensic experts. It was a formidable work of reconstruction. Paul and his two colleagues had painstakingly identified 256 human bone fragments, including 111 smashed-up sections of skull and 47 bits of teeth. Yet the report was also obscure and sometimes misleading about what this mass of evidence potentially signified.

The lack of clarity was evident on the first page, where the authors noted that Bonin had commissioned them "to examine the fragments of bone, teeth etc. discovered during the search made at the suspect's house in the oven, beneath the hangar and in the garden." This sentence gave the impression that some of the human bone fragments came from the garden and the oven. In fact, human skeletal debris had only been discovered beneath the pile of leaves in Landru's hangar, mixed up with animal fragments (a point that the experts also did not make clear).

From one perspective this confusion did not matter, because the human fragments seemed to provide persuasive evidence of murder. Yet a reader of the report could easily miss several other important details that had some bearing on what to make of this sinister evidence. Measured by weight, only one-quarter (1.1 kilograms) of the total material was of human origin and in the absence of pelvic bone parts, the experts could not confirm that all the original corpses had been female. The only certainty was that the charred debris came from three or more skeletons, based on careful examination of duplicate and triplicate fragments.

The burnt scraps of women's apparel also found beneath the leaves pointed strongly to all the human debris being female. Yet there was another question the experts did not address, either because it fell beyond their remit, or because it did not occur to them: Why had Landru left this highly incriminating evidence beneath the leaves at all, rather than scatter it in the woods and fields around Gambais?

There was a deeper conundrum, which Bonin and the police do not appear to have considered. Since the debris had come from at least three skeletons, it was logical to suppose that some or all of the fragments were the remains of the last three victims on the charge sheet: Louise Jaume (who vanished in November 1917), Annette Pascal (April 1918) and Marie-Thérèse Marchadier (January 1919). If this was true, Landru had been a remarkably insouciant killer, happy to forget about the debris beneath the leaves for months and even years.

***

Another expert report landed on Bonin's desk in the summer of 1920, easier to read but just as perplexing.

Ten months after their original commission, the psychiatrists Vallon, Roubinovitch and Rogues de Fursac finally produced their submission on Landru's "mental state". The doctors' slim, 13-page report included a three-page summary of the case, which had no clinical relevance, plus Landru's edited personal memoir, written in September 1919 and therefore not a current representation of his state of mind. The rest of the document amounted to little more than a brisk *tour d'horizon* of Landru from "a psychiatric point of view".

The doctors began by noting their tentative conclusion in 1904 that Landru had been possibly "unbalanced" with diminished responsibility. They did not repeat Vallon's striking phrase about Landru being "on the frontiers of madness".

Next, the psychiatrists observed that Landru's maternal great-grandfather had been committed to an asylum and that his mother had become seriously depressed after the death of a baby son in 1867. With no supporting evidence, Vallon and his colleagues also remarked that Landru's elder sister Florentine was a "neuropath", a label that could have indicated a mental disorder or just that she was highly strung.

A physical examination of Landru followed. The doctors recorded the two serious head injuries that Landru had suffered, without exploring how these accidents might have affected his mental faculties. In the same superficial fashion, the authors merely reported Landru's complaints about severe headaches "at the top of his skull", accompanied by dizzy spells and disturbed vision.

Viewed in the round, the doctors thought Landru resembled "a minor employee whose eyes are full of intelligence, with correct manners, neatly dressed, his hair and beard well groomed". They did not see him as prone to euphoria ("*un excité*"), or depressed or delusional. On the other hand, "conversation with Landru is interesting because of its richness and variety."

They arrived at the delicate matter of Landru's "morals". Landru insisted that he had never indulged in "sexual excesses"; nor did he have "impulses of a sadistic nature". Rather than discuss his sex life, Landru much preferred to talk about his family, displaying "affectionate feelings" for his wife and children:

"On several occasions he set out for us his ideas on the rights and duties of the father of a family, with the clear intention of proving to us that he was imbued with the patriarchal principle."

Once again, Landru denied that any of the missing women had been his mistress. "What a joke!" the doctors quoted him as saying, "Look at my ugly head."

Abruptly, the psychiatrists delivered their verdict on Landru's mental state in four emphatic sentences. Landru had "no trace of psychosis, obsession or pathological impulsion, of a weakening of the intellectual faculties or a state of confusion". His mentality was "in all points normal, once all questions of criminality are excluded", a strange caveat that was not explained. They concluded: "Landru is not affected by any mental illness. He must, in consequence, be considered as responsible for his acts."

In effect, the psychiatrists were asking the court to trust their judgement that a man on the threshold of insanity in 1904 was perfectly "normal" sixteen years later, even though he had been charged with 11 murders. Only one point was clear at the end of their unsatisfactory report. Vallon, Roubinovitch and Rogues de Fursac had given Bonin the answer he wanted. Moro's attempt to get Landru committed to an asylum had failed.

***

On the morning of 1 August 1920, a trunk arrived at Nancy station on the overnight train from Paris, travelling first class. Since no passenger claimed the trunk, a porter took it to the station's left luggage depot. Though Bonin did not yet know it, the trunk was about to disrupt his plans to conclude the investigation of Landru.

Two days later, the left luggage clerk noticed red stains seeping through the joints of the trunk, which had also started to smell. The trunk was prised open, to reveal a decomposing male corpse, shot through the head. Because the body had begun its journey in Paris, the forensic pathologist Dr Paul was summoned from the capital to Nancy.

So began *l'affaire Bessarabo*, featuring a minor writer and journalist called Héra Mirtel, who was charged by Bonin with murdering her second husband, a rich Romanian emigré called Bessarabo. Mme Bessarabo and her daughter by her first marriage had bundled the body into a trunk and put it on the train to Nancy, in the futile hope that no one at the other end would be able to identify the corpse.

The challenge of dealing with both Landru and Mme Bessarabo (who was also arguably insane) may explain why Bonin made a seemingly strange decision in early September. He formally concluded his investigation of Landru and went on holiday for several weeks to Corrèze. Meanwhile, Bonin assigned another government lawyer called Gazier to draft the *réquisitoire définitif*, the key judicial text that would set out the case against Landru.

It was quite common for a busy *juge d'instruction* to delegate this task to a so-called "substitute". Yet *l'affaire Landru* was no ordinary case, as Gazier could tell when he surveyed the mass of paperwork in Bonin's office. At the latest rough count, more than 7,000 pages of material had piled up in the year and a half since Landru's arrest: everything from witness statements and medical reports to police expenses claims. Even with Bonin's guidance, Gazier faced a daunting task.

Gazier finally delivered his 364-page *réquisitoire définitif* in December 1920. From the outset, it was impossible to disguise the gaps and inconsistencies in the case. In the preamble, Gazier declared that Landru was a monster in human form, endowed with a "savage energy"; and yet, he was "not at all deranged", ruling out any suggestion of madness. One by one, Gazier considered the missing fiancées, trying his best to stick to Bonin's theory that Landru had killed all of them for financial gain. Gazier finally tripped up when he came to penniless 19-year-old Andrée Babelay, who had vanished in April 1917. The reason Landru killed her "escapes us", Gazier noted tersely.

Probably on Bonin's advice, Gazier implicitly acknowledged that the charred bone debris could not be directly tied to any of the seven women known to have disappeared at the Villa Tric. The *réquisitoire* did not mention the key forensic evidence in the case until page 161, and only then in the form of a rhetorical question about Anna Collomb's disappearance in December 1916:

"Will we really need now to confirm her death and her murder by joining the experts in searching the calcified bone debris in the garden at Gambais, where some parts cannot fail to arise from her corpse?"

The next reference to the debris came on page 322, when the *réquisitoire* incorrectly stated that "a little bone from a human foot" had been discovered in the oven. In another error, Gazier asserted that human bone fragments had been found in the garden as well as the hangar.

A bound copy of the *réquisitoire* was sent to Landru's defence counsel, as required by law. Moro's copious notes in the margin told their own story. Overall, the case against Landru did not seem "definitive" at all.

***

Moro was intent on delaying the trial for as long as possible, for two reasons. Firstly, Moro hoped that Landru might start to exhibit such obvious signs of madness that he would have to be sent to a mental asylum. Secondly, with the passage of time, witnesses would find it harder to remember the events in question, offering Moro the opportunity to cast doubt on their testimony.

In the autumn of 1920, Moro launched a drawn-out appeal against Landru's sentence in 1914 to exile with hard labour on the island of New Caledonia. The appeal was bound to fail, but until it had been completed, Landru's murder trial could not take place.

At the hearing in February 1921, the press and the public got a taste of Landru's caustic wit.

"Why were you living under a false name in 1914?" the prosecutor asked at one point.

"When one is sought by the police," Landru shot back, "one is not in the habit of leaving one's calling card at the *préfecture*."

Several journalists were shocked by Landru's appearance. After almost two years in prison, his beard had gone grey, his muscles had wasted away, and despite his scrawny physique, he had the beginnings of a pot belly. It was hard to imagine that such a wreck of a man had seduced so many women.

The appeal failed. Landru would still be bound for exile with hard labour, even if he was acquitted of all pending 11 counts of murder and associated thefts and frauds.

More delays followed, as the authorities in Paris and the department of Seine-et-Oise argued over where the trial would be held. Eventually a compromise was reached. The trial would take place in Versailles, the largest town in Seine-et-Oise, before a local jury and a presiding judge from Paris.

In June, Landru was transferred from the Santé to the Prison Saint-Pierre in Versailles, next door to the Palais de Justice. Landru was incensed.

He had grown to like the Santé and took a dim view of the whole idea of a trial. It was clear he was the victim of a "judicial error", Landru told the prison governor on his arrival. The governor thought differently, dumping Landru in a cell reserved for prisoners awaiting execution.

Landru set about trying to postpone the trial forever. He insisted on his right to scrutinise every single item of evidence in the case, by which he meant all 7,000 pages of documents, right there in his cell. Through the summer and into the autumn, the documents kept arriving, organised by Landru into a special filing system, which he repeatedly adjusted.

At the end of September, he complained that his spectacles were too weak for the "work of rehabilitation" he was undertaking. A stronger pair was brought for him.

The opening day of the trial was finally fixed for Monday, 7 November; Landru objected that he had barely begun to master his brief. When this delaying tactic failed, Landru wrote to the judge at the end of October to explain that he was too ill and weak to appear in court. Dr Paul conducted one of his useful medical examinations and declared that Landru was fit enough to face justice. As a precaution, the prison put Landru on a special diet with plenty of meat to keep up his strength.

On Monday, 31 October, *Le Journal* splashed with its curtain-raiser for the trial. "This is not a novel," Landru's mistress Fernande Segret informed the newspaper's one million readers across France. "It has seemed right to me to pull out from my memories the personality of a Landru unknown to all, except me, and to shed light on a personage whose case, unique in judicial annals, has spilt so much ink and provoked so much curiosity."

Fernande's ghostwritten memoir, *Souvenirs of a Survivor*, ran for the rest of the week, as she poured out a torrent of "secrets" from her "intimate life" with Landru: "the most seductive companion, the most fervent and attentive lover one could possibly find".

Rival newspapers ignored Fernande and focused on Landru's chances of avoiding the death penalty. *Le Gaulois*, a right-wing daily, had no doubt concerning the verdict. "Conscience recoils before the image of such a monster," it commented. "Eleven lives" had come to Landru "full of strength, confidence, even sometimes love, only to be annihilated abruptly without leaving the shadow of a trace."

Unintentionally, *Le Gaulois* had made the defence's argument. Here was a case with no bodies, no "definitive proof", nothing but "presumptions", Moro told the colonial *L'Echo d'Alger*, one of the few newspapers to keep an open mind.

On Sunday, 6 November, the eve of the trial, Moro travelled to Versailles to check that Landru really was prepared for what lay ahead. He found Landru in one of his upbeat moods. "Never has my confidence in a happy outcome to my trial been so great," Landru enthused to a guard after Moro departed. "You will see that everything will be resolved."

Next morning, in freezing, overcast weather, Moro's chauffeur-driven car arrived at the Palais de Justice just before noon. Moro stepped out, greeted the waiting press, and was ushered with Navières through a side door reserved for lawyers and witnesses.

Moro knew exactly how he would construct Landru's defence. He would not dispute the many charges of theft and fraud, even though Landru maintained that he had not stolen anything from the missing women. True to his hatred of the death penalty, Moro's sole aim would be to save a man he despised from the guillotine.

PART THREE

THE TRIAL
7 – 30 November 1921

Chapter 13

Chivalry No Longer Exists

A little door, almost hidden behind the defendant's bench, pops open and the man everyone awaits is there. The public lets out an "Ah!" of satisfaction; everyone stands up to catch a glimpse of the accused. Landru appears flattered by this curiosity; he smiles, strokes his beard and obediently follows the three gendarmes who direct him to his bench.

Le Petit Parisien

Day One: Monday, 7 November

He laid out his colour-coded dossiers on the bench, next to his bowler hat and thick, steel-framed glasses. He took out his pens, leaving one in the left breast pocket of his tunic as a back-up. And then he surveyed the scene before him.

The jurors sat directly across the well of the court from Landru: 12 men drawn from the villages and small towns of the department of Seine-et-Oise. They were farmers, shopkeepers and municipal officials who the previous Friday, in the same court, had found a cobbler guilty of setting fire to a haystack, believing his wife and her lover were concealed in the bales.

To Landru's left, the press sat on several rows of reserved benches at the front of the audience. All the reporters were men apart from the novelist Sidonie Colette, swathed in furs, who had been commissioned by *Le Matin* to write a profile of Landru. Colette could already imagine Landru at work on the bodies of his victims, carving up the bones; "then, his job done," she whispered to another journalist, "his tools wiped and cleared away, going out to feed some bread to the little birds gathered by the door."

When Landru looked up from his notes, he could see the audience taking their places in the two-tier public gallery, which had seats for about

250 spectators; among them his recently divorced former wife, come to observe him discreetly.

Most of the lower gallery had been set aside to accommodate 153 prosecution witnesses and six defence witnesses who would be individually sworn in before the hearing began. They looked grim, as if to remind Landru of all his alleged atrocities against their loved ones since he first romanced Jeanne Cuchet in 1914.

Philomène and Georges Friedman sat near to Andrée Babelay's mother Mme Colin, who sobbed noisily into her handkerchief at the memory of her lost teenage daughter. Célestine Buisson's housemaid sister Marie and Anna Collomb's sister Ryno, whose joint detective work had finally trapped Landru, nodded when they recognised each other. Only Fernande Segret, basking in her new-found fame, seemed happy to be in court; she wore the "beatific expression of a showgirl", one reporter noted unkindly.

No one noticed the absence of witnesses whose stories did not fit the prosecution case. Jeanne Cuchet's shirtmaker friend Pierre Capdevieille, who had first-hand knowledge of her poverty, had not been called. Nor had Mme Hardy, Jeanne and Landru's inquisitive neighbour in the village of La Chaussée, whose recollection of the couple's movements in the summer of 1914 contradicted the Friedmans' account. One potential witness had never been located by the police, a shopgirl who had faithfully tended the grave of Berthe Héon's daughter Marcelle. Juliette Auger's moment would nonetheless come.

To the jury's left, the chief prosecuting attorney Robert Godefroy, dressed in scarlet robes, sat hunched over his notes. Born in Le Havre, Godefroy, 54, was a steady barrister on the Paris circuit whose solid, thickset appearance hinted at his ponderous style in court. He seemed a safe pair of hands to guide the jurors through the case set out in the *réquisitoire définitif*, which he had read and annotated in great detail. Godefroy was not without a little vanity. He had a coiffed goatee beard and during the trial would assemble a thick volume of press cuttings as a personal souvenir.

Yet Godefroy was not Landru's main adversary, as would soon become clear. Under the French judicial system, the presiding judge Maurice Gilbert would lead the examination of Landru and the witnesses, exposing the strengths and weaknesses of their testimony for the benefit of the jury. Gilbert, 50, and Moro went back a long way. In 1912, Gilbert had been the investigating magistrate who constructed the false case against the entirely innocent anarchist Eugène Dieudonné, represented by Moro. Since then,

Gilbert had risen to become a senior judge in Paris who looked the part, with a waxed moustache, luxuriant beard and an Olympian manner in court.

Gilbert had done his best to satisfy the needs of the press. Nine telephone booths in the corridor outside the courtroom would enable reporters to dictate their copy back to Paris in time for the overnight editions. Gilbert had also admitted press photographers to the hearing. Two of them were already snapping Landru from directly in front of the judges' bench.

A photograph of the court taken from the upper gallery, minutes before the start of the trial, showed Moro gazing nonchalantly at one of the chandeliers suspended from the ceiling, his mind seemingly elsewhere. It was a performance, like everything Moro did in court, designed to show the jurors that he had done his homework and had no need even to consult his brief.

This illusion was sustained by Navières, sitting to Moro's left, who was busy making the first of hundreds of notes that he would slide across to Moro during the trial. Directly behind Moro and Navières, Landru was also scribbling away in his colour-coded dossiers. From Moro's point of view, Landru's absorption in these files was desirable. Over the next three weeks, the scheduled duration of the trial, one of Moro's main challenges would be to make his volatile, caustic client keep his mouth shut.

It was 12.30 pm. Gilbert called the court to order.

***

Gilbert read out to the jurors the oath that each of them had to swear. They must listen to the evidence "without hatred or malice, fear or favour" and reach a verdict "following your conscience or your intimate conviction (*'intime conviction'*) with the firmness that becomes an upright free man".

As each juror stood and raised his right arm to take the oath, Moro inspected them through his tortoiseshell spectacles. Behind Moro, Landru leafed through his dossiers, making notes, his glasses suspended at the end of his beaky nose, oblivious to the photographers jostling to take his picture.

The clerk of the court now read out the *acte d'accusation*, a 76-page charge sheet that catalogued in exhaustive, repetitive detail the 11 counts of murder and 37 related counts of theft and fraud. After half an hour of this tedium, the novelist Colette's patience snapped. She was here to write about Landru for *Le Matin* (edited by her husband) and time was short if she wanted to get a good look at the Bluebeard of Gambais. While the clerk droned on, Colette strolled across the well of the court and sat on a step in front of the jury box, straight opposite Landru. Godefroy flapped furiously at Colette to go back to her seat and when she ignored him, he signalled to an official to make her move:

"Mme Colette protests; she can only get a good view of Landru from here. The official insists. However, out of deference to her, the clerk of the court stops reading his enormous dossier."

At last, Colette grudgingly agreed to return to the press benches where she soon fell asleep, snoring loudly.

The reporter from *Le Figaro* was struck by Landru's equanimity in the face of the terrible crimes that the clerk was slowly itemising:

"Sometimes he looks in his pocket for the new spectacles that his doctors have prescribed for him. He puts them nearer or further from his notes in order to clean the lenses... Then he settles back, joins his hands together and listens to the charges that he must know by heart."

The communist daily *L'Humanité*, keen to attack the government, deplored the "poverty of information" and "puerile editing" of the *acte d'accusation*. The mass market daily *Le Journal* thought the charge sheet was "littered with sententious phrases and melodramatic paragraphs".

Such press commentary was a particular concern for the prosecution because the jurors were not cut off from the outside world in any meaningful way. At the end of each day they were free to go home, some of them travelling on the same train as journalists covering the trial. Next morning, the jurors would be free to read the newspapers and discuss the case with their families and friends.

Colette's sketch, cobbled together once she had woken up, left *Le Matin*'s readers no wiser about what Landru was really like. She had "searched in vain for any sign of cruelty in his deeply entrenched eyes", Colette reported, but all she had found was "the same unfathomable disdain one sees in caged beasts". Confusingly, Colette also felt that Landru resembled a tailor's dummy in a shop window.

***

At 4.15 pm the clerk sat down, his voice hoarse with the effort. Moro rose to make his first intervention.

He wished to alert the court to a strange piece of news that had come to light in the past few days: a chambermaid called Désirée Guillin had also made contact with Landru during the war. "In the interests of justice", Moro could refute press speculation that Landru's missing fiancée Marie-Angélique Guillin might have been found. The shared surname was just a coincidence.

Speaking for the defence, Moro was struck by how Désirée Guillin's belated emergence illustrated the gaps in the police investigation. Moro could have also pointed out that Désirée Guillin was living proof that the police had *not* traced all the women who had contacted Landru during the war, as the prosecution suggested. Yet Moro refrained from drawing this inference, since it was bound to lead the jurors to wonder whether Landru had killed more fiancées than the ten names on the charge sheet.

Gilbert thanked Moro and turned to Landru: Did the defendant have anything to say in answer to the charges? Landru stood up; he did indeed have something important to announce to the court:

"I will only say a simple thing. I have always protested my innocence. I have never ceased to do so since the first day. Always in the absolute secrecy to which I was bound, I have demanded proofs. I have received no reply. You have just heard an eloquent submission, but of proofs, not a single one! With the greatest energy, I maintain my innocence and count on the hearing to establish it."

Landru had said too much. In referring to his duty of "absolute secrecy", he had hinted that he knew more about the fate of the missing women than he was willing to reveal. With their lawyers' eyes, Godefroy and Gilbert had also gleaned a useful fact from Landru's verbose statement. Moro evidently had no control over Landru, who would have been better advised to declare his innocence and say nothing else.

***

Day Two: Tuesday, 8 November

Light snow fell overnight, turning to slush in the morning. Moro arrived half an hour late for the start of the second day's session, hurrying into the courtroom with Navières in tow. His car had broken down en route from Paris, Moro explained. He apologised in turn to the jurors, Gilbert,

Godefroy and Landru, adding that if he was late in future the hearing should begin without him.

Moro began to sketch cartoons of the press photographers, seemingly indifferent to the first moment of real danger for Landru as Gilbert began his examination of the defendant.

Moro's powerlessness to intervene was underscored when he tried to stop the judge from asking Landru about his early criminal career, on the grounds that it was irrelevant to the present case.

"I register your objection," Gilbert replied smoothly, "but I believe it necessary, for the clarity of these debates and the edification of *messieurs les jurés*, to recall the methods Landru used to attract dupes, methods which he subsequently perfected but which were always the same."

Gilbert ordered Landru to stand up.

"Your parents were honest workers," Gilbert began. "Not far from your home there was a Mme Rémy, who had a daughter."

"She even had two," Landru corrected Gilbert.

"Let us say two then. In any case, you married one of them, Marie-Catherine." Rapidly, Gilbert ran through Landru's descent into petty crime and lack of a regular, respectable profession.

"That just shows the police didn't research me properly," Landru retorted.

"You're incriminating the police?"

"Only their prestige," Landru replied cryptically. "Did they ever discover me during the war? No, it was the alleged victims who found me."

"It is worth remembering that this entire investigation was conducted in spite of you. When *monsieur le juge d'instruction* [Bonin] informed you about the evidence gathered by the police, you said nothing."

"It isn't for me to enlighten the police or guide this court. For the past three years I have been accused of things that the missing women never did."

"You perhaps made it impossible for them to complain. But let us not get too far ahead of the story," Gilbert went on, riled by Landru's pedantry.

Gilbert reached the 283 women who the police estimated had made contact with Landru during the war, via lonely hearts adverts and matrimonial agencies. Why had Landru, a husband with four children, pretended to be interested in marrying them?

Landru had already figured out his answer to this inevitable question:

"*Messieurs les jurés*, it was an innocent, little commercial ruse. Because of the war, many single women who were hard up were looking to sell their furniture, just as many people in the occupied zone would be looking for second-hand furniture after the war. Here was an opportunity for me to exploit. But lots of these women were embarrassed by their situation. Discussing marriage was a simple way to introduce myself to them, after which it became easy to get down to business."

Several jurors could not help smiling as Landru ploughed on:

"In commercial matters, any publicity is permissible in order to attract customers. My advertising system was matrimonial notices."

The same "simple" system explained the suspicious, neatly written list of ten women, plus one young man, in his *carnet*.

"It was a list made by a good merchant, or rather, a personal indication allowing him to remember the clients with whom he had business," Landru said.

Why, then, Gilbert asked, did Landru use code names for three of the women: "Brésil", "Crozatier" and "Havre"?

"When I forgot the woman's name, I wrote down the name of the street or the country where she came from."

Landru was into his stride, acting as his own defence counsel, while Moro sketched frenetic cartoons as a distraction.

"Only these 11 names count," Landru carried on. "One hasn't wished to seek any other victims, but perhaps there are some," he smirked.

Laughter rippled around the public gallery, prompting Moro to protest about the noise. Gilbert ordered silence in court and the examination resumed.

The judge read out one of the pre-written love letters that the police had found in Landru's garage in Clichy. Were these really just a furniture dealer's calling card? Gilbert asked.

"They're just drafts. Show me one which is signed by me."

"You were quite the cavalier, Landru," Gilbert persisted.

"Chivalry no longer exists," Landru replied, as if he was stating the obvious.

***

Mme Jeanne Isoré from Lille was ushered into the courtroom, her thin features half-hidden by a black demi-veil. The first witness of the trial had "the air of a provincial haberdasher's wife", *L'Excelsior* observed with Parisian disdain, as Mme Isoré nervously took the oath.

She had remarried since her disastrous encounter with Landru more than a decade ago and did not wish to reveal her new name; nor did she want her picture taken. To cap her misery, Mme Isoré had a heavy cold and several times had to repeat her testimony in a croaky voice because the jurors could not hear her.

In 1909, recently widowed, Mme Isoré had been seduced by Landru, who had pretended to be a businessman from the northern town of Amiens. Shortly afterwards, Mme Isoré had accepted his proposal of marriage.

Gilbert chose to humiliate her further by reading one of Landru's love letters.

"I hope, my dear Jeanne," Landru had written, "that your good mother lives long enough to be assured that she has consigned her daughter to a tender heart that is worthy of her own."

Foolishly, Mme Isoré had let Landru get his hands on her savings, worth about 10,000 francs, via a bogus premarital "contract". He had been caught almost immediately with her investment deeds when he attempted to cash them in at a bank. Tried and convicted, Landru had spent the next two and a half years in jail on the outskirts of Lille.

"What do you have to say, Landru?" Gilbert asked, once Mme Isoré had finished her testimony.

"It was ten years ago and I repaid the money," Landru remarked, adding that he had "atoned" for his "error".

Mme Isoré was dismissed, having played a minor, but important role in the prosecution's narrative. As cast, Mme Isoré was an early victim of Landru, before he "perfected" his distinctive marriage swindle by killing his fiancées so they could not go to the police. She was lucky, in short, to be alive.

From the defence's perspective, Mme Isoré's survival supported the argument that Landru's fiancées were missing rather than dead. Yet Moro refrained from making this point, aware that Landru steadfastly refused to say what had happened to the ten women on the charge sheet.

***

Amédée Dautel, the next witness to appear, offered Moro his first opportunity to go on to the attack. Visibly nervous, the detective recalled Landru's behaviour in the hours after his arrest on 12 April 1919. Dautel said that when Landru was asked to empty his pockets on his arrival at the police station, the suspect made a gesture to hide his *carnet*.

Landru rose to protest, but Moro waved him down.

If what Dautel said was correct, Moro asked politely, why had he not mentioned this incriminating incident in his original police report? Dautel shrugged; he had no answer, for Moro had caught him embellishing his testimony.

Dautel was followed by his deputy, Jules Belin, well known to the reporters in court as a colourful police source. Moro set about exposing Belin as an unreliable loudmouth, reinforcing the impression left by Dautel that the police could not be trusted to tell the truth.

Belin's credibility collapsed as soon as Gilbert began to examine him. Belin claimed that he had conducted a search of Landru's apartment at Rue de Rochechouart, with Landru in attendance. Moro cut in, accusing Belin of misleading the court. In fact, Moro observed, the official search of the apartment had been conducted by Brigadier Riboulet of the Paris *police judiciaire*, almost a month after Landru's arrest. On the day of Riboulet's search, 10 May 1919, Belin and Dautel had been in Gambais, supervising the drainage of two ponds in the woods near the village.

Belin tried to correct Moro: he had been referring, of course, to his and Dautel's search of the apartment in Landru's presence on the day of the arrest, 12 April 1919.

"Impossible!" Landru barked, wagging his finger at Belin; the record clearly showed that he, Landru, had not returned to the apartment until Riboulet's search on 10 May 1919.

"So did you attend the search on 12 April?" Moro asked Landru.

"Not at Rue de Rochechouart," Landru replied.

For the past twenty minutes, Godefroy had watched Moro's demolition of Dautel and Belin with mounting alarm. Godefroy now panicked, rising to "clarify" Inspector Belin's account, as he put it.

Moro leapt on Godefroy's error. "I am shocked that the prosecution is attempting to pull back the testimony of one of its witnesses," he said pointedly to the jurors.

"I will not permit you to say that I tried to pull back evidence," Godefroy hurled back, enraged by Moro's slur on his integrity.

"If the rights of the defence are breached in this fashion again," Moro warned Godefroy, "I will take my hat and briefcase and abandon the trial."

Godefroy shouted something at Moro, which none of the journalists heard, for "the uproar around the court was intense". It did not occur to the press that Moro had achieved exactly the effect he wanted. Seen through the eyes of the startled jurors, it looked as if the prosecution was trying to undermine due process.

Unable to restore order, Gilbert suddenly called time on the day's session, half an hour before the scheduled close at 5.00 pm.

Moro looked stunned. "*Monsieur le président*, you have given me the floor. I will continue. I will protest in the name of the defence."

Gilbert made clear his decision was final but Landru was still not done. "I accuse this man of having arrested me illegally," Landru yelled across the court at Belin. Then Landru was off, escorted by his three guards, back along the cobbled interior alleyway that led to his prison cell.

Chapter 14

Philomène's Dream

Day Three: Wednesday, 9 November

"Ripped, stained mattresses, an oil lamp and flower vases… dirty linen, pitiful dusty umbrellas": one by one, *Le Petit Parisien* recorded Jeanne Cuchet's meagre possessions, laid out on the evidence table in front of the jurors. Most poignant of all was Jeanne's battered sewing machine, her only source of income before she had met Landru in early 1914.

Gilbert began by drawing a pen portrait of Jeanne for the jury's benefit. Summarising the *réquisitoire*, the judge noted that the widowed Jeanne had discussed her "dream of remarrying" with her sister Philomène and her brother-in-law Georges Friedman. Gilbert chose to ignore Friedman's claim that Jeanne had been worth 100,000 francs, merely commenting that unnamed witnesses put her fortune at somewhere between 30,000 and 50,000 francs.

"Let us just say that she enjoyed an easy situation," Gilbert observed, as if that settled the question.

The judge assumed that Jeanne had owned the substantial sum of 5,609 francs deposited by Landru in a bank in Chantilly in June 1914.

"It is really extraordinary that an orderly man like you did not record the sum in your *carnet*," Gilbert remarked to Landru, forgetting that Landru did not acquire the notebook until 1915.

Landru replied that the deposit represented the "residue" of his legacy from his late father.

"And where was the rest of this inheritance?" Gilbert asked.

"In my pocket!" Landru protested, appealing to the jurors' common sense.

Gilbert turned to Landru's travels on the eve of the war between La Chaussée, Paris, and the farm in Normandy where he installed his family. Landru claimed that he had wanted to get his wife and children to "a sheltered place" when France mobilised at the start of August 1914. The truth was more complicated. Gilbert was apparently unaware that Landru had made an earlier journey with his wife to Le Havre in late July, in order to get her out of Paris during his trial *in absentia* for fraud.

The judge presented Jeanne as a vulnerable woman deceived by a lethal marriage swindler. Landru's pretence that he was only interested in Jeanne's furniture seemed especially weak, given that they had lived together for several months in La Chaussée and Vernouillet.

Gradually he flagged under Gilbert's relentless probing. At 3.15 pm, when Gilbert called an interval, a reporter from *Le Petit Parisien* found that most of the spectators stretching their legs in the corridor thought Landru was making a poor fist of defending himself.

After the break, Gilbert addressed Landru's move with Jeanne and her 17-year-old son André to Vernouillet in December 1914. Landru said that Jeanne had offered to be his housekeeper at Vernouillet because her apartment in Paris was too big for her and André. Gilbert asked why Landru had signed the rental agreement as "Monsieur Cuchet".

"To keep up appearances for André's sake," Landru replied matter-of-factly.

Gilbert got to the point. "How do you explain the disappearance of Mme Cuchet and her son?"

Landru looked up wearily at Gilbert, "visibly tired", according to *L'Ouest-Éclair*. "Suddenly he decided to speak amid a deep silence around the court."

"I arrive at facts that I have never been able to tell the investigation," Landru said melodramatically.

("*Sensation*": *L'Ouest-Éclair*)

"There existed between Mme Cuchet, Monsieur Cuchet [André] and me certain private conventions. We did nothing, neither her nor me, which was contrary to the law or morality."

"You refuse to explain the nature of these conventions?" Gilbert asked.

"But absolutely, *monsieur le président*."

"If you persist with the system of defence that you used during the investigation, the gentlemen of the jury will appreciate your silence," Gilbert observed sarcastically.

("*Sensation prolongée*": *L'Ouest-Éclair*)

Moro stood up, desperate to limit the damage caused by Landru's nonsense about "private conventions".

"If you please, *maître*," Gilbert addressed Moro with silky formality, "let your client reply himself. He is defending himself on his own very well indeed and with great precision when he is able. Any objection that you might be able to produce would only lengthen these exchanges."

Gilbert had no interest in probing Landru's relationship with Jeanne's son André. As portrayed by the *réquisitoire*, André was just a harmless youth whom Landru had killed because the son was a witness to his mother's murder. Yet André had clearly irritated Landru. He sneered at the teenager's "juvenile patriotism", and in particular regarded André's letter in January 1915 to his best friend Max Morin as "badly misjudged". André should not have greeted his imminent call-up with such eagerness, Landru said severely.

***

Jeanne's friend from her married days, Mme Louise Bazire, slim, sombre and dressed in black, came to the witness stand. After taking the oath, Mme Bazire made a point of staring straight at Landru, a procedure she repeated several times during her testimony. She was not going to be intimidated by the man she was convinced had killed Jeanne.

Mme Bazire told Gilbert that Landru had struck her as a well-educated man when she met him at Jeanne's apartment in the autumn of 1914.

Moro stood up, and this time Gilbert allowed him to interject.

"Did Mme Cuchet ever display an intention to go to America?" Moro asked Mme Bazire.

"Yes, she did very often, but she never went."

Moro asked if Mme Bazire could shed any light on the murky issue of Jeanne's financial situation. Mme Bazire explained that she was well placed to answer, because her husband had been one of the administrators of Martin Cuchet's paltry estate, which had been wiped out by his medical and funeral costs. Jeanne did not have a fortune, Mme Bazire stated firmly, yet thanks to hard work she had built up "some savings" after her husband's death.

Moro suggested that Jeanne's savings must have been quite small as a lowly seamstress earning a few hundred francs per month. Mme Bazire tried to be more specific. Jeanne's situation had been "precarious" when her husband had died, but she had still managed to accumulate a modest nest egg.

Albert Folvary, the dress shop manager who had employed Jeanne, was next on the witness stand. He was 55 but looked rather older, with white hair, thick bottle-glass spectacles, and a genial, stooping manner.

Folvary was pleased to assist the court in any way he could, for he had been fond of Jeanne and sorry when she had handed in her notice to live with her fiancé.

"Was Mme Cuchet sincere in her marriage plans?" Gilbert asked him.

"Oh! Absolutely sincere. She loved her son very much and was happy to marry again in order to assure his future."

This was not quite the answer Gilbert had been expecting. According to the *réquisitoire*, Jeanne had pursued Landru because she was naïvely infatuated with him, not on account of André.

Like Mme Bazire, Folvary recalled how Jeanne had often talked about starting a new life with André in America or England. Folvary had never taken Jeanne's chatter seriously, because she could not speak English, and besides, she had possessed "very little savings".

Jeanne's brother-in-law Georges Friedman strode to the witness stand, informing the photographers gathered around that he did not want to have his picture in the newspapers. Friedman could not prevent a courtroom artist drawing him as he testified: a paunchy, balding middle-aged man, with a thick black moustache and a double chin that spilled over his stiff white collar.

Friedman said Landru had made "a poor impression" on him when they had met at Jeanne's apartment in the spring of 1914. Repeating his witness statement, he remarked that he knew Landru was fishy when Landru had obviously lied about doing his military service in Indo-China, where Friedman had also been stationed.

Gilbert took Friedman through his two visits to La Chaussée at Jeanne's request in August 1914, after Landru had vanished. Friedman said that he, not Jeanne, had discovered Landru's identity papers inside the little locked chest and that he and Mme Friedman had advised Jeanne to break off her engagement. Friedman then told a curious story about how Landru had turned up on their doorstep a day or two later, asking after Jeanne. According to Friedman, Landru had been given such an earful by Philomène that he had turned and fled.

At this point, Gilbert asked Landru if he wished to give his side of the story. Landru looked up briefly from a thick red dossier he was annotating and shook his head, as if this was a needless distraction from more important work. Nor did Moro wish to cross-examine Friedman, who was obviously relieved. Friedman was thanked by Gilbert and dismissed.

There was plenty in Friedman's testimony that Moro could have challenged on cross-examination. Friedman's dates for his two visits to La Chaussée, 2 and 9 August 1914, clashed with the absent Mme Hardy's recollection that Landru had returned to the village on 2 August and then driven Jeanne to Chantilly station to catch the train to Paris. According to Mme Hardy, Landru had then spent the night of 2–3 August at the villa.

It was not a trivial inconsistency, because France had mobilised on the weekend of 1–2 August and declared war on Germany on Monday, 3 August. If Friedman's dates were correct, Jeanne must have returned to Paris to be reunited with André before the mobilisation; yet this was certainly not Mme Hardy's memory.

Friedman's story about Landru turning up at his home on 10 or 11 August, asking after Jeanne, also appeared suspect. Jeanne's concierge was sure Jeanne had been at her own apartment on the days in question, and therefore easy for Landru to track down.

None of the inconsistencies in Friedman's testimony, however, had any bearing on whether Landru had murdered Jeanne and André. Moro did not want to give Friedman the chance to express his certainty of Landru's guilt or cast doubt on Mme Bazire's well-founded belief that Jeanne had possessed very little for Landru to steal.

So far, the session had gone well for Moro. He was expecting to do even better with Jeanne's sister Philomène, the next witness to be summoned.

Like her husband, Philomène did not want her photograph in the papers. An artist's sketch for *Le Petit Parisien* showed a homely, middle-aged woman with gentle, rounded features, peeking out from under her bonnet at the court. It was just possible to detect a passing resemblance with her younger sister Jeanne, whose love life had been such a worry to Philomène.

Gilbert asked Philomène whether the tatty furniture next to the witness stand had belonged to Jeanne. Philomène nodded and started to cry silently, her head bowed. Seeing her distress, Gilbert ordered the clerk of the court to bring her a chair, so she could testify sitting down.

Encouraged by Gilbert to take her time, Philomène recovered her composure. She told a story about joining Jeanne and Landru on a day trip in his *camionnette* to the town of Fresnes, 15 kilometres south of Paris, where the two sisters had been born. The car had broken down, and after repairing it, Landru had driven back to Paris at breakneck speed, causing Philomène to express her alarm. Jeanne, by contrast, had not been afraid at all.

"My sister reassured me that with 'Monsieur Diard' one fears nothing," Philomène recalled.

Philomène had either invented or imagined this anecdote, which was not in her witness statement. In fact, she had only met Landru once, during a day trip to La Chaussée in July 1914.

Landru stood up, in the mood to be his own attorney.

"*Madame*," he addressed Philomène, "you told the *juge d'instruction* [Bonin] that you had the impression I had killed your sister."

"That's correct."

"On what do you base your impression?"

"A woman would never abandon her earrings," said Philomène, gesturing at Jeanne's jewellery on the evidence table. "If one sees them here, it's because they were taken from her after her death."

She started crying again. "And because she would be here!" she sobbed at Landru. "Because she would not let a man she loved be condemned! She had a heart, my sister."

Philomène scanned Jeanne's clothes, all in a heap on the table, searching for something she could not see. Her sister had made a scanty sky-blue nightdress "to please this man", Philomène said, pointing contemptuously at Landru. "What became of it?"

Gently, Gilbert informed Philomène that the nightdress had been found in Mlle Fernande Segret's possession.

("*Émotion*": *Le Petit Parisien*)

Moro had so far refrained from cross-examining Philomène about the reliability of her testimony. He decided he could not hold off any longer, despite the agonies she was going through. With Gilbert's permission, Moro asked her about another episode she had described to the police.

"You had a dream, I believe, *madame*. Would you care to tell *messieurs les jurés* about it?"

Philomène seemed puzzled for a moment; a dream – yes, of course:

"I had a dream, and in this dream my sister appeared to me, pale and bloodless. She had been cut – right here." Philomène made a slashing motion across her throat.

"'It was him, Landru, who did this,' my sister told me.

"'Did you suffer?' I asked her.

"'No, I was asleep,' she replied."

Philomène broke down, unable to help herself now.

"Oh, my sister," she wept. "Oh, my poor, poor sister."

Moro had no further questions, realising that he had just made his first serious mistake of the trial. Philomène's dream was exactly that: a fantasy unsupported by any evidence. But the reality Moro had summoned for the jurors was a woman lost in wrenching, uncontrollable grief for a sister whose life she might have saved.

Chapter 15

Her Private Life Does Not Concern Me

Day Four: Thursday, 10 November

Among the reporters covering the trial was Lucien Coulond, a prominent former war correspondent who had travelled widely in the Middle East. Coulond, 38, was married to an actress and had once hoped to pursue a career on the stage. Writing for *Le Journal* under his pen name "Edouard Helsey", he saw the trial as an unfolding drama rather than a dry legal process.

Despite Moro's misstep with Philomène, Coulond thought the prosecution case had got off to an uncertain start. Coulond was particularly struck by the prosecution's failure so far to produce any firm evidence that Landru had killed Jeanne and André Cuchet. It was all just conjecture: "The prosecution has told us nothing about the immediate circumstances of this first disappearance." In Coulond's view, if the case against Landru depended on *l'affaire Cuchet*, then it would be difficult to make the murder counts stick.

Coulond's commentary led the front page of *Le Journal* on 10 November, followed by a long despatch by the newspaper's trial reporter. All the other dailies featured Landru on their front pages, as they would continue to do for the rest of the trial. Even *L'Humanité*, which had initially sneered at the trial as a bourgeois *divertissement*, felt obliged to satisfy its readers on 10 November with a front-page report, illustrated by a cartoon of Gilbert.

Commentators and feature writers, looking for an excuse to write even more about Landru, attempted to invest his trial with a wider significance. The "Bluebeard of Gambais" was variously depicted as a distraction for a nation still in mourning for 1.3 million war casualties, a proxy for France's frustrated need to avenge those deaths, and in the conservative press, a terrible warning of what could happen when the "feeble sex" was led astray.

With his thespian eye, Coulond came closest to the truth. Viewed as theatre, the trial was a lurid, unpredictable show, perfect for selling newspapers. Here was the lumbering Godefroy, out of his depth, "flapping his arms and shouting too loudly in an awkward voice which he quickly stifles." Here was Moro, who "corners, strikes and disarms his adversary". Here was Philomène and her "horrible dream" (*Le Petit Parisien*), weeping for her lost sister. Above all, here was a monster with a "savage audacity", accused of slaughtering ten fiancées, repulsive, volatile and even comic; for when the audience heard that Landru had romanced 283 women, people had "burst out laughing".

***

The star of the show arrived in court just before 1.00 pm on Thursday, laden down with green, red and yellow dossiers. He was soon absorbed in his notes, as the last of the witnesses in *l'affaire Cuchet* came and went in rapid succession.

Jeanne's other brother-in-law, Louis Germain, "podgy and pleased with himself", was soon punctured by Moro. Germain (married to the late Martin Cuchet's sister) denied that Jeanne had ever spoken to him about wanting to leave France with André for a new life in America. Moro pointed out that Germain had reported her comment to Bonin.

"Monsieur Germain was distraught," *Le Populaire* reported. "His whole performance had been wiped out."

Mme Pelletier, Jeanne's former concierge, a short, stout woman in her late fifties, declared bluntly that Mme Cuchet had "worked a lot but wasn't rich". She then told a story about Landru turning up one day at the apartment with two little girls, aged about ten, who he said were his daughters.

"Landru, what do you say?" Gilbert demanded.

Landru ruminated for a moment. It was possible he had made this remark to Mme Pelletier, he said, "but that isn't a reason why they might have been my daughters."

A juror raised his hand, wanting to check something Philomène had said.

"Did Mme Cuchet wear earrings and what were they made of?" he asked Mme Pelletier.

"*Oui, oui*," she replied, "I think they were made of gold."

A thin, grey-haired woman, dressed in full mourning, was next on the witness stand. Mme Louise Morin, the mother of André Cuchet's best friend Max, was allowed to sit, removing her veil and gripping the bar with her black-gloved hand to steady her nerves.

"André wanted to volunteer to fight in the war like my son, but his mother refused to let him go until his contingent was called up," Mme Morin recalled, her voice almost inaudible. "One day, André declared full of joy that an imminent mobilisation law would allow him to go off without his mother's consent. She was heartbroken and it was thus that we knew each other."

Mme Morin told Gilbert how she had warned Jeanne not to marry "such a bandit", following Jeanne's discovery of Landru's identity. "Later, this individual came to tell me that Mme Cuchet and André had left for England, but claimed not to know their address. I never received any more news of the mother. As for my son…"

She paused, sinking back into her misery.

"We know, *madame*," said Gilbert, "that your son fell on the field of honour. Please believe that we too bow before your sorrow."

"The defence, too," Moro added, rising with his fellow veteran Navières.

Max Morin, André's hero, had retrained during the war as an aviator. In March 1918 Max's plane had crashed on take-off, probably from engine failure.

Mme Morin could not continue and was helped from her chair by the clerk of the court. She had offered a glimpse of Jeanne as a more complicated person than the supposedly besotted woman depicted by the prosecution: ambivalent about Landru after discovering his true identity and concerned above all to keep her naïve son André out of the war.

Mme Oudry, the elderly estate agent in Vernouillet, was too ill to testify about how she came to rent The Lodge to Landru in December 1914. Instead, Godefroy read out her witness statement, in which she noted that Landru had signed the contract as "Monsieur Cuchet".

For some reason, Landru tried to deny what he called this "lie" by Mme Oudry. Moro, who had seen the contract, firmly corrected Landru.

"Let me speak!" Landru admonished Moro, who with the help of Navières finally got his furious client to sit down.

One of the jurors wanted to know why Landru had pretended in Vernouillet that he was Jeanne's husband. It was a clever question that tricked Landru into tacitly conceding that he had used the name "Cuchet" on the contract.

"I was being pursued for an 'indelicacy' [criminal offence] and needed a false identity as cover," Landru explained. "It was wartime. A man arriving in a small neighbourhood with a stranger could have seemed peculiar." Landru stared at the twelve solid, provincial jurors and sensed their dissatisfaction with his answer. "Country folk are excessively curious and suspicious," he informed them, with all the *hauteur* of a born Parisian.

***

Landru was beyond Moro's reach for the rest of the afternoon. At 3.30 pm Gilbert moved on to the Argentinian-born Thérèse Laborde-Line, the third of Landru's alleged victims. Thérèse had been 46 when she vanished at Vernouillet in July 1915.

Why did Thérèse's concierge and several neighbours recall her speaking of being engaged to him, a fact that he denied?

Landru smiled: "*Monsieur le président*, here one has to make a little study in feminine psychology."

("Laughter": *Le Journal*)

"Women do not like to admit they are financially embarrassed; they prefer to believe in a beautiful marriage. But this little lie proves nothing."

Where was Thérèse now? Gilbert asked.

"I don't want to know, it's none of my business, I'm just a furniture dealer," Landru snapped. "Don't ask me about matters beyond my station."

"Why, Landru," Godefroy mocked, "you answer very well on certain points, but refuse to respond to others which have the potential to make your head fall off."

Landru leant forward, "very on edge", *L'Ouest-Éclair* reported. "This belongs to the domain of my private life. These women sold me their furniture. I paid them. I do not wish to know what became of them next."

Moro got up, hoping to cut short this disastrous exchange before Landru incriminated himself. Landru had said all he could say about Thérèse's disappearance, Moro observed; perhaps the court should proceed to the examination of witnesses.

Gilbert declined Moro's proposal and returned to his pursuit of Landru.

Why did Landru maintain that Thérèse had never spent the night at The Lodge when a neighbour saw her picking flowers in the back garden?

A night at the Opéra-Comique, 1918: Landru and his mistress Fernande Segret pose for a souvenir snap before heading to their favourite Paris theatre. (Roger-Viollet Collection, Paris)

THE DISAPPEARANCES (1915–1919)

Above left: Jeanne Cuchet, pretty, deaf, and secretive. She declined to reveal why she returned to her fiancé after discovering he was an imposter. (Archives de la Préfecture de police de Paris)

Above right: Jeanne's beloved only son André, who disappeared with her in early 1915. "I could not keep the boy under surveillance," Landru recalled. (Archives de la Préfecture de police de Paris)

Below left: 'Brazil', Landru's codename for the Argentinian Thérèse Laborde-Line. She was last seen picking cherries in his back garden at Vernouillet in the summer of 1915. (Archives de la Préfecture de police de Paris)

Below right: Marie-Angélique Guillin, Landru's third known fiancée, thought she was marrying France's Consul-General to Australia. She never got further than Vernouillet. (Archives de la Préfecture de police de Paris)

Above left: Anna Collomb, thrifty and intelligent, but a poor judge of men. She trusted Landru enough to let him buy her a one-way ticket to his country home at Gambais. (Archives de la Préfecture de police de Paris)

Above centre: Flirty Andrée Babelay, just 19 when Landru spotted her one evening on the Paris metro. "He is my father but I call him 'Lulu'," Andrée told villagers in Gambais. (Archives de la Préfecture de police de Paris)

Above right: Célestine Buisson, homely and naïve, who disappeared at Gambais in August 1917. "If I take a husband it is to cherish him," she told her *monsieur*. (Archives de la Préfecture de police de Paris)

Below left: Louise Jaume, estranged from her husband, sought God's forgiveness for answering a lonely hearts advert. She made Landru pray with her in the village church at Gambais. (Archives de la Préfecture de police de Paris)

Below right: Marie-Thérèse Marchadier, a prostitute who supposedly had a "mania for marriage" and Landru's last known fiancée. She vanished in January 1919. (Archives de la Préfecture de police de Paris)

Annette Pascal found her fiancé almost as terrifying as the German bombardment of Paris. "Be very worried," Annette wrote to her sister on the day she disappeared at Gambais. (Archives départementales des Yvelines)

17 April 1919: Five days after his arrest, Landru poses for a photo in the town jail at Mantes. He found his cell agreeable and resented his transfer to the Santé prison in Paris. (Archives départementales des Yvelines)

Left: The Lodge at Vernouillet, 35 kilometres north-west of Paris, which Landru rented in Jeanne Cuchet's name in December 1914. The pavilion (left) connected with the main villa (centre), while the neighbours lived in the white house (right). (Archives départementales des Yvelines)

Below: From the rear, The Lodge's peculiar construction was more apparent. The villa (left) and the pavilion (centre) were overlooked by Landru's incurious neighbour Mme Picque. (Archives départementales des Yvelines)

15 April 1919: The investigating magistrate Gabriel Bonin (fifth from left) inspects forensic samples taken from the rear garden of The Lodge. Bonin mistakenly thought it would only take a few days to solve the case. (Roger-Viollet Collection)

11 May 1919: L'Étang des Bruyères, near Gambais. The detectives Dautel (left, half-obscured) and Belin listen to Mme Mauguin describe what she saw floating on the water. Her evidence did not fit the prosecution case. (Roger-Viollet Collection)

The Villa Tric, 55 kilometres south-west of Paris, which Landru rented as 'Raoul Dupont' from 1915 to 1919. The village of Gambais (left) is just visible in the distance. (Archives départementales des Yvelines)

The rear of the Villa Tric and its outhouses from a distance, showing the property's isolation. The village church (left) is 250 metres away, while Gambais (right, out of picture) is more than a kilometre in the opposite direction. (Archives départementales des Yvelines)

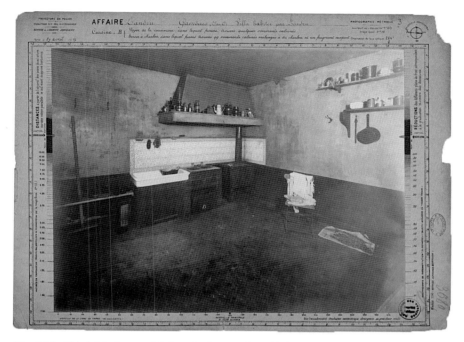

The Villa Tric's kitchen, with Landru's notorious little oven in the far corner. "It is a ridiculous utensil, scarcely bigger than a bedside table," one journalist commented. (Archives départementales des Yvelines)

The Villa Tric's rear enclosure, showing the unearthed grave (left) of Marie-Thérèse Marchadier's three strangled dogs, close to where Landru buried Annette Pascal's cat. (Archives départementales des Yvelines)

The open hangar (left) where Landru stored dead leaves, next to two locked sheds where Célestine Buisson's sister peered through the keyhole at a bundle of indistinct shapes. (Archives départementales des Yvelines)

27 May 1919: Paris, Palais de Justice. Landru, handcuffed to his prison escort, is led away after his first formal interrogation. "It's for you to prove the deeds of which I'm accused," he sneered at Bonin. (Roger-Viollet Collection)

Paris, 18 December 1919: Landru's wife Marie-Catherine, proven forger and liar, looks stern in a police mugshot on the day of her arrest. "My only crime is to have loved him too much," she insisted. (Archives de la Préfecture de police de Paris)

Landru's son Maurice, a convicted swindler, also denied complicity in his father's crimes. Prison was "no hassle", Maurice told a reporter nonchalantly. (Archives de la Préfecture de police de Paris)

"Your proofs, *messieurs*, where are your proofs?" Caustic and volatile, Landru was the despair of his defence counsel during the trial. (Archives de la Préfecture de police de Paris)

Mistinguett ('×'), the queen of French musical theatre, was obsessed by Landru and pretended to be reporting on the trial for an English newspaper. Other celebrities who came to watch included Maurice Chevalier and the film star Sacha Guitry. (Archives de la Préfecture de police de Paris)

Jeanne Cuchet's friend Louise Bazire glares back at Landru while the jury listens to the judge. Inconveniently for the prosecution, Mme Bazire insisted Jeanne was poor. (Gallica, Bibliothèque Nationale)

Above: Célestine Buisson's sister Marie Lacoste, the best detective in the case, glares at Landru. Without her, Landru might never have been arrested. (Alamy)

Left: …and then came Annette Pascal's niece Marie-Jeanne, dressed to kill and intent on humiliating Landru. "The *monsieur* was so gentle in bed with my aunt," she taunted him. (Alamy)

Juliette Auger, plain and shy, who shredded Landru on the witness stand. (Gallica, Bibliothèque Nationale)

Maurice Gilbert (left), the presiding judge, clever and vain, and Robert Godefroy (right), the slow-witted prosecuting attorney. (Archives de la Préfecture de police de Paris and Gallica, Bibliothèque Nationale)

Vincent de Moro Giafferri, Landru's brilliant defence attorney, waits impatiently to launch his electrifying closing address. (Gallica, Bibliothèque Nationale)

30 November 1921, evening: The jurors smile at the camera as they wait to stuff their verdicts in the urn. "They are mostly *petits bourgeois*, with just one timid, moustachioed worker among them." (Archives de la Préfecture de police de Paris)

30 November 1921, evening: Landru waits in a holding cell beneath the court while the jury decides his fate. "On the heads of my family I swear that I have killed no one." (Archives de la Préfecture de police de Paris)

Landru spread his arms in protest: "But it's the pleasure of every *Parisienne* on a day out in the country to pick a flower, to prove that she has been there!"

"Why did you keep her personal papers?"

"It was a sacred deposit."

(*"Rumeurs violentes": Le Gaulois*)

"It's a singular 'sacred deposit' that concerns a commercial matter," Gilbert said. "*Enfin*, do you know where she has gone?"

"I have told you that I did not wish to know anything beyond the commercial sphere. Her private life does not concern me!"

"The same response as for Mme Cuchet."

"And the same reserve, *monsieur le président*," Landru said with dignity. "Her private life, like mine, is a wall."

"Behind which you shelter."

(*"Sensation": Le Gaulois*)

"One last time," said Gilbert, when the noise from the gallery had subsided. "You refuse to say where she has gone?"

"Absolutely."

Mme Tréborel, Thérèse's 34-year-old former concierge, was "thin, aggressive and disagreeable", *Le Populaire* remarked unpleasantly. Moro salvaged something from a terrible afternoon when Mme Tréborel gave an incoherent answer during cross-examination and Gilbert interrupted to "clarify" what she had said.

Moro feigned shock at the judge's intervention.

"I have the right to speak to the witness," Gilbert said calmly.

"Yes, but not to draw conclusions from her evidence!" Moro retorted.

"Come on, *maître*, where have I done that?" Gilbert shot back.

"If you have something to say to myself or the jury, please say it after the verdict," Moro scolded Gilbert, addressing him like a schoolboy caught cheating in class. It was pure flummery, as both he and Gilbert knew. All that mattered to Moro was giving the jurors an uneasy feeling that Gilbert might not be entirely impartial.

Mme Tréborel was followed by Thérèse's only son Vincent, still a postal clerk and "very emotional" about insinuations in the press that he had not cared about his mother. Vincent insisted that if Thérèse had still been alive she would have written to him: "She had great affection for him, despite some differences that had arisen between her and his wife."

No one had the heart to ask Vincent why he had made no further effort to track down Thérèse after she had failed to reply to his last letter.

The detective Riboulet was the final witness of the day, explaining at tedious length how he had established that Landru had given Thérèse the codename "*Brésil*" in his *carnet*. "During this deposition, the public gradually began to leave," *Le Rappel* reported. "It was before an almost empty courtroom that the hearing ended at 5.25 pm."

***

Day Five: Friday, 11 November

Lucien Coulond, the sketchwriter for *Le Journal*, was appalled by how fashionable women, down from Paris for a day out at the trial, were steadily invading the press benches. Coulond did a headcount on Friday: out of 60 seats reserved for journalists, 19 were occupied by "mincing, chattering ladies", he noted in disgust. According to Coulond, these ladies "put their hands to their faces, brandish their *lorgnettes*, titter at every picturesque or scabrous detail and pout disapprovingly when one of the actors in the drama, defendant or witness, delivers a poor speech."

"Parigotte", a columnist for the newspaper *La Justice*, was convinced that most of the women in the gallery were sympathetic to Landru. "In remembering his mysterious history, they are, in spite of themselves, aroused with curiosity, vanity and jealousy; all of which predisposes them to be indulgent."

***

Gilbert turned at the start of Friday's session to Marie-Angélique Guillin, the 52-year-old retired housekeeper who had vanished at The Lodge in August 1915. Marie-Angélique was "uncultured" and foolish, Gilbert said; so stupid that she had fallen for Landru's story about being the next Consul General to Australia, in search of a wife to accompany him to diplomatic receptions. On the evidence table, Marie-Angélique's tatty pyjamas and cheap chestnut wig spoke of a woman more deserving of pity than contempt.

Marie-Angélique had told a neighbour that she had seen other women's clothes and shoes at The Lodge while spying through the keyhole of a locked room. Was she mistaken? Gilbert asked Landru.

"Women always embroider stories because of their vanity," Landru replied knowingly. "Do you really believe I would have left a woman's clothes lying around if I was bringing another one to see me?"

("Laughter": *Le Petit Journal*)

Landru refused to say what had happened to Marie-Angélique, citing his familiar "wall" of privacy. However, he did wish to make an observation about the police.

"It has only been three years since the police began looking for Mme Guillin," Landru said. "Give them a bit more time and perhaps they will find her!"

("Laughter": *Le Journal*)

He dismissed as absurd the allegation that he had forged a letter by Marie-Angélique to her bank in order to steal her savings. Regarding her possessions, he had not paid much attention to what she was selling him.

"Even her wig?" Gilbert enquired. To drive his point home, Gilbert ordered a court official to bring Marie-Angélique's hairpiece to Landru.

"I don't remember it," said Landru, refusing to look at the wig. "When you're buying *en bloc* you don't open up everything to inspect the goods."

Godefroy asked Landru why he would not reveal Marie-Angélique's whereabouts.

"If I know something on this matter, it's a secret that is not mine to share," Landru said, giving Godefroy exactly the answer he wanted.

"You are not forgetting that your head is at stake, are you?" Godefroy taunted Landru.

"You have threatened me with my head!" Landru shouted back. "My only regret is that I have just the one head to offer you."

"*Messieurs les jurés*," Moro said, "you will understand that regardless of my client's attitude, you will have to judge whether there is sufficient proof to cut off the only head that he possesses."

It was a feeble witticism, but Moro had at least reminded the jury that Landru's wild behaviour did not prove he was a murderer.

***

Moro's point was underscored by the witnesses who followed, none of whom had any evidence that Landru had killed Marie-Angélique. A woman who lived in the same apartment block recalled seeing Marie-Angélique and Landru walking arm in arm along the street below. Another neighbour remembered warning Marie-Angélique not to hand over her savings to her fiancé. Marie-Angélique's estranged daughter admitted that she and her husband had not worried too much when they heard no more from her mother. They had decided that her boat to Australia with her new husband might have been sunk by a German torpedo.

Gilbert came to Landru's theft of Marie-Angélique's sizeable investments following her disappearance.

Monsieur Lesbazeilles was the bank manager who had allowed Landru to withdraw part of Marie-Angélique's savings in November 1915, three months after she vanished. A tall, thin man in his forties, Lesbazeilles became flustered when Moro asked why he had agreed to bring the cheque to an address in western Paris that Landru had given him.

Lesbazeilles denied the whole visit, claiming that Landru must have withdrawn the money at the bank. Moro read Lesbazeilles' witness statement back to him, making sure the jury grasped an important detail. Lesbazeilles had also recalled seeing a middle-aged woman in the little apartment on Avenue des Ternes when he handed Landru the cheque. This woman must have been Marie-Angélique Guillin, Lesbazeilles had told the police.

Landru had been waiting for this moment. The witness was correct, Landru remarked courteously to Lesbazeilles; his companion had indeed been Mme Guillin. Landru could even refresh Lesbazeilles' memory about the apartment's location: "45 Avenue des Ternes, ground floor, to the left of an interior courtyard, reached via two or three steps beneath a canopy". At Moro's invitation, Landru drew a precise sketch of the apartment.

All the newspapers grasped the significance of this exchange. If Lesbazeilles' deposition was accurate, then Marie-Angélique must have been alive at 45 Avenue des Ternes several months after Landru allegedly killed her. In the circumstances, Gilbert could not refuse Moro's request for further enquiries by the police at the address.

***

Day Six: Saturday, 12 November

Landru was on perky form when he entered the court on Saturday, flanked by his usual escort of guards. "He takes off his bowler hat and gives the jurors a pleasant wave… a nice, friendly one," *Le Gaulois* remarked.

Moro was late and missed the first hour, which was devoted to the final witnesses in *l'affaire Guillin*. None of them had any first-hand knowledge of what had happened to Marie-Angélique when she left Paris.

Finally Moro bustled into court, full of apologies, just as Gilbert began examining Landru on a critical issue: Why had he terminated his lease at Vernouillet in August 1915 and then rented the Villa Tric outside Gambais four months later?

"Was it because the house where you lived in Vernouillet was squeezed between two other buildings?" Gilbert enquired, alluding to a murderer's need for privacy.

It was partly a matter of cost, Landru replied carefully, and partly because The Lodge had been too "dark" for his taste. "Note as well that I rented at Gambais with an option to buy the property. Now, someone who commits a crime – I am being modest, since I'm accused of committing seven crimes at this place – seeks to flee as quickly as possible from the theatre of his exploits."

Gilbert let the jurors dwell on Landru's supercilious reply while officials spread a plan of the Villa Tric's layout on the evidence table. Once the jurors had inspected the plan, Gilbert resumed.

Why had Landru used the name "Dupont" when he had signed the lease on the villa?

"What do you expect?" Landru said, amazed at the judge's obtuseness. "I often changed my name because I was being pursued by the law."

"This sally by Landru prompted a burst of giggling from some fashionable ladies," *Le Journal* reported. Several of them had even crept to the front of the gallery to get a better sight of the defendant. As an official shooed the women back to their seats, Gilbert threatened to clear the court if he heard more laughter.

Gilbert wanted to know why Landru had bought his little oven for the villa.

"The court insinuates that I bought this oven in order to burn my victims," Landru said. "Here, I appeal to the good sense of the jurors. It was winter; I couldn't just die of cold and not be able to cook a hot meal."

It was a good riposte, but Landru could not resist spoiling the effect with an irrelevant complaint about how "persons unknown" had stolen most of his coal. "I didn't go to the police, for reasons you will understand."

Pierre Vallet, the cobbler in Gambais who had doubled up as the villa's janitor, was the next witness. He was a lean artisan in his early fifties with a hunted, defensive manner. Vallet had seen more of Landru than anyone else in Gambais, yet he seemed confused about what he could recall and his testimony made no sense. Vallet's son Marcel, who had also visited the house regularly, was scarcely more coherent. Marcel said he remembered almost nothing about Landru, and certainly nothing sinister or suspicious. It was hard to tell whether the Vallets were as dim as they seemed to be, or accomplished actors who wanted nothing to do with the trial.

Auguste Tric, the owner of the villa, broad-chested, frock-coated and possessed of a splendid waxed moustache, was a well-to-do provincial businessman who had made his money as a shoe manufacturer. Monsieur Tric was also long-suffering, his former home a ruin, repeatedly ransacked by souvenir hunters.

Like the Vallets, Tric appeared keen to get off the witness stand as quickly as possible. He told Gilbert that he had no complaints against his former tenant, save one. There had once been a muddle about whether Landru was really called "Dupont". Landru had admitted to Tric that his real name was "Guillet", in business with a man called "Dupont". Tric had let the matter drop.

***

At the start of the mid-afternoon interval, the singer and film star Polaire, renowned for her tightly corseted waist and bizarre publicity stunts, saw a chance to get into the next day's newspapers. She left her seat in the VIP section of the gallery, walked straight past the soldier guarding the well of the court, and approached Landru as he was about to leave the defence box with his prison escort.

"Landru shot her one of his enigmatic and intriguing glances which from time to time seems like a lamp that illuminates his soul," *Le Siècle* remarked. "Polaire instinctively withdrew, struck by her encounter."

***

After the break, Gilbert examined Landru about Berthe Héon, the 55-year-old cleaning woman who had disappeared at Gambais in December 1915. Gilbert related Berthe's "cascade of sorrows" in the decade before she met Landru, losing her two legitimate children, her long-term partner, her son-in-law, and finally, in the spring of 1915, her adored natural daughter Marcelle in childbirth.

Landru was still incensed by his first sight of Berthe, when she opened the door of Marcelle's apartment one summer's day in 1915.

"As soon as I saw her, I could see she had lied about her age," Landru recalled. "She had counted her years from the date of her first communion."

("Laughter": *Le Petit Parisien*)

Landru insisted that he had only been interested in selling Berthe's furniture and that his lonely hearts advert had merely been a subterfuge to get his foot in her door.

"Didn't you object when Mme Héon presented you as her fiancé?" Gilbert asked.

"Absolutely not. Why should I contradict her? It did not worry me at all."

"Mme Héon told her friends that you would take her to Tunisia after her marriage. Is that why she wanted to get rid of her furniture?"

"You will see very soon that she did it because she had debts," Landru replied. "I even had to settle 260 francs in rent arrears that Mme Héon owed to her landlady."

This was true, but Gilbert ignored the oddity of a marriage swindler settling his victim's debts.

"Where did Mme Héon live after you sold her furniture?" asked Gilbert, closing in on Berthe's disappearance.

"I will not allow myself to reply to you. Here, we come back once more to the same question."

"Your private life, no doubt."

"If you wish. I arranged the sale of Mme Héon's furniture, that's all. If we wanted to go further, we would have to discuss the whole basis of the charges."

"But that's what we're here to do!"

"In these conditions, *monsieur le président*, I will reiterate my entreaty to you. It is now three years since I was charged; let the proofs be brought before me."

"It's not a question of that," Gilbert objected. "Can you indicate, yes or no, what became of Mme Héon?"

"I have nothing to say."

Landru denied he had taken Berthe to Gambais in early December 1915. He also had an ingenious explanation for why, on the day in question, he had written down the price of a return train ticket and a one-way ticket in his *carnet*. He was new to the area and had wanted a reminder of how much it would cost him to use the different stations that served Gambais.

"It is curious to consider how my unfortunate *carnet* is the prosecution's breviary," he remarked.

At the end of the session, the journalist Lucien Coulond reflected on the prosecution's "particularly nebulous evocation" of Berthe, the only alleged victim for whom there was no known photograph. No one had brought this lonely, bereaved woman to life, Coulond thought. "The widow Héon appears among these ghosts of the missing women like an indeterminate shadow."

Chapter 16

You Accuse Me, You Prove It

Day Seven: Monday, 14 November

Germaine Soubray, a young actress at the Grand Guignol theatre, swept into court on Monday morning with her VIP pass, dressed up warm against the cold, misty weather. Max Viterbo, a theatre critic covering the trial for *Le Siècle*, watched her being shown to her seat.

"Perhaps she dreams of incarnating one of Landru's victims in her next show at the Grand Guignol," Viterbo mused to his readers. "One would burn her totally nude. It would be superb."

Viterbo continued to scour the gallery for any other starlets, amid the "chattering" women whose presence in court he and the other male reporters deplored. Over the weekend, *Le Journal* had attacked these female spectators who were turning the trial "more and more into a spectacle". Meanwhile on its front page, *Le Journal* ran a cartoon showing Landru roasting a body on a skewer.

"For her engagement present, she asked me for *une broche* [brooch or cooking spit]," Landru sniggered, as human fat dripped into the fire.

***

The real Landru had spent much of Sunday in a special room set aside for him at the Palais de Justice, working through the case files on the typist Anna Collomb, who had disappeared at Gambais in December 1916.

"You will be rid of me in a fortnight," Landru remarked to his guard. "Have patience, my innocence will soon be proclaimed."

Gilbert summarised 44-year-old Anna as "thrifty" but with "loose" morals, giving both Godefroy and Moro an opening. Godefroy planned to portray Anna as silly and vulnerable, an easy target for a marriage swindler such as Landru. Moro intended to suggest that Anna had been a slut who had slept with plenty of other men; this "Anna" might easily have tired of her family and Landru and gone off to fresh pastures, probably abroad.

Gilbert failed to mention all the factors that had caused Anna to make a mess of her unhappy life: her bankrupt, alcoholic husband, her abandonment by the father of her illegitimate daughter, her dread that her parents might get to hear about the little girl. In his glib account, Gilbert merely remarked Anna had been determined to "remake her life" after the break-up of her affair with a man called Monsieur Bernard, the girl's probable father.

Gilbert began his examination of Landru by observing that Anna had lied about her true age when she answered Landru's lonely hearts advert in May 1915.

Landru was shocked by the judge's lack of gallantry. "That is something I would never have said, *monsieur le président.*"

Gilbert tartly reminded Landru of his complaint that Berthe Héon had also lied about her age.

("Laughter": *Le Petit Parisien*)

Landru denied that Anna had ever been his mistress. The question did not arise, he explained wearily, because he had only been interested in selling her furniture.

"But you brought her to Gambais."

"She was aimiable, educated, even literary. It was perfectly natural that, taking pleasure in her agreeable company, I thought of bringing her to the country on public holidays."

Landru refused to accept that Anna had ever slept at the apartment they had shared in the summer and autumn of 1916 on Rue de Châteaudun, near the Gare du Nord. "If she ever came there, it was only to get a little rest and certainly without spending the night," he declared. He insisted that Anna had introduced him to her family as a furniture dealer and "comrade", not as her husband-to-be. "It made no difference to me if she gave strangers the impression that I was her fiancé, but to her family, ah! *non!*"

Landru claimed to have no memory of Anna's last visit to Gambais on Boxing Day, 1916. Gilbert remarked that Landru had noted the purchase that day of two train tickets to Houdan, the station nearest Gambais.

Landru thought for a moment. "It's possible," he conceded.

"Can you explain why you bought a return ticket and a single ticket?"

Landru stretched his arms in front of him, palm down, as if he were inspecting his fingernails. Finally he looked up. He had bought a return ticket because his business commitments prevented him staying longer in Gambais. However, "it wasn't the same situation for Mme Collomb. At that moment, she did not have an apartment. To purchase a return for her would have been impolite."

"Did she remain in Gambais?"

"No, she left, but I can't remember when."

"You returned to Gambais on 3 January [1917]."

"It's possible, I don't remember," said Landru, irritated by Gilbert's forensic enquiry. "I never suspected that a day would come when I'd be asked such precise questions about matters I consider of no importance."

"*Eh bien!*" Gilbert exclaimed. "It appears that Mme Collomb disappeared on 27 December. So, precisely on that date, one finds the figure '4'. What does that mean?"

"It was a mnemotechnical indication, useful at the time, but I cannot remember what it signified."

Landru heard some stifled laughter coming from the gallery. This disturbance was too much, he protested, when he was doing his best to put the record straight.

"Each time the prosecution finds a figure in my *carnet*, this figure corresponds to a murder," he went on. "One finds the number 4 and that's it: Landru killed at 4 o'clock. Well, permit me to tell you, *monsieur le président*, it's a singular interpretation."

Landru would not reveal what had happened to Anna because it was a confidential matter. "The wall is closed, *monsieur le président*," he cautioned Gilbert, as if he were standing on high principle. "I will not say any more."

Gilbert pressed Landru about his attempts in early 1917 to fool Anna's friends and family into believing she was in southern France.

Landru said it had been Anna's idea to repay the small debt to her friend who ran a liquor store. "She had a fertile imagination," Landru explained, "and it was me who got my son [Maurice] to execute the commission in the way that Mme Collomb had indicated."

According to Landru, Anna had also dreamt up the ruse of placing a basket of flowers with her name card outside her family's apartment. Landru said he had merely been obeying her orders when he enlisted his younger son Charles to deliver the package.

Gilbert said that the "Nice" postmark on the package was a fake. The whole confection, including Anna's visiting card, had been assembled in Paris, Gilbert suggested to Landru.

Entirely wrong, Landru replied; he protested most earnestly against this misrepresentation of the facts.

"So Mme Collomb was therefore in Nice at this time?"

"Maybe."

Step by step, Gilbert worked through the financial records Landru had kept in his *carnet* during the months leading up to Anna's disappearance. Gilbert showed how the sums entering Landru's account exactly matched the sums leaving Anna's bank, with her written consent.

Godefroy requested the floor, granted by Gilbert. It was true, was it not, Godefroy asked Landru laboriously, that Mme Landru had forged Anna's signature on some of the bank documents.

Mme Landru was none of the court's business, Landru objected.

"Don't complain about justice in regard to your wife, Landru," Godefroy warned. "She has been treated with indulgence."

"How dare you pursue a woman who was only acting on her husband's orders." Landru stood to attention like a soldier and thumped his chest. "The wife owes obedience to her husband."

("Laughter": *Le Petit Parisien*)

***

After the interval, the court wrestled once more with the identity of the mystery woman seen with Landru at 45 Avenue des Ternes. Lesbazeilles, the bank manager, returned to the witness stand, looking nervous. Having checked his original police interview, Lesbazeilles conceded that there had been a woman with Landru in the apartment when he delivered the cheque for Marie Angélique Guillin's cashed-in investments. However, Lesbazeilles did not recognise her from Marie-Angélique's photograph.

Moro used Lesbazeilles' correction of his testimony to draw some "troubling" inferences for the jury. It was not simply that the police, to whom Moro paid "full tribute", had failed to establish the woman's identity. They had failed as well to track down Anna's former lover Monsieur Bernard, or even her illegitimate daughter, supposedly placed in a convent in San Remo.

"What is more," Moro continued, "the police have failed to find a single one of the missing women. I do not draw from these failures, for the moment, any conclusion, but I have the right to say that these uncertainties will, most definitely, make an impression on *messieurs les jurés*."

***

The court returned to the case of Anna Collomb. Mme Davril, Anna's friend in the insurance company typing pool, added force to Moro's thrust about the gaps in Anna's case by confirming that Monsieur Bernard had "flesh and bones". She reiterated: "He exists, I have seen him."

"And even he can't be located by the police!" Moro exclaimed. "It's not just Landru's fiancées that they can't find."

Anna's younger sister Ryno, who had combined with Célestine's housemaid sister Marie to force Landru's arrest, was the next witness. In a possibly deliberate *coup de théâtre*, Ryno was dressed in full mourning – not for Anna, but for her recently deceased father. She refused to be photographed, but when she flung back her veil, an artist drew her profile as she looked up towards the judges' bench. Her eyes were half closed, her lips were half open and her dark, straight hair fell back from her exposed neck; the picture was deliberately sexual.

Ryno wanted to show that she had no fear of Landru. After taking the oath, she looked coolly across at him, challenging him to hold her gaze. He turned away, avoiding her eyes throughout her testimony, which she delivered "with dignity", *Le Journal* reported.

She wished to tell the court the story of Anna's relationship with Landru from her point of view.

"Very soon, I noticed a great change in the character of my sister," Ryno said. "She seemed to be under Landru's influence."

Moro demanded the floor. Gilbert yielded, assuming that Moro wanted to object to Ryno's subjective remark. Instead, Moro shifted the discussion on to sensitive territory for Ryno.

"Your sister, *madame*, did she not have a relative in San Remo?" Moro enquired, alluding to Anna's illegitimate daughter.

Ryno hesitated. "I don't know," she lied, contradicting what she had told the police.

"It is possible for me to insist," Moro said firmly. He looked at Ryno, who stared straight back at him. Moro sat down, prudently deciding he had nothing to gain from bullying Ryno.

Nudged by Gilbert, Ryno explained why she rapidly realised that the basket of flowers left outside her parents' apartment was a trick to make the family believe that Anna was in southern France.

"This delivery of flowers gave me an apprehension that my sister was dead," Ryno declared. "There was no reason why she would have left us with no news for we had the tenderest of relations with her."

Moro could have asked Ryno what first-hand evidence she could produce that Anna was dead. He held back, sensing that Ryno had the jury's full sympathy. For the prosecution, Godefroy chose not to question Ryno about her patient detective work in pursuit of Landru, which reflected so badly on the authorities. She was thanked and dismissed, making way for her widowed mother.

Mme Moreau, dressed in full mourning, bore the twin loss of her husband and eldest daughter heavily. She was 68 but looked much older, as she sat down uneasily on the chair that was brought for her. When she lifted her veil, her face creased with anxiety at the spectacle around her. She began to cry.

At last she pulled herself together, waving aside Gilbert's suggestion that the court should adjourn. There was really only one thing she wanted to say, Mme Moreau murmured:

"My daughter [Anna] had a premonition that something bad would happen to her because the last time she came to see me at Christmas 1916, she left sobbing. She complained that her fiancé owed her money."

At the same Christmas lunch, Mme Moreau experienced her own "premonition" about Anna when she learned that Anna's fiancé used a false name to claim his refugee's allowance. Her fears had not been mistaken, Mme Moreau said. "My daughter was murdered on 26 or 27 December."

Godefroy chose this unsuitable moment to ask the clearly distressed Mme Moreau a delicate question about Anna's "loose" morals.

"Were you aware that your daughter had another liaison?" Godefroy enquired, alluding to the elusive Monsieur Bernard.

"She would never have told me," Mme Moreau retorted. "Besides, I wouldn't have tolerated such a thing."

In truth, Mme Moreau had her own secret, known only to her family. As a young woman, she had had an illegitimate daughter, born almost five years before her marriage to Eugène Moreau. She and her lover, probably Eugène, had called their baby girl Anna.

Mme Moreau was gently led from the court. The next witness, Anna's former concierge Mme Leffray, was quite old, very deaf, and talkative.

"Did Mme Collomb have a 'moral interest' in San Remo?" Moro asked, referring obliquely to Anna's little daughter.

"*Oui!*" Mme Leffray shouted.

With Gilbert's permission, Moro approached the witness stand to explain to Mme Leffray that he wished to ask her about the various men whom the concierge had seen spending the night with Anna. It would be kind if Mme

Leffray could lower her voice a little to spare the feelings of Mme Moreau and her daughter.

"Immediately, the honest chatterbox cupped her left hand and gesturing with her right, began to relay us with a series of tales which – *hélas* – did not reach the ears of the press benches!" the correspondent from *L'Humanité* lamented.

***

Day Eight: Tuesday, 15 November

Freezing rain swept across Versailles on Tuesday morning, drenching the crowds on the street outside the Palais de Justice. Each day the queues to attend the trial had steadily lengthened, far beyond the court's official capacity of about 250 seats. At midday, when the doors opened, people began jostling and shoving, desperate to gain an entry ticket to watch the Bluebeard of Gambais fight for his life.

Today, Gilbert reached Andrée Babelay, the 19-year-old nanny who had vanished at Gambais in the spring of 1917. Gilbert hinted that this extrovert girl might have been open to offers from strange men. "She had no money," *Le Journal* reported, picking up on Gilbert's insinuation, "yet when she went out, her get-up was extremely elegant and one could mistake her profession very easily."

Landru presented himself in relation to Andrée as a benevolent gentleman helping a young woman in distress.

"I met her on the metro, I saw she was sad, almost crying," Landru told Gilbert. "She said that she was all alone in the world, having quarrelled with her mother, and that she had just left her job. I tried to comfort her with kind words."

He had taken Andrée "out of charity" to an apartment he rented near the Gare du Nord. There, she had "fallen ill" and Landru had thought that a few days in the country might do her the world of good. "Andrée was suffering," he explained. "She was still half child, half young woman; the idea of the countryside delighted her."

Gilbert asked the familiar question: Why did he buy a single ticket for Andrée and a return ticket for himself?

"Because she needed to rest there."

What of the "fatal" entry in Landru's *carnet* on 12 April 1917: "4 o'clock, evening"?

Landru said he had merely noted the time of the cab service from Gambais to Houdan.

Gilbert corrected him; the cab did not leave at this hour.

"Did Andrée come back to Paris?" Gilbert asked.

"Yes, and then she got another job as a maid through an employment bureau. I don't know exactly where."

Gilbert pressed Landru further. Why had he kept Andrée's birth certificate, her family papers and various sentimental possessions? Surely, she would have taken these items to her new place of employment.

"She feared the indiscretions of the other servants," Landru replied. He paused a moment and then decided to embellish his answer:

"Andrée was indiscreet herself. One day, she opened a little chest in which I had placed the papers of other people who had confided them to me. This was what gave her the idea to entrust her own documents to me."

Moro could not disguise his shock at Landru's rash disclosure, while Godefroy also gave a start. Gilbert carried on, apparently unaware of Landru's blunder, even as Landru "paled, and tried to stutter back" what he had just said.

It took Gilbert several minutes to realise his oversight, possibly following a note from one of his assistant judges.

"You have just told us that Andrée had the curiosity to look in your chest at the papers of earlier missing women," Gilbert remarked. "Perhaps the court will find that this imprudence by her was not unconnected with her disappearance."

Landru repeated that he did not know where Andrée had gone.

The foreman of the jury, a farmer from a village near Gambais, had a question for Landru: "Why did you bring home with you, without any further formalities, a young woman whom you did not know?"

"Because her sorrow had moved me to sympathy."

"Why didn't you ask for Mlle Babelay's address when she left you definitively?" the juror followed up.

"Out of a sense of delicacy," Landru said. "She owed me money."

Godefroy got up, exasperated by Landru's evasions. "Andrée Babelay looked through your papers and she is dead. Jeanne Cuchet also looked through your papers and she is also dead."

For an instant Landru wavered; and then in an "exquisitely courteous" voice he said:

"Will you allow me, for my part, to ask why the police have not been able to find the employment bureau where Mlle Babelay went?"

"It is for you to say," Godefroy said angrily. "You alone are in a position to know."

"*Non!* I will say nothing. I have nothing to say. You accuse me, it's for you to prove it!"

Godefroy slammed his fist on the lectern. "But you don't even reply to the jurors who are your judges! That is more serious. I will provide the details and I will demonstrate them to you," Godefroy added with heavy menace.

"I'm looking forward to it," Landru replied.

Gilbert stilled the laughter from the audience at Landru's riposte and asked the clerk of the court to bring Andrée's mother to the witness stand.

Mme Victorine Colin, dressed in her best coat and hat, had trod a terrible road following Andrée's disappearance. She had repeatedly visited the central Paris morgue, demanding to see the latest unidentified female corpses in the hope that one of them was Andrée. Eventually the morgue had lost patience with this woman who would not take no for an answer. An official had shown Mme Colin photographs of 67 anonymous female corpses deposited at the morgue since 1914. Mme Colin was sure that one of the faces staring blankly back at her was Andrée. She was wrong. The police eventually identified the body as a suicide who had thrown herself into the Seine.

She stood to take the oath, declining Gilbert's offer of a chair, for she was determined to show a brave, unyielding face to Andrée's killer.

"May I know how Landru came to know my daughter?" Mme Colin asked Gilbert politely.

"Landru, you heard the question," Gilbert said. "Do you wish to reply?"

"I will leave you with this responsibility, *monsieur le président.*"

Gilbert recapped Landru's testimony, including Andrée's alleged row with her mother, making clear this was not the prosecution's narrative.

"It could not have happened like that," Mme Colin said firmly. On the day Landru met Andrée, she had gone out to the cinema with her mother and sisters, a picture of happiness.

"I have the absolute conviction that my daughter has died and that she has been murdered. She would not have left us without any news for the past four years. She adored her little sister too much. For sure, my daughter is no more!"

Mme Colin turned to address Landru, returning his glare across the well of the court:

"My daughter was not ill and she was not afraid of coming home. She visited us every Sunday, for I had the greatest indulgence for her. She had a good heart and deserved pity."

Landru carried on staring at Mme Colin.

"My daughter has been murdered and I am not frightened of looking you in the face." She would not move, her hands gripping the bar, summoning all her courage to keep on holding Landru's eye. And then she broke down, still clenching the bar, and wept.

Chapter 17

Let Us Not Look for Tragedy

Day Nine: Wednesday, 16 November

Mistinguett, the reigning queen of French musical theatre, her 46-year-old legs reportedly insured for 500,000 francs, glided into court on Wednesday morning. She was covering the trial for an English newspaper, Mistinguett announced to her new colleagues on the press benches. She pulled out a large notepad and began to jot down her first impressions.

Gilbert opened his brief on Célestine Buisson, the eighth alleged victim, last seen at Gambais in August 1917. Célestine, 44 at the time she met Landru, "was the epitome of a good little housewife, barely knowing how to read or write," Gilbert told the jurors. Various other details about Célestine seemed relevant to his pen portrait: she had a wig, a policeman lover who had died in the war, an illegitimate son and the "thoroughly creditable desire" to make a new home, using her nest egg of about 10,000 francs, a substantial sum.

Gilbert asked Landru why Célestine had met him in May 1915 via one of his lonely hearts adverts.

"She considered me as a brother, our relations were purely commercial."

("Laughter": *Le Petit Parisien*)

"She addresses you in one letter as '*mon chéri*'."

"It's a family term."

"She says in the same letter: 'I would like to be alone with you.' That's tender for a sister. She writes: 'I love my son, but you, you surpass him.'"

"Mme Buisson was a vulgar woman," Landru explained patiently. "She did not have a precise notion of the meaning of words."

"So, your advert was a ruse to disguise your business from her."

"Ruse is much too severe a word!"

"You used it yourself during an earlier examination."

Gilbert asked why Landru had not seen Célestine for six months, following their first meeting in May 1915.

"According to the prosecution, I was at this time in the process of murdering Mme Laborde-Line and Mme Héon. I must have been a very busy man."

In this roundabout exchange, Gilbert kept making Landru repeat his absurd claim that he was like a "brother" or "comrade" to Célestine. Moro was just as keen to make Landru stay quiet, even if it meant acknowledging that his client was a liar.

"*Messieurs les jurés*, there are two kinds of men," Moro interjected: "Those who, having never had lovers, nonetheless try to dishonour women; and those who, having perhaps had mistresses, refuse to say so. I am sure your choice is made."

It was a weak intervention, since Landru had just dishonoured Célestine by calling her vulgar.

Gilbert asked Landru to confirm that he travelled to Gambais with Célestine on 19 August 1917. Landru made a show of consulting one of his dossiers before agreeing with Gilbert. However, he added, "I am astonished that you have not pointed out that on the day in question, I bought a return and a single ticket."

"I was waiting for you to indicate this fact and for you to provide an explanation," said Gilbert, content to let Landru dig himself into a hole.

"*Eh bien!* It's really very simple. I bought a return for myself because I was coming back to Paris on business, while Mme Buisson was staying in Gambais, so only needed a one-way ticket."

Gilbert noted that Landru had written "10.15" in his *carnet* on the page for Saturday, 1 September 1917, the same day Célestine had vanished, according to the charge sheet.

"What became of Mme Buisson after that date?"

"What became of her?" Landru considered the matter for a moment. "She stayed in Gambais until the 10th or 11th of September."

"How do you explain the leap in your *carnet* accounts on 1 September from 88 francs 30 centimes to 1,031 francs?"

"These financial details escape me," Landru said airily. "I believe I recall that on 1 September I received 1,000 francs from a client."

"*Messieurs les jurés* will appreciate that," Gilbert remarked. "What about the recording of the hour on 1 September?"

Landru's patience was exhausted. "I am ashamed to have to tell you once again that it referred to the time of the cab from Gambais to Houdan."

"That's wrong, the police checked."

166

Landru tried another tack, asking how the prosecution could say Célestine had disappeared on 1 September when the police had found postcards she had subsequently written from Gambais.

"Witnesses will contradict that statement," Gilbert instructed the jurors.

Moro finally saw an opening in this difficult exchange for Landru. Raising a point of order, Moro suggested to Godefroy that Landru's noting of the hour on 1 September 1917 was not itself evidence of murder.

"Will you produce the proof that Landru committed a murder on this date?" Moro asked Godefroy.

Godefroy framed his response carefully. "I am persuaded that the women disappeared on those days, at the hours indicated," he said.

"I was asking for certainty and you reply with possibilities," Moro countered.

Gilbert asked Landru why he had withdrawn the remainder of Célestine's investments after she disappeared. Landru was ready for this question, claiming that Célestine had owed him money.

Why, then, had Landru used his wife to fake Célestine's signature on the bank authorisation papers?

Landru had also scripted this answer: "*Monsieur le président*, I have a particular conception of the law. For me, no offence has been committed when it causes no harm. So, Mme Buisson was travelling at the time, but the assets belonged to me."

"That's your opinion, not mine," Gilbert said sharply.

Landru bowed his head in mock deference to the judge. "Your opinion must be more enlightened, *monsieur le président*."

One of the jurors, a businessman from the suburbs of Versailles, asked Landru why Célestine had not taken her trunk with her when she left Gambais.

Landru gestured at Célestine's battered brown trunk, placed in the well of the court for the jury's inspection. "It was the war, luggage was a nuisance to carry around, especially a great big trunk like this one."

Godefroy wanted to read more extracts from Célestine's letters to Landru. "'My little angel, you will come and wake me – '"

"If I had been her lover," Landru interrupted, "she would not have asked me to come to her home to wake her up. I would have been sleeping with her."

"Look, Landru, you are too intelligent –"

"*Oh! monsieur l'avocat-général*, you are too generous towards me, for I'm really not that intelligent."

Moro had had enough of Landru's banter, which he could see was irritating the jurors.

"Landru," he warned, "don't have any illusions. You have tested the indulgence of the prosecutor to the limit."

Still Landru refused to desist, grumbling loudly about Godefroy's "iron fist inside his velvet glove". Gilbert cut in, ordering Landru to heed the wise words of his counsel. At last Landru sat down and to Moro's relief, returned to his colour-coded dossiers.

***

Célestine's younger sister Marie Lacoste was called to testify. She accepted a seat, not because she was in tears, as *Le Petit Parisien* mistakenly reported, but because she was lame. A photograph in *L'Excelsior* showed a sombre young woman in a wide-brimmed hat and fur stole, clasping her walking stick as she glared disdainfully at Landru.

Marie was the strongest prosecution witness to appear so far in the trial. She testified "with emotion and firmness", waving her stick from time to time at "this individual", as she referred to Landru. In telling detail, Marie recalled how Landru, alias Georges Frémyet, a rich industrialist, had duped Célestine into handing him almost all her savings. Marie described the layout of the Villa Tric, its grim interior and suspicious outbuildings. She also catalogued Landru's recurring visits to the Paris house where she worked as a maid, following Célestine's disappearance in 1917.

Landru had assured her that Célestine was alive and well, but always came on his own, Marie said. "I asked him why and he told me vaguely, 'Oh, she is staying in the country.'"

Moro declined to cross-examine Marie; he had nothing to gain. Neither Godefroy nor Gilbert asked Marie about her crucial role in bringing Landru to justice, assisted by Anna Collomb's sister Ryno. It was not in the prosecution's interest to have the police exposed to further ridicule for their failure to follow up Marie and Ryno's detective work.

Instead, Marie took it upon herself to deliver a final, withering statement to the jurors directly to her left. "I am convinced that if my sister were still alive, she would not have left her son without any news, a poor child who is blind," she declared. "My sister was murdered."

She stood up, shot Landru one last look of contempt, and limped out of court, her duty done.

***

Day Ten: Thursday, 17 November 1921

Fresh from *"Paris en l'Air"*, her latest show, Mistinguett arrived next morning for her second day's reporting in a black dress set off by a little white ruff in pleated muslin and "a superb pearl necklace".

"In my opinion he is guilty," she told her friend Max Viterbo, the theatre critic for *Le Siècle.*

"So you would convict Landru?" Viterbo asked.

"I didn't say that!"

Viterbo was confused. "Then you would not convict him?"

Mistinguett looked archly at Viterbo. "I didn't say that either!"

With that, she pulled out her enormous notebook and got to work.

Félix Belle, the correspondent for *Le Gaulois*, could just about tolerate Mistinguett, but he wanted all the other women attending "the Landru theatre" thrown out.

"Everywhere there are painted faces, plunging necklines, bare arms, jewellery and pearl necklaces," Belle complained. "Drenched by this flood of silk, the unfortunate chroniclers of the judicial process are submerged like shipwrecks."

The correspondent for *L'Intransigeant* agreed with Belle, deploring the "open cleavages" and "naked arms", which he claimed had turned the press benches into a "feminine" stage pit. "Never, at the height of his conquests, did Landru dream of such a success."

***

Louise Jaume, the devout 38-year-old dress shop assistant who had disappeared at Gambais in November 1917, was the next missing woman on the charge sheet. Louise was "gentle, a little *coquette*, and quite avaricious", in Gilbert's muddled pen portrait. Her estranged sister and father in southern France might have provided a more rounded picture of Louise, but they had declined to cooperate with the investigation. Even after her disappearance, they had shown no interest in Louise's fate.

It rapidly became plain that the prosecution had nothing to tie Landru to Louise's presumed murder apart from the notes in his *carnet*. Furthermore, Louise had been poor, once again casting doubt on the prosecution's claim that Landru had only killed for money.

"Are you going to speak again about my greed?" Landru taunted Gilbert and Godefroy. "Is that still the motive for this alleged murder, which you can't prove any more than the others?"

As usual, Landru refused to fill in the details: "Why hasn't the judiciary done its own research? It's always the same thing; you advance facts which you can't prove. *Moi*, I cannot tell you at all."

"You cannot say anything or you will not say anything?" Gilbert asked.

"Put down that I cannot, it's more polite."

Gilbert focused on Louise's last journey with Landru by train to Houdan, the nearest station to Gambais, on 25 November 1917.

"You say you only bought a single fare for Mme Jaume because she was staying on at the Villa Tric."

"And I will prove it."

Gilbert pointed out that on 26 November, Landru had written "5 o'clock" in his *carnet* beneath the date and that Louise had not been seen since.

"That's wrong. Mme Jaume came back to Paris several days later."

Gilbert asked Landru why he, not Louise, had given a friend of Louise a box of chocolates on New Year's Day, 1918. Landru said that the chocolates must have been bought by Louise, because he had not written down the cost in his *carnet*.

"Tell me rather where Mme Jaume was at this time," Gilbert interjected.

Landru stayed silent.

"Do you not wish to reply?"

Landru bowed his head. "*Non, monsieur*," he said quietly and sadly.

("Stupefied murmuring": *Le Petit Parisien*)

Gilbert applied more pressure. "Why, in the *carnet* for 26 November 1917, did you write '*récuperation Lyanes*, 274 francs 60'?"

"No, really, if we're going to carry on like this, I'd prefer to leave," Landru lashed out, turning towards the exit. Landru's guards blocked him, just as Moro was rising to restrain his client. Landru collected himself and then said in an injured tone: "I am truly sorry to see you attach such importance to my *carnet*. These are personal notes."

Gilbert moved on to the story Landru had given Mme Lhérault, Louise's former employer at the dress shop, about Louise going to America to take a job.

"Had she departed when you said that?" Gilbert asked.

"Ah! *monsieur le président*, here we arrive at a moment where I can no longer say anymore what Mme Jaume has done."

"For what reason?"

"I don't have the right to say," Landru said, as if this was obvious. "She sold me her furniture, it was mine. One point, that's all."

Godefroy remarked on Landru's refusal to say what had happened to Louise: "I am warning you that I will be making a powerful argument on this matter."

"Well, *monsieur l'avocat général*, I thank you for having the charity to notify me in advance."

("Laughter": *Le Gaulois*)

Suddenly Landru raised his right arm in the air and held it there, waiting for the court to fall silent. "I request a delay of 24 hours, *monsieur l'avocat-général*, to give you the address of one of the missing women," he announced.

Landru's declaration, "launched out of the blue, and for no apparent reason, caused a sensation," *Le Journal* reported. Gilbert took note of the request, without granting Landru's wish: if he had news to relate to the court, he could offer it at any time.

Godefroy plodded on with his questions about Louise.

"You lifted the 274 francs from the body of Mme Jaume after you killed her at 5.00 pm, as written in the *carnet*," Godefroy accused Landru.

"Prove it," Landru hit back.

Many of the audience were on their feet, trying to get a better view of this latest bust-up between Landru and Godefroy, while a few bolder spectators crept forward to the gangway at the front of the gallery. Gilbert called an interval, hoping to calm things down.

***

Gilbert was losing control of the court, with each new breach of protocol encouraging another one. "During the break, ladies' sleeves are emptied of their contents which, for once, are not make-up boxes," *Le Populaire*'s reporter commented. "Flasks of *chocolat au lait* and *café-crème*, brioches, madeleines and nougats all appear; tomorrow, no doubt, Landru will be judged in champagne."

***

Mme Eugénie Lhérault, the *patronne* of the dress shop where Louise had worked, took the oath. She remembered Louise telling her one day: "'My fiancé is a real homebody and yet he is very bizarre around the house and garden; at Gambais he sweeps up dead leaves and puts them in a hangar.'" This was as close as Mme Lhérault could get to proving that Landru had murdered Louise.

Brigadier Riboulet returned to testify about the suspicious notes in Landru's *carnet* for the date 26 November 1917, the day Louise had disappeared. In his considered view, Riboulet thought there was a "correspondence" (*"rapport"*) between the hour that Landru had noted, 5.00 pm, and the time of the murder.

"What *'rapport'*?" Moro asked Riboulet sharply. "There is a *rapport* which indicates nothing apart from the *rapport* between the note and the hour."

("Laughter": *Le Populaire*)

***

Day Eleven: Friday, 18 November 1921

By noon on Friday, the reporter for *L'Ouest-Éclair* reckoned there were around 500 people queuing outside the Palais de Justice, double the court's seating capacity.

Among those locked out when the doors slammed shut was an old lady from a remote village in Auvergne. Back home, she explained, nobody believed in the existence of the Bluebeard of Gambais. Her fellow villagers thought he was a myth, invented by the authorities "to distract the public from the general situation".

Only she had believed in this Bluebeard, the widow said proudly, and to prove her neighbours wrong, she had travelled all the way to Paris and queued for three days running in the hope of gaining admission.

"All I want is to see Landru for five minutes to confirm he is flesh and bones."

Overhearing her tale, several people persuaded a court official to give her a special pass to sit with the VIPs, who today included the Duke and Duchess of Valentinois.

***

"He [Landru] made his *entrée* and doffed his bowler hat at the jurors in such a studied, ceremonious fashion that the audience burst out laughing," *Le Petit Journal* reported. Landru halted for a moment, taken aback by this affront to his dignity.

Moro was late again, a recurring pattern in the trial, because he generally spent the mornings in Paris dealing with other legal and political commitments before travelling down to Versailles. He and Navières probably had no idea that the statement Landru now asked the court's permission to make about Berthe Héon, who had vanished at Gambais in December 1915, would lead the defence into a trap.

"One has searched in vain for Mme Héon, following her so-called disappearance," Landru declared to the hushed court. "One has searched for her in a 'very meticulous' fashion in all quarters. She was however living very close to her apartment at 159 Rue de Rennes, at the Hôtel du Mans, in a little room overlooking the courtyard for which I could draw a plan, as I did for 45 Avenue des Ternes."

"That's interesting, particularly interesting," Gilbert remarked knowingly.

"It's even more interesting than you think, Landru," Godefroy added with relish. "We will pursue further investigations immediately."

The press was one step ahead, with reporters already calling into their news desks from the phone booths in the corridor to get the Hôtel du Mans checked out.

***

Moro arrived just as Gilbert began examining Landru about Annette Pascal, the dressmaker who had disappeared in April 1918. Annette was "likeable" but "loose", Gilbert said, making her sound like a warm-hearted tart.

"Was she your mistress as soon as you met her?" he asked Landru.

"I am silent."

Gilbert pointed out that Annette's niece Marie-Jeanne and several of Annette's seamstress friends all said that Landru had proposed marriage to her.

"They were just cackling like women together always do," Landru remarked dismissively.

Why, then, had Landru taken Annette to Gambais at the end of March 1918?

"Mme Pascal was a little nervous about the bombing raids," Landru said. "It was an agreeable *détente* for her."

He said he had bought Annette a one-way train ticket for her next visit, on 4 April 1918, because her departure was "definitive" – and no, regrettably, he could not recall why he had written "17h 15" in his *carnet* under the date for 5 April.

Gilbert came to the letters Annette had written on 5 April to her sister Louise in Toulon and to her friend Mme Carbonnel, a seamstress. Landru said he had no idea why the letter to Louise had been crudely post-dated in another hand to read "19 April".

"What became of Mme Pascal?"

"But she stayed at Gambais."

"And perhaps she is still there. For since April 1918, a death-like silence has enveloped her, as with the other missing women."

"Let's not look for tragedy in all this history."

Gilbert tried again. "Why did nobody hear anything more from Mme Pascal after 5 April 1918?"

Landru said nothing.

Why had Landru sold all Annette's modest valuables and personal effects, right down to her denture?

"*Pardon*," Landru corrected Gilbert, "this denture belonged to my father. It was very old and had rubber mountings, not gold ones. I sold it for less than 35 francs. A modern denture like Mme Pascal's would have fetched a much higher price."

***

In her despair, Annette's older sister Louise, Annette's "*maman*", had filed her own civil suit against Landru, even though she had no chance of obtaining any financial compensation from the bankrupt defendant. Louise's counsel now intervened for the first time in the trial.

Maître Louis Lagasse, 61, tubby, bald and irascible, was a prominent *avocat* at the Paris Bar. Lagasse wanted to know what had become of Annette's fluffy white cat Minette, which she had brought with her to Gambais.

"It's no longer me who has to reply here, but the correspondence of Mme Pascal," Landru declared. "She said that the cat was very homesick."

("Laughter": *Le Petit Journal*)

Landru denied that the "vicious stray" he had strangled and buried in the villa's garden was the same creature as Minette. Lagasse sat down after this odd exchange, which got the jury no closer to the truth about Annette's fate.

Mme Dèves, a seamstress who had worked for Annette, was asked by Gilbert if she recognised the defendant.

"Yes, I recognise the murderer Landru," she said, jabbing her finger at him.

Moro objected immediately to the witness's prejudicial language. Gilbert upheld the objection, reminding Mme Dèves that she was here to testify, not to accuse. She pondered Gilbert's advice for a moment and then turned to face Landru.

"Murderer!" she screamed at the defendant.

Annette's older friend Mme Carbonnel, a big, blousy woman, knew little about court procedure. After taking the oath she turned her back on Landru and introduced herself to the jury in a loud "mezzo-soprano" voice.

Once Gilbert had called her to order, Mme Carbonnel repeated a lurid tale from her witness statement. Annette had come back from a night with Landru at Rue de Rochechouart, terrified out of her wits. According to Mme Carbonnel, Annette said Landru had put her into a hypnotic trance, from which she had awoken to find his hands around her neck. Here, Mme Carbonnel pretended to strangle herself and faint.

Moro said Mme Carbonnel's anecdote was pure hearsay and should be dismissed as such by the jury. However, a reporter from *Le Gaulois* newspaper thought enough of her tale to call Dr Gustave Geley, director of Paris's Institut Métaphysique, for an expert opinion.

Geley rejected the notion that Landru might have exercised an "occult", hypnotic power over Annette and his other fiancées. The reason why so many women had fallen for Landru was obvious, Geley opined: "the natural curiosity of all daughters of Eve, their desire for fresh sensations, and the feminine attraction to horror".

***

Day Twelve: Saturday, 19 November

The temperature plummeted overnight, shrouding Versailles in icy fog. Next morning, a reporter for *Le Paris Parisien* estimated there were about 1,000 people trying to bluff or shove their way into the Palais de Justice for Saturday's session. Inside the overfilled courtroom, Lucien Coulond of *Le Journal* decided that most of the audience had come purely to amuse themselves.

Coulond thought that Landru, the star of the show, was on the brink of collapse, after almost a fortnight of relentless examination:

"He no longer has the studied calm of the trial's first days. He is febrile. He makes brusque starts. He springs to his feet like a jack in the box. And when one hits him with one of those questions that he has so much trouble answering, one can see his temporal artery quivering like a compass needle."

***

Gilbert began the hearing with a change to the schedule, for a reason that only became evident at the end of the afternoon. Instead of calling the rest of the witnesses in Annette Pascal's case, Gilbert moved to the last alleged victim on the charge sheet: 37-year-old Marie-Thérèse Marchadier, who had disappeared in January 1919.

Gilbert made Marie-Thérèse sound like an easy target for Landru: a career prostitute looking to better herself through marriage, with stacks of furniture that she wanted to sell. Yet Gilbert's portrait of Marie-Thérèse, based on the *réquisitoire*, failed to answer two questions:

> Why had Landru picked up a debt-ridden prostitute at a time when he was reduced to borrowing small change from his wife?

> Why had an experienced street girl like Marie-Thérèse allowed herself to be hoodwinked by an obvious crook?

Landru claimed he had wanted to rent a room from Marie-Thérèse as a workshop to make the automobile radiator he had invented. Somehow, the negotiation had progressed to buying her furniture.

"I believe that, according to your custom, you spoke as well of marriage to Mlle Marchadier," Gilbert said sarcastically.

"It's not impossible, but it was above all with a view to 'psychological studies'."

Gilbert asked Landru about Marie-Thérèse's two visits to the Villa Tric in January 1919. Why had Landru borrowed money from his wife and the cobbler in Gambais to pay for the train tickets?

"My wallet had been stolen."

"Why didn't you report the theft?"

Landru was incredulous: "Can you seriously see me, on the run from the law, presenting myself to the police?"

Gilbert wanted to discuss in more detail the second of Marie-Thérèse's visits, on 13 January 1919, after her apartment had been cleared by Landru. According to Landru's *carnet*, he had returned alone to Paris on 14 January.

"What became of Mlle Marchadier?"

"She remained in Gambais."

"For how long?"

"Four or five days, perhaps. I wasn't paying attention," Landru shrugged.

"For the last time, do you wish to tell us what became of Mlle Marchadier?"

"I don't have to immerse myself in her private life."

"Oh! Mlle Marchadier's profession was fairly public," said Gilbert, referring to her career as a prostitute.

Landru now changed his story, effectively admitting he had just lied. He said that he had returned by train to Paris with Marie-Thérèse Marchadier and parted company with her outside the station. He regretted that he could not remember Marie-Thérèse's new home in Paris. However, he was sure her friends could give the court "this luminous address", a snide reference to the lights that prostitutes kept on when they were open for business.

Landru found it easier to explain why he had killed the three little griffon dogs that Marie-Thérèse had brought with her to the villa. He said she had "formally ordered" their destruction because she could not afford to feed them or pay for dog licences.

Why had he hung the dogs with a cord? Gilbert asked.

Landru paused, as if he did not wish to answer. At last he looked up and told Gilbert that strangulation was "the gentlest of deaths", drawing gasps from the audience.

A juror stuck up his hand. Why had Landru killed the dog that Marie-Thérèse had borrowed from her friend Mme Poillot?

Landru stuttered that Mme Poillot must have left Paris, having fallen ill, and no doubt her dog would have been a nuisance to her.

Moro had had enough of jurors asking alarmingly pertinent questions. "In a very moderate harangue", Moro put the jurors on guard against "certain forms of questions" that presumed Landru's motives. For once Gilbert supported Moro, reminding the jurors "not to betray their sentiments" about the case.

On that note, Gilbert called a brief interval.

***

At 3.15 pm, when Gilbert returned to the court, he put Marie-Thérèse's case temporarily to one side and went back to Annette Pascal's disappearance.

Brigadier Riboulet appeared for his familiar turn on the witness stand, explaining how all the police's efforts to trace Annette had failed.

Rather than take another general swipe at the investigation, Moro made a more pointed attack on Riboulet's detective skills. Moro observed that there were "contradictions" in Riboulet's analysis of Landru's notes in his *carnet*. In particular, Moro wished to know why Riboulet thought there was a "*rapport*" between Landru's noting of the hour on 5 April 1918 and the alleged time of the murder.

With Gilbert's permission, Riboulet brought the *carnet* over to Moro, so the two of them could go through the relevant pages together.

At this moment, Louise Fauchet's barrister Louis Lagasse began to ask Riboulet a question, which was instantly drowned out by Moro's protest to Gilbert. Moro was adamant that a lawyer representing a civil plaintiff – in this instance, Lagasse – had no right to ask a witness follow-up questions after the defence.

Nothing had prepared Gilbert for Moro's next remark. "I am now withdrawing from the case for as long as the civil party [Lagasse] is engaged in this part of the trial," Moro announced. He stuffed his notes into his briefcase and strode ostentatiously towards the exit in a swirl of flowing robes.

Just in time, Gilbert summoned Moro back for a hasty conclave with Lagasse by the judges' bench. Lagasse grudgingly gave assurances of his "good intentions", ceding a minor victory to Moro, and the hearing resumed.

Moro was still not done with putting Lagasse firmly in his place. A few minutes later, Lagasse tried to ask a handwriting expert about the alteration of the date on Annette's last letter to her sister Louise. It was a legitimate question, but again interrupted Moro's cross-examination. This time Moro carried out his threat, flouncing out of the courtroom, his face "very pale", followed by Navières.

Seeing his barristers abandon him, Landru shouted: "I demand that the trial is declared in default, since I no longer have a lawyer!"

Landru picked up his colour-coded dossiers, grabbed his bowler hat and made ready to go, in his own mind a free man at last. Gilbert snapped at Landru to stay in his seat, while the guards blocked the defendant's exit route. The judge then called a recess, gathered up Godefroy and Lagasse, and went off to find Moro.

Moro soon returned, beaming broadly, along with Navières, Godefroy, Lagasse and Gilbert. There had been a "misunderstanding", Moro explained to the jurors, perhaps "a little too lively", but he was happy to take his place again alongside Maître Lagasse. Moro sounded as if he was making a generous concession.

Lagasse probably knew Moro's courtroom tricks well enough to realise that the whole fracas was a mark of respect. Unlike the pedestrian Godefroy, Lagasse was a skilful *avocat* who had the potential to cause trouble for the defence when his client, Annette's sister Louise, was finally summoned to testify.

***

Louise had waited a long time for her settling of accounts with Landru. From her home in Toulon, she had chivvied Bonin with peremptory notes, handed over all Annette's correspondence, given her witness statement, consulted with another sister in Tunisia, and via her capable daughter Marie-Jeanne (who wrote much better French) kept up the pressure on the authorities in Paris for more than two years. Louise wanted revenge on the killer of her little sister Annette, who had called her "*maman*" and had never really grown up.

Shortly before 5.00 pm, the reason why Gilbert had delayed Louise's appearance in court became clear. She sat in a chair on the witness stand, sad and frightened, staring blankly around her. Through glazed eyes, Louise saw the judges, the jury, the lawyers and Landru and froze, too nervous even to take the oath. A quick nod of agreement from Lagasse, Moro and Godefroy, and Gilbert took pity on her. The trial would be adjourned till Monday.

Chapter 18

You Cannot Live With the Dead

Day Thirteen: Monday, 21 November

The trial had become "a nauseating spectacle", Lucien Coulond, the sketchwriter for *Le Journal*, decided on Monday. As soon as Landru entered the courtroom, the audience let out "oohs" and "aahs", craning to get a glimpse of the "wretched, emaciated" defendant.

Today, it was not just Landru whom the public had come to ogle. Fernande Segret, Landru's mistress and self-styled "survivor", was due to testify. She had already confided to a journalist who had taken her out to lunch that some of her evidence might need to be heard in closed session because it was so shocking.

"Closed session," the reporter exclaimed, as Fernande tucked into a *crème caramel*.

"Yes. I believe they want to ask me some delicate questions about Landru's physiology. They have used the word 'sadism' but this is not true at all. He is an attentive man, very normal, who goes to bed early and sleeps like a baby."

Fernande's *entrée* was scheduled for later in the day. The hearing began with Godefroy making what he called "an important announcement" about the cleaning woman Berthe Héon, who Landru said had stayed at the Hôtel du Mans in the autumn of 1915, shortly before she vanished.

There was "a parcel of truth" here, Godefroy told Landru, for the police had established that Berthe did stay briefly at a hotel in October 1915 after Landru had sold her furniture. However, Berthe had soon moved on Landru's orders to a more interesting address.

"I would request in relation to this matter that the court should now hear a witness," Godefroy declared, labouring to build the suspense. "You believe, Landru, that the dead don't leave their tombs. *Eh bien!* The person is going to come before us who will speak for one of your victims."

181

She came to the witness stand with her hands stuffed into a muff, her chubby face framed by a wide-brimmed velvet hat. Juliette Auger, 27, was not required to take the oath because she had been summoned personally by Gilbert. A few days earlier, Gilbert had received a letter from Juliette and now he asked her to tell her story.

She spoke in a flat, monotone voice, as if she had learned her lines by heart in order to quell her nerves. Juliette explained that she had been the best friend of Berthe's daughter Marcelle, who had died in childbirth in the spring of 1915. Many times, Juliette had visited Marcelle's rough, unkempt grave in southern Paris, keeping her promise to Berthe to lay flowers while Berthe was away in Tunisia with her new husband. Over the years, Juliette had often wondered why this man, whom she had met, had not honoured his parting pledge to buy a nice, marble tombstone for Marcelle.

In April 1919, Juliette had seen a newspaper photograph of Landru and realised that he was Berthe's fiancé. Juliette had thought about going to the police, but as she had noted (a little disingenuously) in her letter to Gilbert, she had assumed that other witnesses had known where Berthe had gone in October 1915. Besides, Juliette had not wanted her name in the press.

She had decided to come forward after reading about the confusion over the identity of the mystery woman in the apartment at 45 Avenue des Ternes. Juliette knew for certain that the woman seen by the bank manager Lesbazeilles had been Berthe, not Marie-Angélique Guillin, as Landru had claimed:

"Mme Héon came to see me as the month of November 1915 approached and announced that she had moved and was now living in a hotel on Rue de Rennes, opposite the Gare Montparnasse. She told me that her fiancé Monsieur Petit [Landru] did not wish her to stay there. Finally, she gave me a rendezvous for 8 November at her new address, 45 Avenue des Ternes."

Juliette recalled that Berthe had been alone when she arrived at the apartment. Berthe had told Juliette that she had just laid fresh flowers on Marcelle's grave and then spoke of her "joy" at sailing soon for Tunis with Monsieur Petit. It would be a whole new life after all her sorrows, Berthe had said.

Landru, alias Petit, had then returned, just as Berthe was giving Juliette some jewellery that had belonged to Marcelle:

"All of a sudden she began to sob, as she talked about the death of her daughter. Monsieur Petit interrupted and remarked to her that one could not live with the dead who did not leave their tombs. I was deeply shocked by his comment."

Berthe had obediently wiped her tears away but Landru, alias Petit, had not finished chastising her. He told Berthe that they would be in Tunisia for at least three years before his next trip back to Paris, so there would be no chance for her to visit Marcelle's grave in the meantime. Berthe had begun to cry again.

A few minutes later, Berthe had accompanied Juliette to the nearby metro station. Before saying goodbye, Berthe had told Juliette that her fiancé had promised to pay for a marble headstone for Marcelle's grave. Berthe had asked Juliette to look after Marcelle's grave, a commission that Juliette had gladly fulfilled.

Juliette's story, heard in silence, was over. Landru rose slowly to his feet and nodded courteously at her:

"I do not doubt the sincerity of the witness but I take note that she is the only witness who has come to speak of Mme Héon having lived at Avenue des Ternes."

"Do you recognise the witness?" Godefroy asked Landru.

"Not at all."

"Do you recognise nonetheless that Mme Héon lived at Avenue des Ternes?"

"I never saw her there." Landru suggested that perhaps the witness was confused about events that had happened seven years ago.

Moro tried to contain the severe damage caused by Juliette's exposure of Landru's lies and cruelty towards Berthe. Overruling Landru, Moro said the defence accepted that Berthe had lived with Landru at 45 Avenue des Ternes. Moro would add only one comment: the police had failed to trace Landru and a woman to this address and it was not the defence's task to fill the gaps in the investigation.

***

Annette Pascal's elder sister Louise Fauchet returned to the witness stand, determined to keep her palpable anxiety at bay for long enough to give her evidence. In a faltering voice, Louise recalled how she had invited Annette to come to Toulon in the spring of 1918, when the Germans were bombing Paris. Louise had even sent Annette 80 francs for the train ticket.

"I had brought her up and she used to call me her 'little *maman*'," Louise explained, adding bleakly: "I never received a reply."

Gilbert thanked Louise for her helpful testimony and moved on to the next witness.

So far, the women witnesses had worn sober shades of grey, brown and black. Louise's daughter Marie-Jeanne came dressed to kill in a tight-waisted skirt cut just below the knee, high-heeled laced boots and a dazzling white stole, the whole ensemble set off by a sombrero in honour of her late aunt. Marie-Jeanne took the oath, flashed an icy glance at Landru, and looked up at Gilbert. She was ready to answer any questions he might wish to ask her, Marie-Jeanne announced to Gilbert in her sing-song Mediterranean accent – "like a little bird", according to *Le Figaro*.

"This gentleman was very gallant," Marie-Jeanne said, flicking her little finger in Landru's direction. "He used to bring us cakes."

"*Monsieur Mystère*", as Marie-Jeanne called him, had for a long time refused to give Annette his address. He had also declined to sleep with Annette at her apartment while Marie-Jeanne was there.

"He once took her off to a hotel to spend the night with him," Marie-Jeanne remembered. "Next morning my aunt told me he had been – oh! *so* gentle with her." Landru's love letters to Annette, which Marie-Jeanne had also enjoyed reading, had been "oh, *so* beautifully written".

"He asked me, 'When are you leaving Paris, little Marie?'" Here, she mimicked Landru's suburban drawl.

("Laughter": *Le Petit Parisien*)

She waved her hand at Landru. "It is perhaps because I knew too many things about the *monsieur* present here that he paid the cost of my journey home."

("Laughter": *Le Rappel*)

Marie-Jeanne recalled how she had visited Rue de Rochechouart in January 1918, bearing a note from Annette for the man they had known as "Lucien Forest"; how she had learned from the concierge that he used another alias, "Lucien Guillet"; and how she had slipped the note under his door, without knocking – a mistake, Marie-Jeanne acknowledged.

Lagasse, the lawyer acting for Marie-Jeanne's mother, asked whether they would have heard from Annette if she had still been alive.

"*Oh! monsieur.* She would have written to us even if she could only have used her blood."

("Murmuring": *Le Rappel*)

Moro stood up, tired of Marie-Jeanne's deliberately provocative performance.

"Was it true, *mademoiselle*," he enquired blandly, "that you visited Gambais with Landru?"

"There was never any question of me going to Gambais with the defendant," Marie-Jeanne retorted.

Clearly, then, Moro continued, she had no first-hand knowledge of the house where Annette had supposedly vanished.

Marie-Jeanne could not deny his point. With one simple question, Moro had exposed to the jury that she knew nothing about what had passed between Landru and Annette in Gambais.

***

Having dealt with *l'affaire Pascal*, Gilbert went back to the interrupted hearing on Marie-Thérèse Marchadier, the last of the missing fiancées, who had vanished at Gambais in January 1919. Several of Marie-Thérèse's friends, all middle-aged prostitutes, were called in turn to testify.

The first, Adrienne Poillot, had gone to great trouble to make sure the authorities could obtain her testimony. In the spring of 1919, after giving a statement to police, Adrienne had left Paris for Strasbourg, her home city, where she had been admitted to hospital for an operation on her leg. While she was convalescing, Adrienne had been interviewed again by the Strasbourg police about her friendship with Marie-Thérèse.

Nine months later, Adrienne was told that the investigating magistrate Bonin wished to interview her in Paris. Adrienne had written to explain that she could not afford the train fare, but could answer Bonin's questions by letter and would of course testify at Landru's trial.

And here she was, mustering all her dignity as she took the oath.

Gilbert treated Adrienne as a necessary evil, in the absence of more respectable witnesses. He scarcely bothered to question her about why she had lent Marie-Thérèse one of her griffon dogs to take to Gambais, even though Adrienne's testimony contained a curious detail. According to Adrienne, Marie-Thérèse had promised to return the dog in a few days' time. If true, Marie-Thérèse's pledge cast some doubt on whether she had seriously intended to settle in the country as Landru's wife.

Adrienne was dismissed and a muddle ensued, as the court bailiff mistakenly summoned Fernande Segret rather than Marie-Thérèse's best friend Yvonne Le Gallo. Fernande tottered to the witness stand, already in tears, and apparently on the verge of fainting. A chair was brought and in a shaky voice she took the oath, confirming she was "Fernande

Segret, 28 years old, *artiste lyrique*". At this point the clerk realised the bailiff's error. Offering the court's apologies, Gilbert told Fernande that her testimony would be heard tomorrow and she was led away, "amid 'ahs!' of compassion and disappointment from the audience".

Yvonne Le Gallo, 48, now took the oath, describing herself as a seamstress. Moro decided to have some fun at her expense.

"Mme Le Gallo has indicated that she exercises the profession of dressmaker," Moro remarked. "Does she perhaps have another profession?"

"Mind your own business!" Yvonne shot back.

("Laughter": *Le Gaulois*)

Like Adrienne, Yvonne was on and off the witness stand in a few minutes, despite knowing far more about Marie-Thérèse's rackety life than anyone else. The only subject of interest to Gilbert and Godefroy was Yvonne's remark that Marie-Thérèse had displayed "a mania for marriage". Still smarting from her needless humiliation by Moro, Yvonne did not explain exactly what Marie-Thérèse had meant.

***

Day Fourteen: Tuesday, 22 November

"It is a ridiculous utensil, scarcely bigger than a bedside table," Lucien Coulond wrote of Landru's rusty little oven, plonked on Tuesday morning in front of the jury box. Coulond thought the oven was far too small to burn human corpses.

The prosecution had hoped to call Mme Falque, the comfortably off widow who had lent Landru money at an extortionate rate in the winter of 1918–19. However, Mme Falque was ill, so Gilbert referred to her witness statement, in which she remembered being unimpressed by Landru's oven (*cuisinière*) during her only visit to Gambais.

According to Mme Falque, Landru had retorted that one could burn anything in his *cuisinière*. His remark was relevant to the case, Gilbert suggested to Landru, who objected that "upwards of 5,000 Parisian concierges" might say the same thing when showing a new tenant around their apartment.

Fernande now made her second appearance of the trial. Mistinguett, once again in the audience, watched agog with the rest of the gallery as

Fernande walked unsteadily to her chair on the witness stand, looking at any moment as if she might faint.

"What is your profession?" Gilbert asked Fernande.

"*Artiste lyrique*," she murmured.

Encouraged by Gilbert, Fernande recalled her literary discussions with Landru on a boating pond in the Bois de Boulogne, their evenings out at the Opéra-Comique, his proposals of marriage; and then suddenly she clutched her throat.

"I'm choking! I'm choking!" Fernande gasped, subsiding backwards into the arms of the clerk of the court. He whipped out a bottle of smelling salts that he had secreted in his robes, having observed Fernande at close quarters the previous day. A doctor came forward from the audience and Fernande gradually came round, watched intently by Landru.

After twenty minutes, she felt strong enough to answer more questions from Gilbert.

Yes, she had visited the Villa Tric six or seven times and had seen the rifle that Landru kept there, plus some cartridges. No, she had never noticed any strange smells or fumes at the property. Yes, she had seen other women's clothes in the bedrooms. She had accepted Landru's explanation that they belonged to an occasional female tenant.

Gilbert asked Landru if he had anything to say to the witness. Landru shook his head. Moro stood up, exuding geniality. He had a question for Mlle Segret, if she could oblige him.

"One day, at Gambais, you cooked a meal in this oven, did you not?" Moro enquired, pointing at the *cuisinière*.

"*Oui, maître*," Fernande replied meekly, using Moro's formal title.

"What did you see when you opened the oven door? A human skull, some bone fragments, perhaps?"

Fernande smiled nervously.

"This is my client's trial" Moro said coldly, all courtesy gone. "You have to answer my question. Did you see bone fragments in the *cuisinière*?"

"*Non, non*," Fernande mumbled, looking as if she might faint again.

Moro sat down; he had no further questions. Fernande was led out of court, still muttering "*non, non*" through her tears.

***

Fernande's exit marked a staging post in the trial. Behind lay all the relatives, concierges, friends and acquaintances who had testified to the women's disappearances. None of them had any direct evidence of murder to offer the court – not even Célestine Buisson's sister Marie, who had visited the Villa Tric. Still to come were the experts who the prosecution hoped would add some essential forensic ballast to the case.

Lucien Coulond of *Le Journal* was no longer the only reporter struck by the dearth of firm proof that Landru had killed the missing women. In a report with the telling headline "The Enigma of Gambais", Félix Belle of *Le Gaulois* noted that the prosecution's case rested "on one thing only: the discovery of the bone fragments and the confirmation by experts that they are indeed human bones". Yet it was impossible to say conclusively that the fragments had come from the skeletons of any of the seven women known to have vanished at the Villa Tric.

Under the French criminal code, the jury could convict Landru of murder purely on the mass of circumstantial evidence that pointed to his guilt. Léon Bailby, editor of *L'Intransigeant*, went further in a front-page commentary. Bailby did not know "for a fact" that Landru had murdered the women but argued that a "presumption" of guilt was good enough to send him to the guillotine. In Bailby's view, the war had killed so many young men who should have lived that "one's scruples have become blunted".

No other journalist dared go as far in dismissing due process as Bailby, who two decades later would become a leading propagandist for the Vichy regime. What the press wanted was hard evidence that situated Landru at the scene of a murder. Instead, Godefroy kept promising "proofs" and "powerful arguments", which he had so far conspicuously failed to deliver.

***

Dr Charles Vallon, 69, was a slight man with a grey beard and a pronounced limp, the result of a knife attack by a patient at his mental asylum in 1904, shortly after his first examination of Landru. The inmate had stabbed Vallon in the neck, leaving him partially paralysed. Despite his frailty, Vallon spoke with the clinical authority of a criminal psychiatrist accustomed to delivering opinions in court that brooked no argument.

Vallon reminded the jury that in 1904 he had been clear that Landru had not yet crossed the "frontiers of madness". He did not mention his warning to Landru's wife about her husband's future behaviour. On the contrary, Vallon maintained that he and his fellow psychiatrists were sure Landru was now completely "normal". After Vallon, his colleagues Dr Joseph Rogues de Fursac and Dr Jacques Roubinovitch confirmed his diagnosis, having examined Landru "from head to toes".

Gilbert and Godefroy did not ask the three psychiatrists why they had excluded "all questions of criminality" from their diagnosis. More curiously, neither did Moro.

The inconsistency between the doctors' assessment of Landru's mental state in 1904 and 1919 looked at first sight like an ideal opportunity for Moro to revive the whole question of whether Landru was fit to stand trial. It was plain from Landru's erratic behaviour in court that he was not "normal" in any common understanding of the word. Yet Moro did not cross-examine the psychiatrists. Moro perhaps feared that if he suggested Landru was mad, the jury might infer that the defendant was a deranged serial killer and convict him anyway.

Landru grasped this point with impeccable logic. "I wish to thank *messieurs les experts*," he observed, "because the crimes of which I am accused are so monstrous and perverse that only a madman could have committed them. Since they have declared me of sound mind, then I could not have committed these crimes."

***

Day Fifteen: Wednesday, 23 November

Maurice Chevalier, currently starring with Mistinguett in *Paris en l'Air*, made his first appearance at the trial on Wednesday. The 33-year-old singer and actor took his seat just as Gilbert made an extraordinary admission.

"In all honesty, the prosecution acknowledges that it is unaware of the means by which you committed the deeds of which you are accused," Gilbert told Landru. "It is reduced to hypotheses."

"False hypotheses," Landru remarked.

Gilbert ignored this counter-thrust and proceeded to speculate for the jury's benefit about how Landru might have killed his victims. The judge referred to Landru's rifle, which he had kept at the Villa Tric, while at Rue de Rochechouart the police had found a book about notorious female poisoners.

"One does not kill someone with a book," Landru retorted.

Gilbert observed that glass phials had been found in the cellar at Vernouillet, supporting the theory that Landru might have poisoned his fiancées. Finally, Landru had let slip that strangulation had been "the gentlest of deaths" for the dogs he had killed in the garden at Gambais.

"Oh, look!" Landru exclaimed, incredulous at Gilbert's theorising.

Gilbert moved on to how Landru had disposed of the women's remains. The judge said the prosecution took it as "a given" that Landru had burnt his victims; indeed, several witnesses had noticed "a suspicious glow and smell" while passing the Villa Tric.

Landru raised a bony finger: "I would very much like to know what distinguishes a suspicious glow and a suspicious smell from glows and smells that are normal." Furthermore, why had he not been allowed to witness the experiments on his oven conducted by the forensic scientists?

Gilbert stated that it was not the "custom" for the accused to be present at such experiments and that the court had full confidence in the experts' integrity.

"That's not what Landru is protesting about," Navières said, making a rare intervention. According to Navières, the key issue "was the origin of the bone fragments that were collected in his absence".

Navières had touched on an extremely sensitive subject for the prosecution. On 13 April 1919, the day after his arrest, Landru had attended the detective Dautel's initial "survey" of the villa. However, Landru had not witnessed the full-scale official search of the house and grounds on 29 April 1919, when the bone fragments and charred scraps of women's clothing had been discovered beneath the leaves. In the meantime, the police had failed to attach seals to the property, as required by law. It was a bad mistake, allowing the defence to argue that the fragments might have been planted as false "proof" of murder.

Gilbert sidestepped Navières by noting irrelevantly that Landru had attended Dautel's "investigation" of the villa on 13 April 1919, whose purpose had been "to find the corpses".

"What is surprising," said Landru, "is that one has not recovered a single one of my supposed victims."

Gilbert replied that the bone debris represented calcified human remains.

Landru now fell into his familiar trap of saying too much after scoring a point. He added pedantically that the police had only found an "infinitesimal" quantity of human material. It was "easier to believe" that he had not killed the missing women and besides, "it appears they are not exactly bone fragments, but phosphate of lime."

"It's the same thing, according to the experts," said Gilbert.

"*Eh bien!* I will discuss this matter with the experts."

"One has also found the charred remains of hair clips, suspender hooks and porcelain buttons," Gilbert added.

"Just rubbish that I threw on the fire."

"You drove around in your car at night and a witness saw you get out of it by a pond and drop a heavy package in the water". Gilbert added that several other witnesses who would shortly appear had noticed dubious objects, possibly human flesh, floating around the same pond in the forest just east of Gambais.

***

After the interval, a parade of witnesses testified to mysterious goings-on at Landru's house in Vernouillet, which he had rented from December 1914 to August 1915.

Mme Corbin, who lived on the same street, recalled the summer's evening in 1915 when she saw thick, odorous smoke billowing out of Landru's chimney. "I suspected espionage and alerted the local constable," she said.

"Landru, what do you have to say?" Gilbert demanded.

Landru spread his arms. "I don't know what to say. The summer of 1915, that's really vague! I could have been burning some dirty old rubbish around the time I was moving out."

Mme Picque, Landru's immediate neighbour on the higher side of the property, remarked that he went out a lot in his car. "One morning he drove off carrying a heavy trunk," she declared. Neither the car nor the trunk had been mentioned by Mme Picque in her original witness statement.

Émile Mercier, the elderly constable in Vernouillet, insisted that when he had visited The Lodge to follow up Mme Corbin's complaint, a woman at an upstairs window had told him to go away.

"If, the previous evening, I was 'incinerating' a woman," Landru said, "it is really astonishing that this woman was found alive and well next day by the constable."

("Laughter": *L'Ouest-Éclair*)

Ernestine Guillerot, the maid who worked for Monsieur and Mme Vallet on the other side of The Lodge, remembered seeing a bonfire blazing in Landru's rear garden. Ernestine said she and Mme Vallet had wondered whether Landru might be burning one of the ladies who visited his house. Neither woman had mentioned this conversation when they were originally interviewed by Dautel in April 1919.

Back then, Monsieur Vallet had told Dautel that he had not seen the bonfire because he was at his butcher's shop in Vernouillet. Yet on the witness stand, Vallet recalled with disgust the fire's nauseating stench. "In our trade," Vallet added authoritatively, "we are familiar with this particular sickly, insipid aroma" of burning flesh.

Moro bided his time until Gilbert called a series of witnesses from Gambais who had similarly sinister tales to relate.

Two peasant women, Mme Auchet, who was very old, and her friend Mme David, a little younger, recalled how one day in late October or early November 1918 they had separately passed the Villa Tric on their way back from the village bathhouse. Each of them had seen horrible, foul smoke churning out of the chimney.

"That must have smelt terrible," Moro commiserated with Mme Auchet. As Moro pointed out, Mme Auchet and Mme David's timing of this incident did not fit the date of any of the alleged murders on the charge sheet. Their testimony was therefore worthless.

The two old ladies left the court, looking rather crestfallen. "The jurors are people of good sense," *Le Journal* commented, "and will know how to identify the large part inevitably played in such depositions by gossiping in the village, scandal-mongering and imaginative hindsight."

There was only one witness from Vernouillet or Gambais whose testimony directly corroborated the prosecution's timing of a murder. Gustave Andrieux, the butcher in Gambais, was cycling home past the villa at 9.00 pm on 18 January 1919 when he saw a glow in Landru's rear kitchen window. Looking up, Andrieux noticed foul smoke wafting out of the chimney. If the butcher's date was correct, Andrieux made this sighting five days after Marie-Thérèse Marchadier's disappearance and the same day that Landru's *carnet* indicated that he had returned to the villa from Paris.

***

The detective Dautel was the last witness of the day, called to testify about the discovery of the bone fragments during the official search of the villa on 29 April 1919. Moro preferred to focus on the events leading up to this search.

"*Monsieur le commissaire de police*, I am astonished by one thing," Moro began. "The villa at Gambais was searched for the first time on 13 April 1919. Why were the police seals not attached to the property until 25 April?"

"*Bah!* But what guarantees would the seals have provided?" Dautel replied scornfully.

Moro paused, allowing the court to absorb what Dautel had just said. Finally, Moro turned to the jurors:

"Permit me to put on record my great concern at seeing a police commissioner asking what purpose the seals would have served. *Enfin*, it is because 150 people were able to visit the villa between 13 April and 25 April."

The jurors needed to pay attention to realise that Moro was only saying it had been possible for 150 people to visit the villa during this twelve-day period.

"Monsieur Dautel, tell us," Moro continued, "did you conduct searches during the first investigation of the property?"

Dautel replied that he had only conducted a limited "survey" (*"sondage"*) on 13 April.

"'Search' and 'survey' are different words for the same thing. Do you want proof?" Moro read out extracts from Dautel's report on his "survey" of the villa, when he had also used the word "search" (*"fouille"*) several times.

"During the first descent on the villa by the police, no seals were attached. Grave omission!" Moro chastised Dautel. "A second investigation was conducted without the presence of the suspect. Another irregularity!"

Moro turned to Godefroy:

"*Monsieur l'avocat général*, I will not hide from you that in my closing speech I intend to report on the singular difference between the negative result of the first investigation and the discoveries made during the second."

Next, Moro addressed Gilbert:

"In the light of what *monsieur le commissaire de police* Dautel has just told us, I now request that the four workers who were put at his disposal for digging during the first investigation should be summoned to testify."

Gilbert agreed to Moro's request and ended a session that had gone better for the defence than the prosecution. Ominously for Godefroy, the press was starting to doubt his chances of securing guilty verdicts on the 11 counts of murder.

"The more the trial advances," the evening daily *La Justice* remarked, "the more one realises that the investigation has remained powerless to produce material proofs."

Chapter 19

A Veritable Puzzle

Day Sixteen: Thursday, 24 November

On Thursday morning, *Le Petit Parisien* ran a cartoon on its front page showing two little children stuffing a doll into an oven while their mother glared down at them. "We're only playing at being Landru," they explained.

Gaston Bayle, the senior forensic chemist at the Paris police laboratory, had played the same game with Landru's real-life oven, using the decapitated head of a sheep. It had taken only 45 minutes to incinerate the head, allowing Bayle to conclude that a severed human head would have burned just as easily.

"Fatty flesh is an excellent fuel," Bayle explained to the jurors, several of whom looked queasy. "It's like 'putting oil on the fire', as the vulgar expression goes."

Landru initially declined Gilbert's invitation to put questions to Bayle, saying he would leave the task to Moro.

"No, speak Landru," Moro said. "For reasons that I will make known when I deliver my closing speech, I will only take the most minimal part in the debates from today onwards."

Moro started doodling cartoons, apparently oblivious to the hubbub provoked by his announcement.

Landru did a poor job of cross-examining Bayle. He began well enough, forcing Bayle to concede that the bloodstains in the cellar were of animal origin. Landru then speculated ludicrously that the bone debris beneath the leaves could have been blown into the open hangar by "the four winds" and that the scraps of burnt women's apparel found in the same place could easily have belonged to a man.

Moro suddenly stood up, alarmed that Landru might incriminate himself.

"I am abandoning my somewhat grumpy silence," Moro declared.

"I thought that wouldn't last," said Gilbert tartly.

Moro plunged into a contemptuous cross-examination of Bayle and his colleague Dr Kling, who had helped Bayle conduct his grisly experiments with sheeps' heads and other animal parts. Moro argued that these tests were meaningless, because the prosecution had no proof that Landru had burnt any human remains in his oven.

Godefroy reminded Moro that the prosecution was only "imputing" this fact to Landru.

"Precisely," said Moro, seizing on Godefroy's blunder. "And will you not tell us where the other remains are to be found?"

"Landru only has to say the word."

"*Non!*" Moro was outraged, or certainly looked so to the jurors. "He has nothing to say, it is for the prosecution to produce the evidence. *Messieurs les jurés*, who are people of good sense, will reckon that this question of 'flesh combustion' is a matter for the chimney trade, not forensic experts. God help me if I ever confuse the two professions."

Gilbert called an interval.

***

"The hearing resumed amid a certain tumult," *L'Excelsior* reported. "The whole courtroom was completely overrun as people waited for Dr Paul's deposition." The public, like the press, was anticipating a mighty confrontation between Moro, France's most famous defence barrister, and Dr Paul, the country's leading forensic pathologist, over the significance of the bone debris found at Gambais.

"Dr Paul wears a gallant face, a swaggering moustache and a cavalry officer's jacket," *Le Petit Parisien* noted. "He seizes the bar with both hands, like a horse's reins, tips backwards, bends his legs, stands up again and smiles."

For the record, Paul confirmed that the three dead dogs found in Landru's garden had been strangled. He proceeded to the human bone debris.

As in his report, Paul conflated the total volume of animal and human fragments discovered in various locations with the human debris that had only been retrieved from the ashes in the hangar. Paul also said that bone debris had been sifted from cinders in an oven drawer, without making clear that he was only talking in this context about animal matter. He had not lied, but nor had Paul made it easy for the jury to understand the origin of the charred fragments that court officials had arranged in trays on the evidence table.

Landru listened closely to Paul's fluent presentation, "not a muscle trembling on his impassive, mysterious face", *Le Figaro* observed. *Le Temps* sensed "relief" rippling around the court, as at last the trial entered "the domain of the real and the certain".

This was not quite true. In his closing remarks, Paul described the task of identifying all the human skeletal fragments as a "veritable puzzle" and cautioned the jury "not to ask him for conclusions that were more affirmative than those he could deliver 'in all conscience'".

Moro took note of Paul's remark and drew the jury's attention to the absence of pelvic bone matter. Grudgingly, Paul acknowledged that he could not confirm with "absolute precision" that the debris had come from female skeletons.

"You do not know, in other words, if any of the skeletons are female," Moro stated as a matter of fact.

"Everything leads one to believe that the corpses were of the female sex."

"Why?"

Paul replied unconvincingly that the teeth from one of the skeletons were quite small, suggesting that they had belonged to a young woman.

Moro could have asked Paul whether he could confirm that the debris came from the skeletons of women on the charge sheet, knowing the forensic pathologist would have to say no. But Moro refrained from scoring an easy point, since it would raise another possibility: that the fragments came from other, unknown victims.

Paul remained on the witness stand as Gilbert asked Landru why he had recorded several times in his *carnet* that he had purchased metal saws.

He had needed the saws for various "industrial" enterprises at the villa, Landru said.

Why, then, had part of a saw blade been found in the cinders in the oven drawer?

Nothing was more easily explained, Landru replied. The saw had snapped while he was repairing the iron grille on the front gates to the villa. "I imagine the fragment that I threw away was not the only one I picked up."

Landru declined Gilbert's invitation to say something about the bone fragments, remarking that he had confidence in the competence of Dr Paul. "I am in agreement with what he has stated," Landru declared, forgetting that Paul had confirmed the presence of human bone matter.

Godefroy now asked Paul an obviously pre-scripted question, designed to block a potential opening for Moro.

"Are you astonished by the complete absence of human blood in the villa and on the clothes of the accused?"

Paul admitted that the lack of blood had "perplexed" him for several weeks. Eventually, he had found a recent coroner's report that explained how a corpse could be dismembered with no trace of blood, provided the stains were washed away rapidly. In effect, Paul was asking the jury to believe that Landru had performed this "rapid" clean-up seven times at the villa, without leaving even the tiniest bloodstain.

For once, Godefroy had outwitted Moro, who should have asked Paul about the absence of blood. Perhaps realising his mistake, Moro changed the subject, asking Paul whether any of the human bone fragments had saw marks.

No, Paul replied tersely.

Moro smiled at the jury. "*Eh bien!* That's Landru's answer as well."

Landru threw "an anxious glance at the jurors' bench at this exclamation from his lawyer", *Le Journal* reported. "It was as if he wanted to scrutinise the soul of those who hold his fate in his hands."

***

Days Seventeen and Eighteen: Friday, 25 November; Saturday, 26 November

The next two days were an anti-climax, as the public and the press waited for the trial's grand finale: the closing speeches for the prosecution and the defence, followed by the jury's verdict. First, though, Gilbert had to clear the rest of the hearing's unfinished business.

On Friday the remaining witnesses were called, including three for the defence (from an original list of six), all requested by Landru. They were a gardener who had seen nothing amiss at the villa when he mowed the lawn; a local official in Gambais who was supposed to confirm that the villa had not been properly guarded by the police (he said the opposite); and a man who claimed Landru had defrauded him when he enquired about subletting the villa in the summer of 1918.

For the prosecution, Godefroy read a witness statement by a young army doctor called Jean Monteilhet who was reportedly ill and could not testify in person. On paper, Monteilhet told a vivid and sinister story.

He had been cycling back to his barracks one evening, past the Villa Tric. As he approached the house, Monteilhet had seen a glow that he had thought at first were car headlights. He had stopped outside the front gate, where a grey *camionnette* van was parked, and realised that the light was coming from the house. At this moment, Monteilhet had also noticed thick, foul smoke belching from the chimney and wondered what dreadful meal was being cooked. Then he had continued on his way.

About an hour later, Monteilhet had been repairing a tyre puncture by the pond in the forest beyond Gambais when he had seen the same *camionnette* approaching from the village and pull up by the side of the road. Without noticing Monteilhet (who was hidden down a bank), a man matching Landru's description had lugged a large package to the far side of the pond and dumped it in the water. The man had then returned to the *camionnette* and driven back to Gambais.

Le Petit Parisien assumed that Monteilhet was a self-publicist who wanted to get his name in the papers. Furthermore, Monteilhet's testimony did not fit the prosecution's chronology for the murders.

"What crime do you situate at this time?" Moro asked Godefroy.

"None," Godefroy had to say.

Inconveniently, Monteilhet had originally dated the incident in late May or early June 1915, six months before Landru had rented the Villa Tric. Monteilhet's aunt, whom he had been visiting, had then confirmed that he had seen her in late May or early June 1916. But this revised date still did not help the prosecution, which maintained that Landru had not killed anyone between December 1915 (Berthe Héon) and December 1916 (Anna Collomb).

Godefroy conceded this point to Moro, ensuring that the absent Monteilhet's statement would have no influence on the jury.

On Saturday, the whole session was set aside for the lawyers representing the civil plaintiffs to deliver their closing speeches, called *plaidoiries*: first Robert Surcouf, an accomplished, well-known barrister representing Jeanne Cuchet's sister Philomène, who had decided to file her suit halfway through the trial; and then Louis Lagasse, acting for Annette Pascal's sister Louise.

For almost four hours Surcouf and Lagasse thundered away, as Philomène and Louise wept on the benches beside them.

"Stand up, Landru," Lagasse snarled, "and tell us where she [Annette] is." Head down, Landru carried on scribbling in his colour-coded dossiers, studiously ignoring this rude interruption to his labours.

***

At the end of Saturday's hearing, a reporter for the highbrow *Journal des Débats Politiques et Littéraires* watched Landru as he prepared to leave the court:

"Slowly, Landru closes his dossiers, wipes his pen and puts his pencils in his pocket, with the attention to detail of a meticulous bureaucrat who, on Saturday evening, orders his office accessories with greater care than on other days. For almost four hours by the clock, two orators [Surcouf and Lagasse] have called for his head. This head he now inclines graciously towards the jurors, in a gesture which says quite simply, 'Till Monday, *messieurs*'."

The day was not yet over for Navières. Most evenings for the past three weeks, a young woman with "a bitter mouth, creased forehead and feverish eyes" had waited in a little anteroom for Navières to brief her about the latest session.

On this Saturday evening, Navières would have been careful not to give Landru's daughter Suzanne false reasons for hope. Her father was destined for the horrors of a penal settlement in Guyane even if he was acquitted of the 11 murder charges; and the circumstantial evidence that Landru had killed all 11 individuals was substantial. Everything pointed to his guilt, from the missing women's silence and the telltale notes in the *carnet*, to Landru's theft of their assets and above all, the charred bone debris.

Yet Navières, taking his cue from Moro, was still cautiously confident that Landru could avoid the guillotine. Throughout the trial, Moro had repeatedly reminded the jury that a death penalty required them to be *certain* of Landru's guilt, because the sentence could not be reversed. Moro had shown how doubt, ambiguity and police incompetence lurked in every corner of a murder case with no bodies. Even Dr Paul, the prosecution's star forensic expert, had conceded that the bone fragments were a "puzzle".

Only one fact was clear. That Sunday, as Godefroy worked on his closing speech, he was under more pressure than Moro, the acknowledged master of the *plaidoirie*; for Godefroy would have to prove the prosecution case beyond all reasonable doubt.

Chapter 20

You Have Death in Your Soul

Nineteenth Day: Monday, 28 November

Godefroy caught flu over the weekend. In chilly weather, he arrived at the Palais de Justice on Monday with a fever and a rasping cough, determined to read every word of the *plaidoirie* he had laboriously written. Shortly after 1.00 pm he stood up, lent heavily against the lectern, and surveyed the tumultuous scene before him.

On Gilbert's authority, the press was camped in the well of the court, allowing more spectators to cram into the gallery. It was standing room only in the gangways and aisles, while "elegant ladies [had] clambered up to the high window ledges, shamelessly displaying their legs to the spectators placed beneath them," *Le Journal* reported in dismay.

Mistinguett and her one-time lover Maurice Chevalier were back, seated near General Robert Nivelle, author of the deranged military offensive in 1917. Gabriel Bonin, the investigating magistrate, had also come to watch Godefroy, adding to the prosecutor's nerves.

Godefroy coughed twice, looked down at his script and began.

L'affaire Landru was not "a political invention" aimed at distracting public attention from the grave problems of post-war France, Godefroy said. Nor was Landru a comic figure, a criminal Charlie Chaplin.

"You know the character of this man, his cheating ways, his downcast look like a hunted fox," Godefroy told the jurors. "For sure, Landru has killed ten women and one young man."

Godefroy "confessed loyally" that the prosecution could not produce any witnesses who could speak to this certainty. "But I consider that the testimony of the experts has made the sliced-up corpses of his victims appear before the eyes of the jury."

Landru was not "devoid of all decent feeling", Godefroy went on, because his infidelity "had not lessened his love" for his wife. "When she was accused of being his accomplice, he strenuously defended her."

Somewhere outside the Palais de Justice a cock crowed. Landru glanced up from his notes, momentarily distracted, and then returned to his meaningless homework, utterly uninterested in Godefroy.

Several reporters were already struggling to pay attention to Godefroy's speech, delivered in a hoarse monotone. "He reads without any *éclat*," *L'Excelsior* remarked. Godefroy was also obviously ill, mopping beads of sweat off his forehead with a handkerchief.

His biggest mistake was to fail to offer the jury a clear line of argument. He deplored Landru's insistence that it was up to the prosecution to prove his crimes, even though Landru was correct in law. Godefroy then wandered back to Landru's early career, seeking to extrapolate clues in the defendant's "true character" to explain the terrible events in Vernouillet and Gambais.

What followed was a mishmash of contradictions. Here was "an accomplished swindler" (prompting a smirk from Landru) who nonetheless kept getting caught by the police. Faced with the "horrors" of deportation in 1914, Landru had decided to assure his "peace and comfort" by resuming a life of crime. So began the "tragic litany of the ten fiancées", robbed and then killed by Landru to prevent them going to the police:

"Before you, *messieurs les jurés*, is a monster dripping with the blood of 11 victims. It remains for me to unmask him completely to obtain from you the suppression of this dangerous, rotting branch of the social tree."

Gilbert called an interval; Godefroy slumped in his seat. He had been talking for more than an hour and had not yet reached the first alleged murder on the charge sheet.

***

"When the session resumes, the din is indescribable," *Le Petit Journal* reported, using the present tense to convey the drama. "The whole audience stands up solely to catch a glimpse of Landru, for it is difficult in such a throng to see him completely, because the crowd in the well of the court is as packed as in the gallery." Spectators had even grabbed the vacant seats of any journalist who had gone off to the lavatory, refusing to budge when the reporters returned.

Once Gilbert had restored order, Godefroy at last turned to the case of Jeanne Cuchet.

"Mme Cuchet, who lived comfortably, was she going to break with her relatives just like that in order to hand her furniture to Landru?" Godefroy asked. "No. She lost her head, fascinated by Landru."

Godefroy reminded the jury that Landru had refused to talk about what happened to Jeanne because he had a private arrangement with her, an excuse he repeated for all his other victims.

"You cannot say anything because you're guilty," Godefroy accused Landru, who was so immersed in his dossiers that he did not notice a large fly had settled on his forehead.

"How can one explain as well the disappearance of young André Cuchet, an ardent patriot who would never have left *la patrie* when it was in danger?"

Failing to answer his own question, Godefroy announced that he would next unveil eight certain 'proofs' that Landru had murdered Jeanne, André and the other fiancées who had vanished at Vernouillet and Gambais.

The first proof was the "fatal list" of 11 names that Landru had written in his *carnet*. The second proof was Landru's purchase of one-way train tickets for his fiancées on their last journeys to Gambais. The third proof was his recording of the time in his *carnet* on the day of each murder: "It is the hour of the crime, indicated by the executioner. How, one will say, could someone as intelligent, informed and methodical as Landru be so imprudent that he inscribed such important annotations in his *carnet*?"

Godefroy merely referred the jury back to famous murder cases in the past where the killer had left a trail of evidence.

His fourth proof was Landru's sale of the womens' assets after they disappeared. It was the "realisation of the booty". To establish his fifth proof, Godefroy asked why Landru had enlisted his wife to fake several fiancées' signatures in order to get his hands on their savings: "If the genuine title holders were living, he would not have needed recourse to the services of Mme Landru." This was a strong point and to root it in the jurors' minds, Godefroy went over in detail all Marie-Catherine's forgeries on Landru's behalf.

By mid-afternoon, Godefroy was "starting to show signs of fatigue", according to *Le Journal*. A photograph of Godefroy, taken at about this time, caught him resting his elbows on the lectern as he hunched over his prepared text. One juror seems half asleep, while a reporter stares away, apparently at a loss about what to write in his notepad.

Godefroy battled on to his sixth proof. After each murder, Landru had returned a few days later to the Villa Tric for some mysterious task; clearly the job in hand was the disposal of the remains of his victims.

Godefroy's seventh proof was Landru's use of cover stories for the missing women: Jeanne Cuchet had supposedly gone to England with

André; Anna Collomb was travelling in the south of France; Célestine Buisson was managing a canteen for American soldiers; and so on.

At this point Godefroy stopped. He admitted to Gilbert that he was extremely tired and asked if he could complete his *plaidoirie* in the morning. Gilbert readily agreed and the hearing was adjourned for the day.

Unintentionally, Godefroy had just sabotaged Moro's planned *plaidoirie*. Moro had constructed his closing argument as a seamless speech to be delivered, with intervals, in one session. He would now have to use whatever time Godefroy left him on Tuesday afternoon to begin his address and then resume on Wednesday at a juncture he could not anticipate. It was as bad a stroke of luck for Moro as the flu had been for Godefroy.

***

Twentieth Day: Tuesday, 29 November

Most of the next morning's newspapers struggled to say anything complimentary about Godefroy's speech. *Le Petit Journal* thought that the jury had paid less attention to Godefroy than to the witnesses in the trial. *L'Excelsior* remarked condescendingly that an "unhappy attack of flu" had deprived Godefroy of some of his powers. By implication, the last part of Godefroy's *plaidoirie* would need to be considerably more persuasive or Landru might yet avoid the death penalty.

The weather on Tuesday was the coldest of the trial so far and the clerk ordered the blow heaters to operate at full blast. Once again, a stream of people flowed into the courtroom, long after all the seats had been taken. A scuffle broke out between two women who had both claimed the same place, and they "scratched each other good and proper amid shouts from the crowd", *Le Journal* reported disapprovingly.

More cries greeted Landru as he arrived in court, flanked by his guards. He glowered at the gallery and started laying out his pens and dossiers, ready for the day's business. Gilbert called for order and Godefroy, still sick, resumed his *plaidoirie*.

***

Godefroy's eighth and final proof was Landru's possession of his victims' goods at his various garages, lock-ups and apartments. "Is this not the best signature of his crimes?" Godefroy asked, conflating Landru's obvious thefts

204

with his presumed murders. The fact that no one had witnessed the murders was immaterial, Godefroy asserted. Landru's strangling of the three dogs was a sure indication of his capacity to kill.

Godefroy came finally to the bone debris: "I do not know – and I have already said so – how Landru killed, but what I can establish is that corpses were discovered at the defendant's property." He observed that it was "scientifically certain" the bone fragments were human and impossible that anyone could have planted this evidence. What was more, Godefroy believed Dr Paul was wrong to say that all the fragments with saw marks were of animal origin.

"We have the right to say that they are human fragments," Godefroy argued, because the jury had the "right" to go "beyond scientific certainty". In one, ill-judged sentence, Godefroy had undermined the credibility of the prosecution's star expert witness.

Godefroy reached his peroration. At repetitive length, he reviewed his eight proofs of murder, committed by Landru solely for financial gain "in order to satiate his desire to live on the margins of society":

"It is the death penalty that I demand for Landru, the murderer of Vernouillet and Gambais. Death, *messieurs les jurés*, is the only punishment which is commensurate with such crimes. It is essential to raise the scaffold because the security of society requires it. I beseech you, *messieurs*, show no pity and strike hard. Landru is guilty, with no excuses, and he knows it."

***

It was 2.35 pm. Moro asked the jurors whether they would prefer to hear the defence's argument in one session tomorrow. This would be his preference, Moro said, but he was in the jurors' hands.

They retired briefly to consider Moro's request and returned with the answer he had been dreading. If it pleased Maître de Moro Giafferri, they wished him to start his *plaidoirie* today. A "great brouhaha" erupted around the courtroom at this welcome announcement. Moro smiled wryly and asked Gilbert for a few minutes to prepare.

At exactly 3.00 pm Moro was ready:

> He stood up, rather pale, his palms resting flat on the bar… He took a long time, and then with the faintest movement, his eyes seemed to alight on something, and he began – not in the grave tone the audience was expecting, but with a feline *politesse*.

Moro wished to discuss the law of 8 December 1897 regarding the right of the accused to hear and see all the evidence against him. "The legislative power in 1897 desired at the same time that the presentation of evidence was open and public, and enjoined the judge to remind the accused that he had the right to remain silent," Moro said, addressing the jurors like a law professor at the Sorbonne.

Moro's immediate purpose was to tackle Landru's repeated refusals to explain what he knew about the missing women's fate. Implicitly, Moro was also putting the jurors on notice that they were here to judge facts, not the accused man's morality.

Moro turned to Godefroy:

"You have demanded a head, *monsieur l'avocat-général*, and I protest. You said: 'I do not fear a miscarriage of justice.' Terrible words!"

"To arrive at the truth one has to doubt it ceaselessly," Moro chastised Godefroy, paraphrasing the nineteenth-century writer Ernest Renan. "And so, when you spoke in order to demand death, I felt as if you had death in your soul."

Moro pointed at Landru, momentarily startled by his barrister's gesture. "This man has struck 11 times. Where, when, how? The prosecution has no idea!"

Moro asked how Godefroy could accuse a man of 11 murders when the prosecuting attorney admitted having no idea how the crimes were committed.

"You cannot escape the obligation to prove your case," Moro told Godefroy, and yet the prosecution's "proofs" were not proofs at all. They were mere hypotheses, bundled together at random.

Moro offered the jurors one example among many to illustrate what he meant. The times of day that Landru had written in his *carnet* on certain dates demonstrated nothing more than a habit of noting the hour. Godefroy's claim that these notes represented "the hour of execution" was empty speculation, not evidence.

Moro turned again to Godefroy, who was listening intently:

"'Landru,' you say, 'one has seen 11 people pass through your hands, they have entered into relations with you and then they have disappeared. Tell us where they are or you will die.' The law forbids you, *monsieur l'avocat-général*, from talking in such fashion to this man, under threat of being charged with felony."

Moro threw in a "confession" of his own for the jurors to consider. He, too, was irritated by Landru's "lying answers, his mediocre facetiousness".

Yet the issue before the jurors was not whether they despised this man. It was whether they respected his legal right to remain silent.

"Ten women and one young man have disappeared," said Moro. "Landru, you knew them. One asks you what became of them and you say nothing. One does not have the right to reproach your silence."

All Moro's rhetoric could not disguise the weakness of his argument. For the past three weeks, Gilbert and Godefroy had used every opportunity to make Landru repeat his disastrous trope about the "wall" of his private life, which supposedly prevented him from revealing what had happened to the women. Yet Landru had insisted on having his say about a host of other details, from the times of trains between Houdan and Paris to the chemical composition of the bone debris.

Moro raised another point of law. In a civil court the 11 missing individuals on the charge sheet would not be regarded as dead unless their bodies had been found and identified. Indeed, the beneficiaries of a missing person's estate could not "definitively" inherit his or her assets until 30 years had elapsed:

"The law tells you: 'Up to 30 years, the fact of a disappearance does not indicate death.' You would be breaking your oath if you pronounced to the contrary. The prosecution demands a head and you will reply, *Non!*"

On that ingenious note, Moro called time on the first part of his *plaidoirie*, to applause and cheers from the gallery. Landru "emerged as if from a dream. It was with the air of a connoisseur that he shook the hand of his *avocat*."

Chapter 21

Do You Feel Nothing in Your Hearts?

Day Twenty-One: Wednesday, 30 November

Prince Murat, proud descendant of the Emperor Napoleon's brother-in-law, had got his hands on one of Gilbert's VIP passes for the final day of the trial. Landru would hear the jury's verdict today, even if Gilbert had to prolong the session into the evening.

Maurice Chevalier was in the audience, along with Mistinguett, who had long since dropped her pretence that she was reporting for an English newspaper. Above the VIP enclosure, women had once again climbed up to the window ledges, dangling their legs over the side. An icy draft filtered through the windows behind them, while the court's fan heaters stank of oil, one reporter grumbled.

No one had a clue how many people had managed to force their way past the guards at the front entrance into the courtroom. Newspaper estimates varied from around 800, a physical impossibility, to about 500, a more likely figure. Meanwhile, the trains from Paris were still disgorging more people hoping to see the Bluebeard of Gambais sentenced to death.

***

At 1.00 pm Landru made his entrance, wearing his familiar tunic and bowler hat, with today's colour-coded dossiers tucked under his arm. He halted on his way to his seat and stared at a group of women near the front of the audience who were complaining that they could not see him above the heads of other spectators.

"If those ladies want my place, they are welcome to it," Landru remarked sourly to one of his guards.

Gilbert cautioned the public that he would not tolerate any disturbance and ordered them to remain calm. Moro waited for the noise to subside and then rose to complete his *plaidoirie*.

209

He confronted a new difficulty as he sought to re-engage the jury's attention. Louis Lagasse, the lawyer acting for Annette Pascal's sister Louise, had placed Louise on the bench in front of Moro, next to Jeanne Cuchet's sister Philomène. Both women, already tearful, were bound to distract the jurors, as Lagasse surely intended.

Moro spent most of the first hour reminding the jurors of the main points of his speech so far. "You told me, 'I will show you the corpses'," Moro mocked Godefroy. "Have you, *monsieur l'avocat-général*, renounced your famous thesis?"

Ashes, charred bone debris and "expert" opinions did not equal corpses, Moro said. Nor did the jury "have the right to suppose" that around 1 kilogram of debris was of human origin, given that more than 4 kilograms had not been identified.

As Moro probably knew, his assertion conflated two separate quantifications by Dr Paul and his colleagues. Paul's report stated that 4.2 kilograms of bone debris had been identified, including nearly 1.2 kilograms of human fragments. Separately, the report noted that an unspecified quantity of charred debris could have been human or animal matter.

Moro returned to the flawed investigation of the Villa Tric. He remarked on the "extreme irregularity" of Dautel's failure to seal the Villa Tric after the police's first, hasty "survey" of the property on 13 April 1919. In Moro's view, the house was as open as "a windmill" during the crucial fortnight between the two searches.

Moro was equally struck by the failure to find any trace of human blood at the villa; not one tiny speck. "You represent this house as a monstrous butcher's slab," Moro ridiculed Godefroy, yet where was the proof to support the prosecution's claim?

Le Journal thought Landru seemed strained and anxious as he listened to Moro - "extremely pale, with pinched nostrils and lifeless eyes".

"He is a crook," Moro stated, nodding dismissively at Landru. "He has all the signs, so be it. But that this man has been able to incinerate calmly 11 victims; that this duffer has the strength of someone who does not fear blood: I do not believe it."

It was 2.30 pm. Moro had been going for an hour and a half and he could see that some of the jurors were drifting. He requested a brief interval, granted by Gilbert.

***

During the break, spectators took out flasks of coffee, lit cigarettes, and ate patisseries. "People even talked about fripperies, since the feminine element dominated," *Le Journal* observed with distaste.

The hearing resumed at 3.05 pm. In rapid succession, Moro revisited The Lodge, the Villa Tric and the ponds in the forest near Gambais, seemingly without notes, as Navières fed him prompt lines out of the jury's sight.

"One has poked through the ashes, dredged the ponds, one has searched everywhere, even the graveyard, and one has discovered nothing, nothing, nothing," Moro reiterated. "One has gone as far as asking the village gossips about nuisance smoke and smells," – an unkind jab at the two old women from Gambais, Mme Auchet and Mme David, who would not be budged from their story.

The *carnet*, described by Godefroy as a "mute witness", was nothing of the sort. What to make, for instance, of Godefroy's vaunted "hour of the executioner", the times recorded by Landru beneath certain dates in the *carnet*? On each occasion, the same *carnet* indicated that Landru had caught the train to Paris almost immediately, leaving him no time to dispose of the alleged corpse.

What, then, of Landru's suspicious bonfire at Vernouillet in the summer of 1915? Moro asked the jurors to consider whether a man in possession of his senses would choose to burn a corpse in a trunk in broad daylight in full view of his neighbours.

"You cannot escape this dilemma: either the defendant is mad, or he has not killed." Yet the psychiatrists had confirmed that Landru was sane.

What of the women's identity papers, which Landru had kept in his garages and lock-ups? "These papers, they were the arsenal of a meat trader, not an assassin," Moro said; in short, Landru was a pimp. "I tell you this, and I feel at this instant Landru detests me with all his heart."

In truth, it was hard to tell what Landru was thinking or feeling. "He has the immobility of a statue," *Le Journal* remarked. "His trunk stiff, he sits up and literally drinks in the words of his barrister."

Moro looked down at Annette Pascal's niece Marie-Jeanne, seated next to her weeping mother Louise. "This charming young woman from Toulon, who testified with such pluck, was not 'disappeared' by Landru," Moro said. "So, did Mlle Marie-Jeanne Fauchet know the secrets of Landru's house?"

It was a crude but effective swipe at Marie-Jeanne, reminding the jurors that she had never been to Gambais, for all her damning evidence about Landru's deceit of Annette.

How, finally, to explain the ten women's silence since they vanished? Moro warned the jurors that he was about to raise a "delicate" subject. The willingness of Landru's fiancées to give him their papers and cut all ties with their families might indicate that he had sold them into the "white slave trade".

"*Abominable!*" Louis Lagasse bellowed at Moro, over the noise from the audience.

"What?" Moro looked in astonishment at Lagasse. "Do not say that I am insulting these women," Moro scolded him.

It was certain, Moro told the jurors, that most of Landru's fiancées had split from their families. Moro's claim was questionable: in different ways, the typist Anna Collomb, the teenage nanny Andrée Babelay, the housekeeper Célestine Buisson and the dressmaker Annette Pascal had all had close relations with parents, siblings or offspring.

According to Moro, most of the missing women had also talked about going abroad after their marriage to Landru to start a new life. Moro asked the jurors merely to note that the law on the white slave trade had been passed to protect respectable women from being drawn into prostitution overseas, on the false assumption that an "honest job" awaited them. If his hypothesis had caused offence, so be it: "I am defending a head and nothing will prevent the defence from doing its duty until the very end."

Moro added other sinister elements to the phantasmagoria he was conjuring up for the jurors. In 1909, a murdered child's skeleton had been washed up on a beach in Normandy, or so the forensic pathologist had concluded. Actually, it was the corpse of an artist's pet monkey. So much for the authority of "experts".

What, finally, of the famous bone debris? Moro observed that the previous tenant of the Villa Tric – a Belgian, no less – had been a funerary mason who designed tombstones. This Belgian had enjoyed access to the ossuary in the village graveyard across the fields from the house. Could there be a connection here, Moro wondered aloud: an innocent, no doubt accidental reason why the debris had ended up in the hangar?

It was almost 6.00 pm. The jurors were starting to look at their watches, aware that Gilbert had ruled that the court would stay in session into the evening, to allow them to reach their verdict. Sensing the jury's impatience, Moro plunged into his peroration:

"*Messieurs les jurés*, it is not your mission to shed light. My mission has been to denounce obscurity to you, and I have done so. From the depths of my heart, I say to you: do not do something irreparable. What if tomorrow just one of the women reappears, just one?"

He paused for a long time, waiting for the audience to fall quiet.

"So, tell me," Moro eventually resumed, looking hard at the jurors, "where is the strength of character that will allow you to confront an icy ghost who appears in the night and tells you: 'I have not killed and you have killed me.' If posterity records, 'They handed down death and they were mistaken', it will not be on my conscience. Look to yours."

Moro sat down. Applause broke out around the gallery. Through the noise, Gilbert ordered Landru to stand up.

"Do you have anything to say?" Gilbert demanded.

"I have a declaration to make," Landru said calmly. "Yesterday, I was accused of all kinds of crimes and misdeeds, but *monsieur l'avocat-général* nonetheless recognised one virtue in me, that of a father and a husband. On the heads of my family I swear that I have killed no one."

Even before Landru had finished, the crowd had started to chatter again.

"This is shameful," Gilbert erupted, threatening yet again to clear the court.

"*Abominable!*" Godefroy shouted above the din.

***

Still the audience carried on talking, with the odd jeer directed at Landru, as Gilbert read out the 48 charges for the jury to consider: 11 counts of murder and 37 counts of theft and fraud. Landru strained to hear Gilbert above "the brouhaha all around the courtroom".

When Gilbert had finished, Moro requested the floor again. He explained to the jurors that if they found Landru guilty on all 48 charges he would be sentenced to death. If, however, they only found Landru guilty of theft and fraud, he would be sentenced to 20 years' hard labour and transportation for life. The subtext of Moro's message was clear. The jurors could either choose to kill Landru swiftly via the guillotine or slowly, breaking rocks and clearing jungle in Guyane.

Lagasse was up the moment Moro was down. Lagasse informed the jurors that if they did as Moro requested, and acquitted Landru on the murder charges, the full 100,000 francs cost of the trial would fall on the civil plaintiffs, Mme Fauchet and Mme Friedman.

"That is not true and it is intolerable that you should introduce such an error into the proceedings," Moro protested to Lagasse. Moro demanded that the prosecution dissociate itself from Lagasse's misinterpretation of the law. Godefroy willingly agreed, appalled by Lagasse's cheap trick. Only the cost of the civil action fell to the litigants, Godefroy told the jurors, who finally retired to consider their verdict.

It was just after 6.30 pm. In two hours' time, Mistinguett and Maurice Chevalier were due on stage at the Casino de Paris for the next performance of *Paris en l'Air*. Reluctantly they slipped out of the courtroom, forced to miss the grand finale.

***

Landru's guards took him down to a holding cell in the vaults of the Palais de Justice to have supper, pursued by several photographers who snapped him after his meal, bowler-hatted and inscrutable. Upstairs, an enterprising reporter fitted a 900-candle-power lamp with a reflector directly above the spot where Landru would stand to hear the verdict: "The brutal light will reveal pitilessly his emotion or his nerve."

While the jurors deliberated, Godefroy retired with the two lawyers acting for the civil plaintiffs. Moro preferred to wait for the verdict in the courtroom, lighting up his pipe and sketching more of his vivid cartoons. A spectator who approached him to ask about the case got nowhere. He had every faith in "justice", Moro said blandly, puffing away.

At 9.20 pm, an official rang a handbell up and down the corridors, the signal that the jurors had reached their verdict.

Moro knew he had lost as soon as he saw the jurors' grim expressions. The jury foreman, Jacques Martin, a stolid farmer with a waxed moustache, frowned at the piece of paper in his hand to make sure he did not fluff his lines. The announcement Martin had to make to the court was not straightforward. By a majority of nine to three, the jury found Landru guilty of all 11 murder charges, Martin said. By a unanimous verdict, they also found him guilty of all the theft and fraud counts, bar two. None of the jurors believed that Landru had defrauded and robbed 19-year-old Andrée Babelay, for the simple reason that she had been destitute.

Gilbert ordered the clerk of the court to bring Landru up from his holding cell. Moro pushed his way past the journalists crowded round the little door where Landru would reappear, determined to be the first to break the terrible news to his client.

"It is bad, very bad, have courage," Moro said to Landru when he emerged with his guards. Landru nodded politely at Moro, as if they had been exchanging courtesies.

DO YOU FEEL NOTHING IN YOUR HEARTS?

He stood beneath the newly installed lamp, his bald head glinting in the light, as Gilbert read the jury's verdicts. Moro clapped his hand over his face in a gesture of incredulity, holding his pose long enough for the photographers to get their picture. By contrast, Landru "seemed not to have heard or understood" what was being said to him, *L'Echo de Paris* remarked.

Gilbert retired again with the two assistant judges to draft the formal sentence. Landru leant over and consoled Moro, who was still theatrically upset, in full view of the jurors. Around the court, spectators cracked open bottles of wine and lit more cigarettes, gossiping and joking while they waited for the climax of the drama.

Suddenly Godefroy smashed his fist on his lectern. "Do you feel nothing in your hearts?" he yelled at the audience. "This man is going to be sentenced to death! Is that what has brought you here? Just shut your mouths, you shameless scum!"

Gilbert swept back into court with the assistant judges. The crowd fell quiet. Once again, Gilbert ordered Landru to stand up.

"Landru," Gilbert intoned, "the court condemns you to death. In accordance with the law, you will be taken to a public place in Versailles where you will have your head sliced at the neck."

The audience gasped. Landru did not flinch.

Moro was busy again, forcing a passage through the crowd in the well of the court towards Godefroy, who shook his hand. Godefroy told Moro he was "very moved".

Calmly, as if it was a piece of routine procedure, Moro handed a pre-drafted appeal for clemency to Jacques Martin, the foreman of the jury. Moro explained patiently to Martin why he believed the jurors should sign the appeal, even though a majority of them had found Landru guilty of murder. Moro reminded them that Landru was destined in any case to spend the rest of his life in the swamps of Guyane.

"You must sign if you have any doubts," Godefroy advised the jurors, assuming that only the three who had found Landru not guilty of murder would do so.

One by one, the appeal was passed around the jurors; one by one, they all signed, as Godefroy looked on helplessly.

Moro marched over to Lagasse, who was as confused as Godefroy by Moro's swift manoeuvring; for having demanded Landru's head, Lagasse now advised Annette Pascal's bewildered sister Louise Fauchet to sign the clemency appeal.

"She hesitates, she cries and *enfin*, she signs," *Le Figaro* observed in astonishment.

Jeanne Cuchet's sister Philomène was not so easily fooled. When Moro approached her, she flapped him angrily away.

Landru was not going to be taken in either. He refused to put his signature on the appeal, which could not go forward without it.

"A man like me would never appeal for clemency or pity," Landru told Moro, who decided to hold off persuading his client until the morning.

Once Moro had returned to his seat, Gilbert informed Landru that he had three days to sign the appeal or his death sentence would be carried out. Landru's guards prepared to take him back to his prison cell. Landru put up his hand; there was something he still wished to say.

"The hearing is over," Gilbert said firmly. "I just told you that you have three clear days to appeal. Once this deadline is passed, the sentence is definitive."

"One minute, *monsieur le président*." Landru stood his ground. "I am sorry for detaining you, but I have just one word to tell you."

"Well, make it quick."

"It's that the tribunal has made a mistake, I have never killed anyone. This is my final protest."

Then he was off with his guards, through the little exit door and into the freezing night.

Chapter 22

A Terrible Doubt Came to You

Landru lost his cool the instant he got back to his cell; not at the verdict, but at the "revolting spectacle" of all the women who had cheered when Gilbert read out the sentence. "Now these women will be able to contemplate at leisure 'Landru the ladykiller'," he complained to his guards.

Over the next few days, the press tried to make sense of why three jurors had acquitted Landru on the murder counts and then all the jury had signed the clemency appeal. The actor and writer Jean Kolb thought the split verdict was entirely due to the brilliance of Moro's closing speech. "I shudder to think what might have happened if the great lawyer had given an even more powerful *plaidoirie*," Kolb remarked in his column for *La Presse*.

Regarding the appeal for clemency, *L'Echo d'Alger* thought the jurors "could not be certain that Landru was either guilty or innocent" and like Pontius Pilate had washed their hands of the case. The jurors stayed quiet, apart from one, who confusingly told a journalist that they had all believed Landru was guilty of murder and had then signed the clemency appeal out of "respect" for Moro's performance.

Landru still refused to stoop to appealing for his life. Moro and Navières visited his cell, with no success. In the end, Moro bought some more time for Landru to reconsider his position by appealing against the sentence itself, with his client's reluctant approval.

As Christmas approached Landru sank into a depression, telling the prison doctor that he had exhausted his energy during the trial. He would not eat and lay all day on his bunk, gazing blankly at the ceiling. Apart from Moro and Navières, he received no visitors from outside.

At his family's apartment in Clichy, Marie-Catherine told neighbours that she and her children had renounced Landru and would be known in future as the Rémys. Landru's former mistress Fernande was more ambivalent. She was still in love with him, so she said, but too busy capitalising on the success of her ghosted memoirs to visit Landru in Versailles. A few days after the trial, a Paris music hall announced that Fernande would be performing "in flesh and bones" in a new revue specially written for her called *Psst! Montez-vous?*

Landru remained inert until the start of February when his appeal against his death sentence was rejected. Surprisingly, this news galvanised him into action. He recovered his appetite and was at last persuaded by Moro to sign his appeal for clemency.

A short hiatus ensued, because Moro was committed to pleading a case in the provinces and would not be back in Paris till 19 February. Landru was unconcerned by Moro's absence, since he felt perfectly capable of handling his own appeal. He went back to work again in his cell, annotating his colour-coded dossiers and endlessly reorganising his filing system, only taking time out to devour the meals that would keep up his strength for the coming battle.

Landru soon arrived at a considered opinion: a mistrial must be declared and the whole process begun again, he informed Navières. On the evening of 16 February, Navières told Landru that this futile request had been rejected. Landru showed no surprise at the decision, while insisting that he was innocent. He spent the next three days compiling a memorandum on the authenticity of the bone fragments at Gambais and the police's failure to attach seals to the Villa Tric. These were both matters of great concern to him, Landru told a colleague of Navières who came to collect his latest submission.

Full of energy, Landru launched a second demand for a mistrial. "You will see," Landru told the prison doctor giving him his daily check-up, "one by one the missing women will be discovered."

On the afternoon of 22 February, Navières brought Landru's sons Charles and Maurice down from Paris to see their father. Charles and Maurice had come to say goodbye, even though Landru's appeal for clemency had not yet been heard. Landru told his boys to be brave.

On 23 February, just after 4.00 pm, Moro arrived by car at the Elysée Palace to plead the appeal before the President of France, Alexandre Millerand. Moro spent 90 minutes closeted with Millerand, telling the press when he emerged that the president had listened carefully to his points.

It took Millerand only a few hours to reach a decision. On Friday, 24 February, Anatole Deibler, France's chief executioner, was ordered to guillotine Landru at dawn on 25 February, outside the prison gates.

***

A TERRIBLE DOUBT CAME TO YOU

Like Landru, Deibler, 58, owned a *carnet* in which he recorded his executions. Landru would be the 147th prisoner Deibler had guillotined.

At about 1.00 am on 25 February, Deibler set off from Paris with his two assistants in his customary horse-drawn black van; inside were the various parts of the guillotine. The night was clear, and Deibler planned to reach Versailles by 4.00 am, two hours before sunrise, allowing ample time to assemble his contraption.

In Versailles, the police were clearing the Rue Saint-Pierre in front of the prison gates where the guillotine would be erected. The street was not especially wide and a packed café opposite the gates overlooked the execution site. The gendarmes moved in, sweeping the press out of the bar and ejecting customers who had hidden in the toilets and the bedrooms upstairs.

Under the normal procedure for executions, Landru would only be told his appeal had failed a few minutes before being marched to the guillotine. In a breach of protocol, Landru had heard his fate by the time Deibler set off from Paris, along with the news that Godefroy would not be attending the execution. Instead, a "substitute" lawyer would represent the prosecution at the scaffold.

Landru could not believe it. Now he would have to go to all the trouble of writing Godefroy a farewell letter.

"Astonished at first (a rare thing in a prosecutor) by the neatness of my replies, doubt came to you, a terrible doubt for you who were responsible for establishing the proof," Landru began. "This doubt, I saw it being born, and you, who scarcely stopped looking at me, you sensed that I understood."

On and on Landru rambled: "you understood that the frightful atrocities of which you accused me could not have happened"; "you had too much good sense to value the gossip of concierges"; "you saw the pathetic little oven, better suited for a toy dinner-set that you must have made as a child with your little sister, and you understood that the appalling atrocities of which you accused me did not, could not, have taken place."

Finally, he ran out of accusations to heap on Godefroy. "*Adieu, monsieur*, our common history will finish tomorrow, no doubt. I die with an innocent, peaceful soul. Please accept, with my respects, my wishes that yours will be the same. Landru".

At 4.00 am, the prison almoner Abbé Loisel, "still young, with a gentle face", rang the bell at the main entrance and was let inside, along with the barber assigned to cut Landru's beloved beard to shreds. Five minutes later, Deibler's horse and cart rattled up to the gates. Deibler got out, set up two portable gas lamps and put on a pair of spectacles. He identified the spot prescribed by law for the guillotine, 3.5 metres outside the prison entrance, and the three executioners, dressed in overalls, began bolting the different bits of the scaffold together.

They finished just before 5.00 am. Deibler checked the base of the guillotine with his spirit level and then retreated with his assistants into the back of the van to exchange their overalls for dark suits and bowler hats. At a word from Deibler, the two assistants went into the jail to size up Landru, while he kept watch on the guillotine.

At 5.20 am, Moro, Navières and Godefroy's "substitute", a government prosecutor called Béguin, were admitted to the prison and taken to Landru's cell.

Landru was roused from his bunk by Béguin, who told him that his appeal had been rejected and that he needed to "have courage". According to Navières, Landru looked indignantly at Béguin and said: "*Monsieur*, you insult me, one doesn't exhort an innocent man to have courage."

Moro and Navières made small talk with Landru while he dressed, watched by Deibler's two assistants. In line with the rules, Landru was made to wear a collarless shirt to ensure the blade met no obstruction before it cut through his neck. He was also told to remain barefoot.

Landru declined Abbé Loisel's offer to take confession; according to one account, Landru told Loisel that while he was "not without religious feelings he did not wish to keep these gentlemen waiting", nodding at the bowler-hatted executioners. He thanked Moro and Navières for all their efforts, expressing regret that his cause had eventually turned out so badly for them.

Deibler's assistants grabbed his wrists and frogmarched him to the prison registry office, just inside the prison gates, followed by Moro, Navières, Béguin and various other officials, including the investigating magistrate Gabriel Bonin. On his arrival at the registry office, Landru was offered the ritual glass of rum and a cigarette to strengthen his nerves, both declined. The executioners now shackled his legs and trussed his arms behind his back so tightly that Landru yelped with pain; at the front, the prison barber sheared Landru's beard to a length where no stray hairs could possibly catch the guillotine.

It was almost 6.00 am. Outside the gates, Deibler was getting nervous about the growing crowd gathered behind the barricade, 30 metres back from the scaffold. Worse, a tram was clattering up the street towards the prison, carrying factory workers on their way to start the morning shift.

Deibler flapped at the guards to open the barricade and the tram rattled past the guillotine, as the passengers hurled abuse at Landru over the prison wall.

At 6.04 am the gates swung open. Landru emerged, a blur of wild eyes, ragged beard and scrawny neck, caught by a newspaper artist as he was bustled towards the scaffold.

Deibler's deputies pressed Landru down on his knees and locked his head in position. If he kept his eyes open, he was now staring at the open wicker basket that would catch his head, lined with cloth to absorb the blood. The assistants withdrew a few paces and waited for Deibler to release the blade.

Nothing happened. Perhaps the tram had disturbed Deibler's delicate mechanism, or perhaps Deibler was in no hurry: whatever the reason, one journalist counted a delay of seven seconds. Finally the blade dropped.

Once Landru's decapitated body had been dumped in a cheap wooden coffin, Moro, Navières and Godefroy's "substitute" Béguin went back inside the prison to complete the post-execution formalities. A few minutes later, Moro re-emerged into a pack of reporters, one of whom asked if Landru had made a last-minute confession.

Moro raised his arm for silence; he wished to answer a different question. "An irreparable verdict presupposes an infallible judge," Moro declared, quoting Victor Hugo. Then Moro got into his waiting car, sickened by what he had just seen.

***

Life went on. That evening, Fernande Segret performed her latest cabaret sketch, *The Survivor*, at a music hall in north-west Paris.

PART FOUR

LANDRU'S SECRET

Chapter 23

The Signpost

Seven months after Landru's execution, Moro gave an interview to a newspaper in Marseille. Inevitably, the reporter asked Moro whether he thought Landru was guilty. To deflect further enquiry, Moro told a story. He said that as he accompanied Landru to the guillotine, he had whispered in his client's ear:

"Look, Landru, I have defended you with all my energy and I'm your last remaining friend. I need to know if I must now defend your memory. Tell me the secret of your life."

"*Non, maître*," Landru had supposedly replied, "my secret is all the luggage that I am taking with me."

There are several reasons for doubting Moro's anecdote. In the final, terrifying seconds of his life, Landru was in no fit state to think up such an elegant metaphor. He had also just written his tirade against Godefroy, insisting on his innocence. And besides, Moro later told a more plausible story to another journalist. Moro spoke of his instant regret that he had bid Landru "*au revoir*" as the prison gates swung open, while Landru, correctly, had grunted "*adieu*".

Landru's "secret" – the truth about what had happened at Vernouillet and Gambais, and why – seemed to have been buried with Landru in the Cimitière des Gonards at Versailles.

***

The Villa Tric, abandoned and derelict, stood as a monument to the official version of Landru's terrible crimes. During the months following his execution, forensic experts returned several times to search the garden, "in the vain hope of finding something more than pebbles". The authorities were still persuaded that more human remains could be found to add to the charred bone debris.

In early 1923, Landru's infamous little oven was sold at auction for 4,200 francs, with the proceeds going to public funds. The entrepreneur who bought the oven hoped to put it on display in the Italian city of Turin, beyond French jurisdiction. However, the Turin police banned this potentially lucrative horror show and the *cuisinière* disappeared, possibly acquired by another private collector.

Shortly after the auction, the government granted the villa's owner, Monsieur Tric, 5,000 francs in compensation for the damage caused to his property by vandals and souvenir hunters. Tric then put the house on the market, but struggled for several years to find a purchaser. In 1930, the villa was finally acquired by a commercially minded young couple who converted it into a Landru-themed restaurant.

"The Kitchen Grill" ("*Au Grillon du Foyer*") offered customers home cooking from an oven located exactly where Landru had allegedly burnt the remains of his fiancées. For a little extra, guests could sleep in one of the bedrooms that Landru had shared with Anna Collomb, Annette Pascal and his other fiancées. The restaurant survived until 1940, exploiting what had become France's most famous murder brand.

Between the wars, the French press regularly stamped Landru's name on any serial killer whose victims were female. There was a "Landru of Nancy", a "Landru of Marseille" and other supposed Landru copycats in Poland, Czechoslovakia, Britain and the United States. Yet the legend of the Bluebeard of Gambais remained almost unknown outside France, largely because almost all the literature on the case was in French.

Somehow the American actor-director Orson Welles alighted on Landru as a possible film project, soon after the release of *Citizen Kane* in 1941. Welles wanted to cast Charlie Chaplin against type as Landru and wrote the outlines of a script for Chaplin to read. Chaplin decided he would rather direct the film himself and bought the rights to Welles's script. The result was a movie that bore almost no relation to the real story. In *Monsieur Verdoux*, Chaplin (playing the title role) reinvented Landru as an unemployed bank clerk who bigamously marries and kills a succession of wealthy widows in order to support his family. *Monsieur Verdoux* was a flop except in France, where the public's appetite for both Chaplin and Landru remained insatiable.

In 1963, the French new wave director Claude Chabrol offered an inaccurate, facetious take on Landru from a script by the novelist Françoise Sagan. Chabrol's Landru, played by Charles Denner, was a bourgeois antiques dealer whose fiancées were all fashionable, moneyed women.

To speed up the action, Chabrol started with Berthe Héon, Landru's fifth known victim, transformed from a humble *domestique* into an elegant *Parisienne*.

A 71-year-old woman saw the film and decided to sue for defamation. For almost four decades, Landru's former mistress Fernande Segret had lived in complete obscurity. Her theatre bookings had soon dried up after Landru's execution and eventually she had taken a job as a children's governess with a French colonial family in Lebanon. At some point in the mid-1950s, Fernande had finally returned to France, having never married or got over the man she still called "Lucien".

Fernande was outraged by her portrayal in Chabrol's film by Stéphane Audran, who was everything Fernande had once wanted to be: sexy, sophisticated, a star in the making (and about to marry Chabrol). In 1964, a civil court refused Fernande's enormous claim for 200,000 francs in damages while awarding her 10,000 francs for several scenes that the judge ruled had invaded her privacy.

Fernande withdrew to an old people's home in the small Norman town of Flers, where she spent her days brooding about the past, afflicted by chronic backache. One day in January 1968, Fernande made her way to the sixteenth-century chateau on the outskirts of the town, entered the park and walked slowly and deliberately towards the castle moat. She carried on, over the edge, and drowned in the freezing water.

***

It had never been clear how much Fernande had glimpsed and understood about Landru behind his self-declared "wall" of privacy. Fernande's *Souvenirs of a Survivor* confused intimacy with knowledge of Landru, while her testimony at his trial was incoherent and self-serving.

Another woman knew more about Landru than Fernande. In the years following Landru's execution, she maintained her own barricade against all enquiries regarding her former husband.

"*Monsieur*, don't speak to me about Landru, it's finished, okay," Marie-Catherine snapped at one reporter in 1924 who doorstepped her at the family's apartment in Clichy. "I was never aware of the business of the father of my children who, besides, did not live with me."

Gradually Landru's family slipped into the shadows. In 1927, the "Rémys" (their new name by deed poll) returned briefly to public view when they declined to renew their five-year concession on Landru's grave in Versailles, pleading poverty. His remains were dug up and discreetly reburied in an unmarked plot on the other side of the cemetery. Six years later, the press descended again on the family's apartment in Clichy, when a skeleton was unearthed by builders working on a site only two doors along the street. Marie-Catherine had no comment on whether this might be another of Landru's victims. Forensic experts soon concluded that the skeleton belonged to a man who had died at least 25 years earlier, long before the family moved to Clichy.

At some point in the 1930s, Marie-Catherine and her eldest son Maurice changed their surnames for a second time in a bid to shake off journalists and blackmailers. They vanished from sight, although somewhere in France's official records the traces of their later lives must exist.

Like his elder brother Maurice, Charles Landru worked between the wars as an automobile mechanic and a taxi driver in Paris. Charles married in 1938 and seems to have lived in and around the city until his death in 1980. Marie, Landru's eldest daughter, married a bank clerk and after a long widowhood, died in 1985 at the age of 94. Suzanne, the younger daughter, lived for many years in French West Africa with her second husband, a colonial soldier. She died in 1986, the last person with any intimate knowledge of Landru.

***

By then, all the leading figures in the investigation and trial of Landru were long since dead and largely forgotten. Gabriel Bonin, the *juge d'instruction*, suffered a fatal embolism only two months after Landru's execution. Bonin was only 43. In 1924, Amédée Dautel, the first detective to interview Landru, was killed by a heart attack at his home in Toulouse, where he had been transferred four years earlier. Dautel's death left the field clear for his former deputy, Jules Belin, to inflate his own role in the case. Over the decades, Belin gave several dramatic and inconsistent accounts of how he finally apprehended Landru, none of them true.

Louis Riboulet, the third main detective in the case, retired from the Paris police in 1926 at the age of 50 and became a private eye. Riboulet was sufficiently adept at self-publicity for one newspaper to hail him in 1931 as the officer whose "implacable logic" had cracked open *l'affaire Landru*. Two years later, Riboulet published *La Véritable Affaire Landru*, a ghostwritten rehash of the prosecution case. Riboulet's book, serialised in *Le Matin*, relied heavily on extensive reproduction of Landru's notes in his *carnet* and a substantial volume of other material from the police and judicial archives that has never been seen since.

Charles Paul, the chief forensic pathologist at the trial, continued to cut up corpses with phenomenal industry. By the time of his own death in 1960, Paul had performed almost 160,000 autopsies, while frequently appearing as a trenchant expert witness in murder cases. Yet on the subject of Landru, Paul remained uncharacteristically tentative. "Does something mysterious surround the disappearance of the ten fiancées?" Paul mused to a reporter shortly after Landru's execution. "With the necessary passing of time, we will judge more calmly this astonishing and shocking case."

Robert Godefroy, the chief prosecuting attorney, maintained till his death in 1935 that his eight "proofs" of Landru's guilt had removed any doubt in the case. Maurice Gilbert, the presiding judge, was also convinced of Landru's guilt, while retaining a dim view of Godefroy's performance at the trial. Before his death in 1937, Gilbert reportedly confided to friends that he thought Moro might have saved Landru from the guillotine if just one of the missing women had turned up alive.

After Landru's execution, Moro resumed his stellar career at the Paris Bar. He continued to campaign against the death penalty and in the 1930s became one of France's most outspoken opponents of the Nazi regime. When France fell in 1940, Moro only just evaded arrest by the SS, joining his wife in the unoccupied zone. They eventually escaped to Corsica, where Moro laid low until the island was liberated in 1943, seething at the injustices he could no longer reach.

He returned to the Paris Bar after the Liberation, nicknamed "the old lion" as he prowled and pounced in the courtroom. Yet still Landru's spectre hung over Moro. In his final years, Moro would smile when inquisitive grandchildren asked him if he believed Landru had killed the missing women. He could not say what he thought, Moro patiently explained, because of his duty of confidentiality to Landru, even beyond the grave.

Moro died suddenly in November 1956 at the age of 78, felled by a heart attack after running to catch a train that was leaving the station. At his funeral in Paris, the speech of honour was given by the minister of justice, an artful, ambitious politician who at this stage in his serpentine career was a supporter of the death penalty. Moro would not have appreciated the irony.

Auguste Navières du Treuil, now 75, was among those who attended Moro's funeral. Before he died in 1967, Navières set down his recollections of Landru in a three-page private memoir. It is a frustrating document, all the more so because Navières was a wonderfully vivid writer. Navières brought to life his first encounter with Landru at the Santé prison, the turmoil of the trial's final day and Landru's last minutes in his cell as he prepared to go to the guillotine. What Navières did not reveal was whether he believed that Landru was guilty.

Navières also refrained from mentioning a piece of evidence in his possession that might have been significant. Sometime between the end of the trial and his execution, Landru had entrusted Navières with a sketch. In 1968, a year after Navières died, his daughter displayed this drawing on French television.

Landru's little picture showed the rear wall of the Villa Tric's kitchen, with his oven in the centre. Beside the *cuisinière* Landru had written: "One can burn anything one wants in there." This was the remark attributed to him by Mme Falque, the wealthy widow who had visited Gambais in October 1918 and then broken off her engagement.

On the reverse side of the page, Landru had written his rejoinder to Mme Falque's insinuation that he had burnt human remains in the oven. "This demonstrates the stupidity of the witnesses," Landru had observed. "Nothing happened in front of the wall, but in the house."

There was no telling whether Landru had planted a cryptic clue or an ambiguous tease. Yet at a minimum his message seemed a signpost, directing his accusers back to the Villa Tric for the key to his fabled secret.

Chapter 24

The Road to Gambais

From the station at Garancières, the road to Gambais has changed little in the century since Landru cycled off to inspect the Villa Tric for the first time. It winds through rolling farmland and then straightens into an avenue that heads south-west for the last four kilometres towards the village.

On the edge of Gambais, a left-hand turn heads into dense woods, the outer fringe of an ancient hunting forest that stretches more than 20 kilometres south-east to the former royal chateau of Rambouillet.

One clear, moonlit night in the late spring or early summer of 1916, a 39-year-old army doctor took this side road, called the Route de Gambaiseuil, as he cycled to his barracks. Jean Monteilhet had just witnessed a strange scene, which he later recalled in the crisp, precise language of a medical man who knew the importance of facts.

Monteilhet had been visiting his aunt, the Mother Superior at the local convent, and had missed the last train from Houdan to his barracks in Versailles, some 40 kilometres away. Cursing his luck, he had ridden back towards Gambais en route to Versailles along the road that went directly past the Villa Tric.

Approaching the house, Monteilhet had noticed a grey *camionnette* parked outside the front gates and thick, nauseous smoke churning out of the chimney. He had stopped by the gates to have a closer look and seen the glow of a fire in one of the windows at the rear. Monteilhet had wondered what dreadful meal was being cooked and then continued on his journey.

About half an hour later, Monteilhet was peddling along the Route de Gambaiseuil, deep in the forest, when his bike got a puncture. Swearing again, he stopped by a pond at the foot of a long hill, pushed his bike down a small embankment, and took his puncture repair kit out of his army satchel.

Monteilhet had just finished mending the puncture when he heard the sound of an approaching car, chugging through the woods from the direction of Gambais.

"I was surprised to see the same automobile I had seen in front of Monsieur Tric's villa," Monteilhet remembered. "This vehicle stopped about 50 metres before the pond and a man got out, rather short, wearing a cap and a kind of chestnut or khaki hunting jacket. He had quite a long beard. As he got out of the car, he was carrying a package on his shoulders. He headed towards a causeway which extended almost to the middle of the pond. When he reached the end of the causeway, I could no longer make out the package, but I heard a 'plosh' noise coming from something which had been dropped in the water. At that moment, I had the impression that he was a poacher who was throwing his cast-net in the pond."

Having dropped his package, the man hurried back to the *camionnette*, still without seeing Monteilhet, who remained half-hidden down the embankment. The man started the engine, turned the car around, and drove off back towards the village.

Monteilhet had thought nothing more about this rather sinister incident until Landru's arrest in April 1919, when the doctor instantly recognised the "poacher" as the same man. At first glance Monteilhet seemed to have come closer than anyone to witnessing Landru in the act of burning and dumping the remains of one of the seven so-called "*disparues*" [missing women] known to have disappeared at the Villa Tric. Monteilhet's testimony prompted Bonin to order the detectives Dautel and Belin to search the pond in the woods, along with a much smaller pond nearby.

On 10 May 1919, in balmy, late spring weather, Dautel and Belin began their investigation, assisted by workers from the local chateau and six officers from the river police. As the temperature rose through the morning, a gathering crowd of villagers bought beer and other cold refreshments from a mobile drinks cart set up by the side of the road.

The spectators saw an operation that bore no resemblance to a modern forensic search. In their superficial fashion, Dautel and Belin settled for a "semi-drainage" of the pond, which was clogged with reeds and thick mud. All day, the river police meandered on a barge around the half-drained pond, casting dragnets to catch any debris, while the detectives directed operations from the bank.

One elderly woman, Mme Mauguin, was certain she had seen a package wrapped in waxed linen floating on the water in the summer of 1918, while picking wild herbs for a pharmacist in Houdan. She had thought it was "a drowned person", although oddly, she had not gone to the police. The searchers found nothing at the spot she indicated or anywhere else in the muddy shallows. At sunset Dautel abandoned the search as futile and returned with Belin to Paris.

Given Monteilhet's vivid testimony, the police should have unblocked the sluice gates and drained the pond completely. Instead, the investigating magistrate Bonin lost interest in the pond as a possible crime scene, because in one crucial detail, Monteilhet's deposition did not fit the prosecution case.

Initially, Monteilhet said he saw the "poacher" in the late spring or early summer of 1915, about six months before Landru rented the Villa Tric. Realising his error, Monteilhet had then checked with his aunt. She confirmed that Monteilhet had seen her in late May or early June 1916, possibly by referring to the convent's visiting book.

Yet this still did not overcome the main problem with Monteilhet's testimony as far as the authorities were concerned. Monteilhet's sighting of Landru at *L'Étang des Bruyères* (Heather Pond), as it was known, fell approximately halfway between the first known disappearance at Gambais (Berthe Héon, December 1915) and the second (Anna Collomb, December 1916). Monteilhet's story was worthless, so long as the investigation stuck rigidly to the assumption that Landru had killed precisely seven women at Gambais, and no more.

***

Standing by the pond today, it is easy to visualise the incident that Monteilhet surely witnessed. Here, a murky expanse of water, about 70 metres wide and 150 metres long, crowded by reeds and ferns and overhung by vast, deciduous trees; there, a small path, leading towards a rotten wooden stump jutting out from the far bank, the last vestige of the causeway that Landru hurried along, lugging his heavy package.

Looking at the pond, it is also possible to sense an altogether darker case, one that Monteilhet saw, smelt and heard that moonlit evening. In this narrative, Landru killed more women than the ten fiancées on the charge sheet (three at Vernouillet and seven at Gambais). It all depended on whether the police had grasped the full extent of Landru's operation.

At Landru's trial, the prosecution implied that the *carnet* was a comprehensive record of his movements during the period between his first meeting with Jeanne Cuchet in early 1914 and his arrest five years later. Godefroy based this assumption on the *réquisitoire définitif*, which claimed that from 1914 to 1919 "he [Landru] was in contact with 283 women, all of whom have been found or their fate is known, apart from the ten whose names appear in the *carnet*." The statement was untrue. In a report sent to Bonin, the police acknowledged that of the 283 women Landru was known to have contacted, "the identity of 72 individuals had not been established".

This was only the start of the slippages in the official record of Landru's activities. The police deduced the figure of 283 women from the notes in Landru's *carnet* and the files in his garage, which contained records of his contacts via matrimonial agencies. However, Landru only acquired the *carnet* and started his filing system in the spring of 1915, after Jeanne Cuchet's disappearance. He did not keep detailed notes in the *carnet* until the summer of 1916, an important fact that emerged in 1933 when Riboulet published his memoir of the case.

At Vernouillet, where Landru rented The Lodge from December 1914 to August 1915, the police only knew about the disappearance of Jeanne and André Cuchet, Thérèse Laborde-Line and Marie-Angélique Guillin. Berthe Héon, the fifth victim on the charge sheet, must have visited Vernouillet, because she joked to a friend in the summer of 1915 about the saucy underwear she had seen at her fiancé's country house. Beyond these five names, the police could not be sure that no other women had visited The Lodge, because the recollections of Landru's neighbours were so hazy.

At Gambais, the investigation confronted a different problem. The police interviewed a number of witnesses in addition to Monteilhet who had very precise memories of Landru behaving suspiciously. Yet like Monteilhet, their testimony jarred with the official narrative of seven disappearances at the Villa Tric: Berthe Héon (December 1915), Anna Collomb (December 1916), Andrée Babelay (April 1917), Célestine Buisson (September 1917), Louise Jaume (November 1917), Annette Pascal (April 1918) and Marie-Thérèse Marchadier (January 1919).

***

In May 1916, around the time that Monteilhet saw Landru, Marie Bizeau was wandering in the woods near the same pond. Mme Bizeau, 46, was the wife of a gamekeeper at the nearby chateau which owned this stretch of the forest. Through the trees, she spotted a bald, bearded man, only visible from the head and shoulders upwards and apparently digging a large hole. The man looked up and Mme Bizeau hurried on her way, not inclined to get too close to this dubious stranger whom she later identified as Landru.

Almost two years later, Mme Bizeau saw Landru again while her husband and other estate workers from the chateau were restocking the pond with fish. Landru was on the causeway, laughing and gesticulating at the men as they stood chest deep in the cold water.

"What numbskulls," he exclaimed, pointing in particular at Monsieur Bizeau.

Mme Bizeau grabbed Landru by the sleeve and suggested that he might like to get in the water and give the men a hand. Landru shook her off and strolled back along the causeway, flicking the water with a makeshift cane as he wandered into the forest.

About two hours later, Mme Bizeau was handing her husband some dry clothes when she saw Landru emerging from the trees with a "rather fat" woman in a fur coat who looked about 30 and two small girls, aged about eight and ten. The woman complained to "Monsieur Dupont" about the cold and told him firmly that it was time to go home.

Mme Bizeau was interviewed by the detective Dautel in May 1919, a few days after the futile "semi-drainage" of the pond. She gave a lengthy deposition and Dautel tried in vain to trace the plump, fur-coated lady and her two girls. Mme Bizeau never heard from the police again and she was not summoned to testify at Landru's trial.

Inadvertently, Mme Bizeau had knocked a hole in the police's reconstruction of Landru's movements during the week before Annette Pascal's disappearance at the start of April 1918. Mme Bizeau saw Landru with the fur-coated woman on 29 March 1918, two days after Landru first brought Annette to the Villa Tric. Annette returned to Paris by train on the evening of 27 March, as confirmed by her concierge. The police assumed that Landru had accompanied Annette back to Paris and then returned with her to the Villa Tric on 4 April, the day before she vanished.

Mme Bizeau contradicted this account. Based on her testimony, Landru must either have remained at the villa on 27 March, after Annette left for Paris, or returned with Annette to Paris and then come back to Gambais on 28 March or the morning of 29 March in time for his walk in the woods with the fur-coated woman. Landru must then have returned to Paris in time to accompany Annette back to Gambais on 4 April, the day before she disappeared.

Yet the *carnet* contained no record of any journeys by Landru between 27 March, when Annette returned to Paris, and 4 April, when she came back to the Villa Tric with him. Landru's notes in the *carnet* did not therefore amount to a complete log of his movements during the last week of Annette's life.

Mme Bizeau saw Landru by the pond for the last time in June 1918, about two months after Annette's disappearance. He was standing bare-headed on the opposite bank, while a blonde woman who looked in her late thirties lay asleep at his feet. The woman had a little pet dog, which began barking when it saw Mme Bizeau. Landru's companion on this occasion could not have been his mistress Fernande Segret, who was staying with relatives in Burgundy at the time. Mme Bizeau had stumbled across another woman the police never traced.

***

On foot, it takes about an hour from the pond to reach the Villa Tric, walking back along the Route de Gambaiseuil towards Gambais. At the village's war memorial, the road swings sharp right past the *mairie* and strikes northwest in the direction of Houdan, seven kilometres away. For a while the road is flanked by modern detached houses and then it gives way to open farmland, with the village church and graveyard visible in the distance. Approaching the church it is easy to miss the Villa Tric, half-hidden on the left-hand side of the road behind a thick, evergreen hedge.

No one lived here when I visited the villa in 2017, shortly before the house was put up for sale. On the rusting iron front gate, a tattered "*chien méchant*" notice warned away intruders; on the roof, a television aerial twisted in the breeze. Despite the boarded-up windows, the house still looked much as it did in Landru's time: nondescript and desolate.

A thin, straggly hedge along the side of the property facing Gambais offered more glimpses of the rear garden. Landru's open-air hangar had gone, as had a couple of other outhouses; otherwise the scene was the same as a century ago. An enclosure with a wash house and outdoor pantry or storage shed opened onto a much larger, unmown lawn, shielded on the side facing the church by a large garage where Landru had kept his *camionnette*.

Bonin saw the Villa Tric as the heart of the mystery he was trying to solve. The house seemed an obvious setting for a multiple murder plot, complete with clues to guide his investigation: the charred bone debris and scraps of women's apparel beneath the leaves, the rusty, tinpot oven, the suspicious smoke.

In Bonin's plot, a man brings seven women to the villa between December 1915 and April 1919, solely to steal their assets and murder them. Only five other women visit the house during this period and survive to tell their story:

the man's wife, his younger daughter, his mistress, her mother, a wealthy widow, and the sister of one of his victims. All the murders are premeditated and follow a barbaric logic. One killing leads to the next murder as soon as the man's funds begin to run low.

Monteilhet and Mme Bizeau were not the only witnesses from Gambais who undermined this narrative. Two elderly women, Mme David and her friend Mme Auchet, were ridiculed at Landru's trial when they testified about passing the Villa Tric one autumn day in 1917 and seeing foul smoke pouring out of his chimney. They were just a couple of "village gossips", one reporter wrote. Yet if Mme David and Mme Auchet were broadly right about the date then the official body count of seven victims at the villa was questionable.

With the confidence of country women who followed the seasons, Mme David and Mme Auchet stuck to their recollection that they had seen the smoke in late October or early November 1917. This was at least two months after the disappearance of Célestine Buisson and almost a month before Louise Jaume vanished.

Landru said that when Mme David and Mme Auchet passed the Villa Tric he must have been burning dirty old rags soaked in automobile oil along with other refuse. "Clearly, it didn't smell of roses," he sneered at the women.

Assuming that Landru was lying, it is arguable he was burning the remains of Célestine Buisson, having stored all or part of the corpse for at least two months. But it appears more likely that Landru was burning another victim's remains.

**

If Mme David and Mme Auchet were reliable witnesses, another plot begins to take shape.

A convicted swindler, on the run from the law, invites an unknown number of women to the villa he rents outside Gambais between December 1915 and April 1919. He finds these women via lonely hearts adverts, matrimonial agencies or by trawling Paris's trams, buses and metro lines. Sometimes the man jots down his companions' names or codenames in his *carnet*, along with a note of his journeys with them between Paris and Gambais. At other times he forgets to keep records, for his schedule is increasingly hectic and his memory is not what it used to be.

In Gambais, the man and his guests are sometimes noticed by local people – in particular, the coachman who operates a cab service between

Houdan and Gambais, and the local shopkeepers. Sometimes, however, they are not seen by the villagers, especially when the man and his latest woman get off the train at Garancières or Tacoignières and walk across country to the house.

The man is not always clear in his own head about why he has invited a woman to the villa. Sometimes he wants to get rid of her because he finds her irritating or deserving of punishment. Almost anything can set him off: a woman lying about her age, going on about God, or having nosy relatives. On other occasions he wants her money and if she balks, he kills her. The only thing he always wants is sex, regardless of whether she is young or middle-aged, pretty or plain. In the spring and summer, he especially enjoys taking his guests to the forest on the other side of Gambais.

When it is time for the women to die he strangles them, "the gentlest of deaths" in his opinion, and also the quietest. Sometimes he notes the hour that he kills them in his *carnet*; at other times he cannot be bothered, especially when he has also failed to log their name or codename. Once he has stripped his victim of jewellery and cash, he drags or carries the body to a locked shed at the end of the garden.

Then he returns to Paris, for up to a week; not so long that the body begins to decompose, but long enough to wonder if it will be discovered by the local cobbler or his son, who are paid by his landlord to keep an eye on the house when it is empty. He enjoys taking this risk, which adds to his sense of power. The cobbler and his son are lazy and not inclined to visit the villa regularly. The man may also have bribed them not to come to the house, for the landlord lives far away and will be none the wiser.

When the man returns to the villa, he waits till nightfall and brings the body back to the house. He cuts off the hands, feet and head, the body parts most commonly used to identify corpses. He is careful to wash away the blood as quickly as he can and he may also take the opportunity to cut up a dead animal – for instance, a chicken bought at the butcher in Gambais – to disguise the source of any tiny stains he leaves behind.

Next, he burns the identifying body parts in his oven, along with the women's clothes. The risk he takes is the noxious smoke billowing out of the chimney that any passer-by will smell. At intervals, various locals see and smell the smoke while he is at work in the kitchen. However, only one witness, the butcher in Gambais, notices smoke at approximately the same time that one of the man's known guests vanishes.

When the man has finished his grisly task, he cleans the oven, scraping out any remaining bone debris or non-combustible items like hair pins and buttons. He conceals these charred fragments beneath a pile of leaves in his hangar, mixing them up with burnt animal bones. His oven is small and time is short, so he dismembers the rest of the body and packages up the sections, which he stores temporarily in the locked shed.

Over the coming nights, the man gradually takes the packages away in his *camionnette*. This is another risky moment, because any civilian driving a car around the countryside after dark in wartime is bound to attract suspicion and the village constable is on the alert for German spies. But the man has a clever cover story. He says he is an automobile trader, and gradually the villagers become accustomed to seeing him driving around the neighbourhood at odd hours.

He disposes of the packages in secluded spots he knows well – notably the ponds in the forest and the surrounding boggy terrain, where it is easy to dig deep holes. The possibilities for concealment are endless, although on one occasion he is nearly detected by a woman walking past one of his burial sites. The police subsequently investigate these ponds, but they lack the resources, the energy and the skill to undertake a comprehensive, systematic search.

The man has an unwitting ally in his efforts to erase the evidence of his crimes. For centuries, wild boars have roamed the forest, rooting through the thick undergrowth for any food they can unearth. The makeshift graves make easy pickings for these ravenous omnivores, which consume everything they find, including the bones.

One day in early 1919, the man tries to tally up his murders by writing a list, but his records are patchy and his memory is "rebellious", as he puts it. He cannot be sure that the list is complete, for as he also notes, his previous life flows past him as if it had been lived by someone else. Fifteen years earlier, a psychiatrist warned the man's wife that her husband stood on the "frontiers of madness". By the time he is caught, he has long since crossed the border.

***

I do not know if all the elements of this alternative plot are true. Landru may never have bribed the cobbler to stay away; Pierre Vallet and his son Marcel may simply have been incurious, never bothering to snoop around the property. The boars in the forest may never have gone near Landru's makeshift graves, which may never have existed; the only circumstantial evidence was the hole that Mme Bizeau thought she saw Landru digging.

Yet not all the elements need to be true for the overall story to hold together. One can remove the greedy pigs, the indolent cobbler and much else besides without the rest of the narrative falling apart. By contrast, Bonin's tightly circumscribed, single-motive plot depends on every element standing up to scrutiny. It relies, for example, on Landru murdering the destitute 19-year-old Andrée Babelay for her non-existent money, an absurdity that the jury refused to believe.

Every pattern that Bonin tried to impose on the case broke down because of the exceptions. Landru's ten known female victims were not all comfortably off, as the prosecution continued to argue at his trial. Three of the women had almost no money at all, while only three had sufficient savings to be attractive targets for a marriage swindler: Marie-Angélique Guillin, Anna Collomb and Célestine Buisson.

To paper over these inconsistencies, the authorities deployed the easy slur that the women were all "besotted" with Landru. Yet I felt only three of the missing women qualified for this description.

Thérèse Laborde-Line, Landru's Argentinian-born fiancée, struck me as achingly lonely when she fell into his clutches in the summer of 1915. She was alone in an apartment she could not afford, estranged from her postal clerk son, and without friends in Paris. Marie-Angélique Guillin, Landru's next known victim, was swept up by the fantasy that she was going to be a diplomat's wife in Australia. Célestine Buisson was in thrall to the idea of making a home with a respectable husband.

None of the other seven women on the charge sheet seemed "besotted" with Landru or even especially fond of him. In their different ways, they were using him for a purpose. For example, Berthe Héon saw Landru as a means to escape the intolerable grief of losing her daughter and stillborn grandchild. Anna Collomb wanted a husband who would adopt and legitimise her little daughter. Even Louise Jaume, the devout, estranged wife of a husband who had run off to Italy, appears to have seen marriage to Landru as a path to regaining God's esteem. Louise kept up her guard till almost the end, refusing to sleep with Landru and finding him somewhat suspicious, as he obsessively swept the leaves at Gambais.

It was these sinister glimpses of the Villa Tric – the pile of leaves, the print of the wolf in sheep's clothing, the four animals buried in the kitchen enclosure – that formed the backdrop to the case that Bonin constructed. Yet the Villa Tric did not hold the key to why the horror began; in that sense, Landru's sketch of his oven was a false signpost. The key lay elsewhere.

Chapter 25

The Road to Vernouillet

It takes a quarter of an hour to reach The Lodge on foot from the station that serves Vernouillet, passing through quiet suburban streets on the outer fringe of Paris's commuter belt. The Rue de Mantes has been renamed since Landru's time and the house has a different street number, but it is still recognisably the same property: an odd, double-fronted residence near the bottom of a steep lane, with a smaller annexe tacked onto the main villa.

The more one looks at The Lodge, the more striking its lack of privacy becomes. Landru's neighbours had a clear sight of the back garden, as did anyone walking across the fields behind the house. It seems an improbable place for Landru to have chosen to kill Jeanne and André Cuchet, quite unlike the isolated Villa Tric at Gambais.

As I worked through the immense file on Jeanne at the Paris police archives, I came to believe that Landru had no plan to murder her and André when the three of them arrived at The Lodge at the start of December 1914. Something happened in December or January to make Landru decide in his desperation that Jeanne and André had to die.

***

"We are in the presence of facts which are reproduced identically." Such was Bonin's accusation against Landru during one of their many interrogation sessions. Yet in almost every detail, the case of Jeanne and André Cuchet differed from the nine subsequent murders on the charge sheet.

Jeanne and André represented the only double murder in the series; two victims at the same property, one straight after the other. André was the only male victim and crucially, he and his mother were the only victims who knew Landru's true identity and were aware of his criminal past. Nonetheless, they came to live with him at The Lodge.

There was another version of Jeanne's strange, sad tale that Bonin either never considered or jettisoned because it was impossible to reconcile with his hypothesis of identical murders. This story told of a humble Parisian seamstress who hated her job and dreamed of a new life abroad with her one true love: not Landru, but her only son André.

Until the outbreak of war in August 1914, Jeanne's relationship with Landru fitted the pattern of a hard-up woman in search of a husband who would provide for her and André, or at least act as her *vieux monsieur* (sugar daddy). Jeanne was poor, a fact proved by her financial records, the will of her husband and the testimony of two well-placed witnesses: her friend Louise Bazire and her probable lover, the shirt-maker Pierre Capdevieille. In 1914, Landru had plenty of cash as a result of his latest swindle and his seizure of his father's legacy. All Jeanne had to trade in return was her sex appeal, which she used to get Landru into bed.

Bonin expended an enormous amount of time trying to make Jeanne fit the template for all the murders that followed. Yet she kept breaking the mould. There was no hard evidence that Landru was after her pitiful savings and plenty of circumstantial evidence that Jeanne was quite unlike her portrayal in the *réquisitoire définitif* as a dim, emotionally vulnerable woman.

Jeanne's sister Philomène and brother-in-law Georges Friedman did their best to suggest to the police that Jeanne was naïve about men. On the contrary, she seems to have been quite calculating in her dealings with potential suitors after the death of her husband, who had left her destitute. Before meeting Landru in early 1914, Jeanne rejected at least two potential suitors, a wine merchant and a commercial traveller, while the only man she appears to have trusted was Capdevieille, who may have been married.

Why, then, did Jeanne "fall" for Landru? Mme Hardy, the nosy neighbour who lived above the couple in La Chaussée, saw a woman who was quite cool, even distant in her exchanges with Landru. Viewed through Mme Hardy's eyes, it appears plausible that Jeanne could have become engaged to Landru to advance a specific project.

Five witnesses recalled Jeanne speaking about her desire to start a new life with André in Britain or America: her friend Louise Bazire, her concierge Mme Pelletier, her former employer Albert Folvary, her brother-in-law Louis Germain and Germain's wife. All five dismissed Jeanne's plan as a fantasy, on the grounds that she spoke no English. Yet it was not so far-fetched.

It is easy to see why a single working-class mother, scrimping a living as a seamstress, might have wanted to emigrate; in *belle époque* Paris, there were plenty of other women in a similar situation to Jeanne who felt the same way. It is also understandable why Jeanne's ambition suddenly became an urgent goal when war broke out in August 1914: for her prime concern as France mobilised was the safety of the one victim on the charge sheet whom the authorities scarcely bothered to investigate.

***

André Cuchet merited just one slim police report in his mother's bulging case file, where he was cast as a mere victim of circumstance, killed because of Jeanne's obsession with Landru. "The son followed the mother to his death," the *réquisitoire* declared, "and an eleventh corpse was added to the mournful list."

André's status as a footnote overlooked the testimony of Mme Morin, the mother of André's best friend Max. Mme Morin remembered how Jeanne was "heartbroken" when she heard a false rumour in the autumn of 1914 that André, still 17, might soon be able to volunteer for the army, without her permission.

Jeanne's behaviour in the war's opening months bore all the signs of a mother who was terrified that her callow son, gripped by military fervour, would soon be killed by the *Boches*. At the start of August 1914, Jeanne rushed back to Paris from La Chaussée, unwilling to leave André on his own. In October, she pulled André out of pre-army training, telling him it was pointless. In November, she forced André to give up his newly found factory job to come and live in cosseted seclusion with her and Landru in Vernouillet.

Jeanne's fears for André were entirely rational because the war was rapidly descending that autumn into carnage. On 11 October, as André began his pre-army training, *Le Journal* published a "bitter, vehement, superb" letter from two sisters who had already lost four brothers at the front; a fifth had been severely wounded. Now they addressed their sixth brother, also mobilised, on behalf of their grieving mother:

"*Maman* weeps, she says you must be strong and wishes you can avenge their deaths... God has given you life, He has the right to take it back, this is *maman* who says so."

Some French families took what the nationalist press called the cowards' option. They emigrated, with distant North America a particularly appealing prospect. During the war, more than 50,000 people left France each year for the United States, many of them speaking little or no English. Jeanne's challenge in following their example was her lack of money and connections. She needed someone who could make possible her and André's escape.

Did Landru encourage Jeanne to think he was that person? A passing remark by Landru to Mme Oudry, the estate agent in Vernouillet who looked after The Lodge, suggests that he might have done. Landru told Mme Oudry that Jeanne worked for a Paris fashion house, a position that required her to make business trips to America.

Why might Landru have encouraged Jeanne's dream of emigrating? I think the reason was straightforward. He enjoyed having sex with her and wanted to keep the relationship going by stringing her along. Landru was besotted with Jeanne, not the other way round.

Until Jeanne prised open his locked chest on 16 August 1914, Landru could use the excuse of his "lost" papers to delay their promised marriage and subsequent emigration, *en famille*. The balance of their relationship changed completely when Jeanne discovered Landru's identity and, critically, the fact that he was a criminal on the run. Based on the evidence in the case archives, I believe she decided to blackmail him. In return for allowing him to sleep with her again, Landru had to get her and André out of the country, with or without him. Otherwise she would have him arrested by the police.

Jeanne does not appear to have reached this decision lightly. Following her discovery of Landru's papers, she confided her misgivings about him to three people: her friend Mme Bazire, Max's mother Mme Morin, and her former assistant seamstress who visited her at the end of August.

Jeanne probably decided to resume her relationship with Landru and blackmail him for two reasons. One was André's incorrigible naïvety about the war, expressed in his letters to Max Morin; the other was the mounting slaughter at the front.

Landru might well have looked like a plausible escape agent to Jeanne. Even his criminality could have appeared an advantage, because here was a swindler loaded with cash, with a car and false identity papers, adept at getting past military checkpoints. In addition, Landru knew his way around the Atlantic port of Le Havre. The point is not that Landru could have engineered Jeanne and André's flight from France. It is that he might have convinced her that he had the means to do so.

Why, then, their sudden move to Vernouillet at the start of December 1914; so rapid, that "everything was rushed through", according to Jeanne? Mme Oudry, the Vernouillet estate agent, may have provided another clue. Mme Oudry recalled that Landru told her he could not sign the rental contract for The Lodge after his first inspection of the property, because his "wife" needed to see the place for herself.

Landru's remark appears unusual, given his repeatedly expressed opinion about the subordinate position of women and their duty to obey men. I have no firm proof, but I suspect it was Jeanne, not Landru, who initiated the abrupt move to Vernouillet, because of some unwelcome development in Paris: perhaps a visit by her meddling sister Philomène to her apartment near the Gare de l'Est.

In this plot, Jeanne panicked at the end of November, ordering Landru to find a discreet base near Paris where she and André could leave France unnoticed – or she would hand him over to the police. Having approved Landru's choice of The Lodge, Jeanne then went to ground. She made no effort to get to know her neighbours in Vernouillet. Over the Christmas holidays, she wrote careful letters to her sister-in-law Mme Germain and to Mme Morin, discouraging them from paying a visit because of the "poor weather".

Jeanne behaved as if she had turned her back on her former life.

***

Landru's lack of urgency in the weeks following the move to Vernouillet reinforces the impression that he had no plan to kill Jeanne and André. His dawdling may also have revived Jeanne's doubts over whether he could be trusted; a dangerous position for Landru, since she only needed to walk up the hill to the police station at the top of Rue de Mantes in order to get him arrested.

Sometime in the first half of December Landru went off for several days to retrieve his car from the farm in Normandy where he had billeted his family. Nothing of any note happened at The Lodge for the next month. And then something did happen.

In the middle of January, André's prospects suddenly changed when the government brought forward the mobilisation of his contingent – the so-called "class" of 1917 – to the summer of 1915. André now knew that his possessive, fretful mother would soon be powerless to prevent him leaving home to fight the Germans. He would shortly be "savouring the pleasures of garrison life", André told Max without irony in his last letter to his friend, dated 20 January 1915.

From Jeanne's perspective, any project to emigrate with André would collapse when André left for barracks. André's impending departure was also bound to alarm Landru because the boy, like his mother, knew Landru's true identity. At his trial, Landru made the curious remark that he could not

245

keep André under "surveillance" after he "left" Vernouillet, purportedly for England. In the same indiscreet aside, Landru also let slip his low opinion of André's final letter to Max.

André feelings about Landru and his mother's liaison with a convicted crook can be deduced from what is known about his character. Monsieur Folvary, Jeanne's employer at the dress shop, recalled that André disapproved of his mother's plan to marry again. André's "ardent" patriotism and boyish sense of honour shone through his correspondence with Max, while his silence about Landru was also eloquent. It was as if André could not bear to write about a man he despised and probably feared.

The situation at The Lodge was already unstable because once André turned 18 in June 1915 he would be entitled to volunteer for military service, provided he had parental consent. However, André's last letter to Max implied that Jeanne would withhold her permission. Her refusal to yield to André's wishes almost certainly explains his excitement about the advancement of his compulsory mobilisation; for Jeanne would not be able to stop him joining Max in the trenches.

By 20 January, when André wrote his last letter to Max, it is possible to imagine several crises erupting in this toxic, combustible household. Perhaps Jeanne told Landru that he had to get her and André abroad in a matter of weeks, if not days, before André received his call-up papers. Perhaps Landru stalled, and Jeanne at last saw through his deceit, telling him she was going to the police. Or perhaps Jeanne told André the full details of her project to get him overseas, before he was killed by the *Boches*; and André, fired up with *esprit de combat*, told his mother and Landru that he was having no part in their illegal scheme.

In all these scenarios, Landru had been cornered by Jeanne and André, who could send him to New Caledonia for the rest of his life. To avoid that fate, Landru had only two options. He could disappear, which would be difficult, although not impossible, as the next four years would prove; or he could kill this dangerous mother and son.

***

How did Landru pull off the only double murder on the charge sheet? The detective Riboulet, who did not attend the police search of The Lodge, thought Landru probably used a gun. This theory falls apart as soon as one looks at the house, hemmed in on either side by neighbours who would certainly have heard the shots.

It seems most likely that Landru strangled Jeanne and André, taking advantage of The Lodge's peculiar two-sided construction to catch each of them in turn by surprise. He could have waited till one of them left the house and then hidden the first body out of view in the garage or the uninhabited pavilion-style annexe, before Jeanne or André returned.

It is an opinion, nothing more, but I decided that killing Jeanne and André gave Landru an appetite for murder and specifically murdering women. Nothing else satisfactorily explains the frenzy of activity that followed, as he bought the *carnet*, opened his filing system and raced around Paris trawling for female targets. I also felt that the act of murdering the Cuchets finally tipped Landru across the frontiers of madness.

Before Jeanne and André's deaths, Landru's actions seem recognisably rational, based on the immoral goals he had set himself. He pursued Jeanne because he found her attractive; he fled his home in Malakoff to avoid arrest; he removed his wife to Le Havre to prevent her testifying at his trial.

Conversely, Landru's behaviour after he killed Jeanne and André appears increasingly wayward. He did not act in his own best interest, pursuing the "logic" of a remorseless, lethal marriage swindler, as described in the *réquisitoire*. Instead, his choice of victims was illogical. He killed the Argentinian-born Thérèse Laborde-Line, who had almost no money, before the relatively affluent retired governess Marie-Angélique Guillin. He then murdered the penniless Berthe Héon while pretending to the relatively well-off Anna Collomb and Célestine Buisson that he was on a lengthy business trip abroad.

I think it is conceivable that Landru got rid of Thérèse because he resented the long climb upstairs to her dingy sixth-floor apartment. During the investigation and at his trial, he was still grumbling about this irksome chore. I also believe that with the same vicious caprice, Landru singled out Berthe for punishment because she had lied to him about her true age.

All of this lay ahead as Landru contemplated the dead bodies of Jeanne and André. He had two corpses on his hands, in a house overlooked by its neighbours. At this critical juncture, he could have done with some help. Did he receive it?

***

On 14 April 1919, two days after Landru's arrest, his younger son Charles told the detective Dautel an intriguing story. Charles said that one day in late 1914 or early 1915, his father summoned him to Vernouillet. According to Charles, he spent the whole day with Landru at The Lodge, but only went into the garage and the kitchen in the pavilion-style annexe. Incredibly, Dautel did not ask Charles to explain the purpose of his visit.

Several months later, Charles provided one more detail about this visit to the detective Riboulet. Charles said that his father had required him at The Lodge for some unspecified "gardening work" ("*jardinage*"). In another extraordinary lapse, Riboulet did not ask Charles to describe the nature and precise location of this "gardening".

Bonin eventually gave up trying to gauge the degree of complicity of Landru's family in his crimes and the task is still just as difficult. At times, as in this episode involving Charles, members of the family are so close to a murder scene that it seems they must have known Landru was a killer. Only Suzanne, Landru's younger daughter, kept her father at a distance, by moving out of the family's apartment in Clichy to live with her fiancé; and it was this young man, an automobile mechanic called Gabriel Grimm, who shed the most light on Landru's overbearing relationship with his wife and children, in a long witness statement that Grimm gave to the police.

In April 1914, soon after his engagement to Suzanne, Grimm visited the family at their apartment in the southern Paris suburbs. "I found them all in tears," Grimm recalled. "They told me that Landru had done some bad business at his garage in Malakoff and had had to flee."

Grimm did not say whether Marie-Catherine and her children were rueing the fact that Landru had committed a crime, or the prospect that he might get caught. Either way, Grimm made clear in his statement that Landru, a fugitive from justice, remained in close, regular contact with his family throughout the war.

Grimm was mobilised in August 1914 and did not see Suzanne again until the autumn of 1915, when he was assigned to work in a factory engaged in war production in the northern Paris suburbs. Conveniently for Grimm, the factory was near the family's apartment in Clichy.

Soon, Grimm asked Landru for permission to marry Suzanne. Landru refused, explaining that he could not do so while he was living under a false identity. Without telling Landru, Grimm and Suzanne decided to rent an apartment of their own in Clichy, so they could live as man and wife. Landru pursued them, insisting that he would "make them comfortable" by providing all the furniture for their new home. Grimm and Suzanne knew better than to refuse this offer from her possessive, interfering father.

On his and Suzanne's frequent visits to the family's apartment, Grimm remembered how Marie-Catherine could not bring herself to escape from

Landru by sueing for divorce: "One day she would appear to have made up her mind, the next she was undecided. It was enough for Landru to make an appearance for only a few minutes for her to excuse his way of life."

Overall, Grimm left an impression of a criminalised household that was complicit in Landru's thefts and frauds, while maintaining a state of wilful ignorance about the rest of his activities. And in the end, that is how I came to see Marie-Catherine and her children.

Charles's "gardening work" at The Lodge illustrates graphically the fine line that the family never dared cross. On a first reading, Charles looks like an accomplice to murder. It seems probable that Landru summoned Charles directly after Jeanne and André's deaths in late January or February 1915 and possible that the gardening work concerned the disposal of some or all of their remains. Yet it does not follow that Charles saw Jeanne and André's corpses or realised what he was doing.

Charles volunteered his disclosure about the visit, suggesting he was unaware that he might be incriminating himself. He was also quite specific about which parts of this lopsided property he had visited: the garage, where he may have helped Landru reassemble the recently dismantled *camionnette*; the kitchen in the side annexe, possibly for lunch; and the garden. All this time, Jeanne and André's bodies could have been stored by Landru in the upstairs bedrooms of the main villa, well out of Charles's view, because the garage offered a passageway between the street and the rear garden.

Did Charles, still only 14, ask his father about the purpose of the *"jardinage"*? He may have done and Landru may have lied in response. However, I think Charles was telling the truth when he said he kept his mouth shut. As he explained to Dautel, he was so afraid of his father's temper that he never dared ask about Landru's "way of life".

***

A century later, we can see how it was not just Landru's family who stepped back from the horror, allowing him the freedom to operate almost at will. So did the mayor and the village schoolmaster in Gambais, who refused to take seriously the exact, detailed enquiries of two sisters of the missing women. The police turned a blind eye, both before and after Landru's arrest, when they pretended in public that they had traced all his female contacts. Ultimately, the authorities cared more about sending Landru to the guillotine than gauging the full extent of his crimes.

Boundless misogyny ran through Landru's dark psyche; it was the thread that tied together all the murders he committed after killing Jeanne and André. Yet Landru appeared "normal" because he operated in a society that took women's inferiority for granted and in the middle of a terrible war, valued men's lives more highly.

Misogyny distorted the prosecution case, reducing the ten women on the charge sheet to chauvinist stereotypes. They were foolish, vulnerable, feeble, loose – never individuals whose personalities deserved any deeper enquiry. The defence case also reeked of chauvinism. Moro seized any chance to portray Landru's victims as promiscuous, as if this undermined the charge that his client was a murderer. In one especially distasteful cross-examination, Moro humiliated Marie-Thérèse Marchadier's friend Yvonne Le Gallo, simply because she was a prostitute.

The press complained about the "invasion" of the courtroom by women spectators, even as journalists at the trial revelled in images of startling sexual violence. One reporter, a well-known drama critic, fantasised about an actress who attended the hearing being burnt, naked, on stage. Newspaper cartoonists drew pictures of female hearts being roasted on a spit or dolls being stuffed into ovens.

This was the world in which Landru thrived and it is not so very distant; for while the past is a foreign country, it has borders with the present.

Afterword

From the Quai de la Pinède to the Jardin des Plantes

Six years after Landru's trial, a middle-aged woman stood in tears on the Quai de la Pinède in Marseille, watching a ship come into harbour. Louise Dieudonné did not recognise her former husband Eugène when he walked down the gangway, but she hugged him all the same and would not let him go. All Louise wanted was to marry her anarchist house decorator again and settle down like a proper couple, with none of this free love nonsense.

Dieudonné had returned to France after 13 years' penal servitude in the swamps of Guyane for a crime he did not commit, only spared the guillotine because of a successful appeal for clemency by Moro. He had escaped twice – once in 1921, when he was soon recaptured, and again in 1926, when he fled from Guyane to Brazil. Now he was back in Louise's arms, having been assured of a full pardon after a campaign led by Moro in the National Assembly.

Louise got her wish and once the pardon was granted she and Eugène remarried at a ceremony in the *mairie* of Paris's 11th *arrondissement*. There was one surprising guest – a juror at the trial in 1913 who had contacted Dieudonné after his return to apologise for wrongfully finding him guilty. In an astonishing gesture of forgiveness, Dieudonné invited the juror to be an official witness at the wedding.

Dieudonné resumed his old trade, opening a small decorating business on Boulevard Saint-Germain, and in 1930 was persuaded to write a book about his terrible years of forced labour. As a token of gratitude, Dieudonné sent a complimentary copy to the lawyer who had saved his life.

"*Mon cher Maître*," Dieudonné wrote to Moro, "you will perhaps feel a little joy in thinking that your efforts have not been in vain. Since, without you, I would not have been able to write this book."

Dieudonné, a man he liked, and Landru, a man he despised, defined why Moro fought all his life for the abolition of the death penalty. By coincidence, on the same day in November 1921 that the newspapers reported Dieudonné's failed escape attempt, Godefroy admitted at

251

Landru's trial that the prosecution had no idea how Landru had killed his victims. All Godefroy could offer was "hypotheses". For Moro, the death penalty was not justifiable even if a defendant was deemed guilty beyond all reasonable human doubt. A higher standard of certainty had to be reached, too high for a jury of fallible mortals, because the sentence could not be reversed.

Moro did not win this argument in his lifetime, but he won it from beyond the grave. Twenty-four years after Moro's death in 1956, the justice minister who had delivered his funeral oration became President of France. In one of his first acts of office, François Mitterrand abolished the death penalty on the advice of his justice minister, Robert Badinter, who as a young barrister had known and admired *"le grand Moro"*.

Moro's legacy was complete.

***

I am also opposed to the death penalty, in any circumstances. For that reason, I like to think that I would have sided with the three jurors at Landru's trial who took Moro's advice and voted to acquit on the murder charges, safe in the knowledge that Landru would have joined Dieudonné in the tropical hell of Guyane. Yet if I am honest, I cannot be certain that I would have had the strength of principle to vote with the minority, rather than send Landru to the guillotine in a spirit of raw, visceral vengeance; for at his trial, Landru's fate was settled by the heart, not the head.

I think the moment when Moro lost the case came early in the trial and had nothing to do with the evidence. It arrived when a woman wept helplessly for a younger sister who, in life, she had found exasperating.

Philomène Friedman was not a trustworthy witness, as Moro wished to demonstrate when he asked her to describe her dream about the ghost of Jeanne visiting her in the night. Philomène's dream was a fantasy, yet unfortunately for Moro, what the jurors saw was a sister lost in grief, alone on the witness stand, beyond any consolation. No normal human heart could fail to be moved.

Again and again, other women bore witness to the sorrow and the pity of losing their loved ones, while Landru tried to glare them into submission: Mme Colin, Andrée Babelay's mother, crying for her poor, foolish teenage daughter; Louise Fauchet, Annette Pascal's elder sister and surrogate *"maman"*, frozen in fear as she gazed at the court; Yvonne Le Gallo, Marie-Thérèse Marchadier's loyal prostitute friend, holding her dignity amid the laughter about her profession.

My breaking point came when Juliette Auger testified about the terrible scene she had witnessed in the little apartment at 45 Avenue des Ternes.

Of all the missing fiancées, the "*disparue*" I admired the most was Berthe Héon, the 55-year-old widow from Le Havre who had lost all three of her children and her long-term lover in the years before she met Landru. Despite this "cascade of sorrows", culminating in her favourite daughter Marcelle's death, Berthe had been determined to pick herself up and start her life again. This was why she had answered the cunning advert from a lonesome *monsieur* seeking a wife to live with him in a "pretty colony".

I see Berthe now, dazed with grief, asking Marcelle's best friend Juliette to take care of Marcelle's grave. I see Landru, alias "Georges Petit", an entrepreneur from Tunisia, sneering at Berthe that she could not "live with the dead". And I see Berthe start to cry.

At that instant, I wanted Landru to go to the guillotine and the feeling never entirely left me.

***

This is not a story with a neat ending. It finishes, if at all, in more ambiguity and confusion.

In the spring of 1958, a builder in Vernouillet accidentally unearthed the partial, headless skeletons of an adult woman and a boy on land that had once formed the end of the rear garden of The Lodge. It appeared that Jeanne and André Cuchet's remains had at last been found but the medical examiner was less sure. He concluded that the woman had been about 30 at the time of her death, nine years younger than Jeanne, while the boy had not reached puberty and was probably about ten or 11. The skeletons were never formally identified.

I think the builder did stumble across Jeanne and André's remains in an area of the garden that Bonin had overlooked during his superficial search on 15 April 1919. The coincidence of the skeletons appears too striking to admit any other explanation, especially as the medical examiner's margin for error was so narrow. Jeanne had not been so much older than the presumed age of the female skeleton, while André had been a slim, weedy youth.

I also think that the burial plot was dug one winter's day in early 1915 by Landru and his unknowing son Charles, summoned to Vernouillet to assist his father with unspecified "gardening work". But it is all conjecture, underlining Bonin's mistake in treating The Lodge as a less important crime scene than the Villa Tric.

***

A few years before the discovery at Vernouillet, the bone debris found at the Villa Tric was removed from the Paris police laboratory and buried in the city's Jardin des Plantes, a botanical garden on the left bank of the Seine, opposite the Gare d'Austerlitz. The transfer prompted a strong protest from forensic pathologists who argued presciently that advances in science might eventually allow some of the fragments to be matched with the missing women.

I went one spring morning to the Jardin des Plantes, hoping to bring some finality to the story of the *disparues*; not a conclusion, but at least the end of a trail. Following the transfer, a story arose that the fragments had been scattered beneath the shade of a weeping willow, a fittingly poetic resting place. For an hour I wandered around the garden, searching in vain for this tree, until I gave up and asked a park official to check the botanical records. There has never been a weeping willow in the Jardin des Plantes. The tale appears to have been a ploy by the park authorities to prevent macabre souvenir hunters from digging up the bones.

I do not mind this last deception. On a sunny day, in the heart of Paris, the Jardin des Plantes makes a peaceful refuge from the teeming, dangerous city. It is a good place to remember all Landru's victims, known and unknown.

Notes

Prologue: Alas I Have Little Hope

p.xi   "with blue eyes and chestnut hair, medium height": Marie Lacoste letter to the mayor of Gambais, 12 Jan 1919, Paris Police Archives, reproduced in *Landru: 6h 10 Temps Clair, Les Pièces du Dossier* (Paris, 2013).

Chapter 1: The Locked Chest

p.3   "a commercial traveller and a wine trader": *La Presse*, 24 Aug 1919.

p.3   "in order to tide her over": 'Renseignements fournit par l'Enregistrement au sujet de la succession de M. Cuchet', 12 July 1919, Paris Police Archives, Carton JA 32. 'Rapport de l'Inspecteur de Police Peretti', 2 July 1919, Paris Police Archives, Carton JA 28, *Dossier Cuchet*; 'Déclaration de Mme Bazire', 28 July 1919, Yvelines Archives, Carton 2U 769/2613, *Dossier Cuchet*.

p.3   "for whom she worked from home": Jeanne Cuchet to Pierre Capdevieille, undated letter, 1912, Paris Police Archives, Carton JA 28, *Dossier Cuchet*.

p.4   "despite taking Cuchet's surname": 'Déposition d'Albert Folvary', 26 July 1919, Yvelines Archives, Carton 2U 769/2605, *Dossier Cuchet*.

p.4   "her plans to find a husband": 'Déposition d'Albert Folvary', 26 July 1919, Yvelines Archives, Carton 2U 769/2605, *Dossier Cuchet*.

p.4   "looking up for André that autumn": In his will, Martin Cuchet recognised André as his son. However, Cuchet was probably living in his home town of Limoges at the time of André's birth in 1897 and did not marry Jeanne until 1904.

p.4   "a gang of older lads":'Audition de Pierre Capdevieille' in 'Rapport sur André Cuchet', 2 July 1919, Paris Police Archives, Carton JA 28, *Dossier Cuchet*.

p.4   "his new friend's condescension": 'Déposition de Mme Morin', 1919 (undated), Paris Police Archives, Carton JA 28, *Dossier Cuchet*.

p.5   "ask any more questions": Jeanne continued to work for Folvary until 18 April 1914, making clothes he had already commissioned from her. *Le Petit Parisien*, 10 Nov 1921.

p.5   "bookstore employee called Georges Friedman": The name "Friedman" was sometimes misspelt "Friedmann" in the police and judicial records of

255

the case. At Landru's trial, some newspapers incorrectly gave Friedman's first name as "Albert" rather than "Georges", because of a clerical error on the original witness list.

p.5 "suspicious of Jeanne's fiancé": 'Disparition de Mme Cuchet et de son fils', Georges Friedman interview, 16 April 1919, Paris Police Archives, Carton JA 28, *Dossier Cuchet*.

p.5 "anywhere near the colony": 'Disparition de Mme Cuchet et de son fils', Georges Friedman interview, 16 April 1919, Paris Police Archives, Carton JA 28, *Dossier Cuchet*.

p.6 "who invited him to eat": Statement of Mme Jeanne Hardy, Gouvieux, 1 Aug 1919, Yvelines Archives, Carton 2U 769/2659.

p.7 "'strong aversion' to Jeanne's disagreeable fiancé":'Audition de Mme Friedman', 16 April 1919, Paris Police Archives, Carton JA 28, *Dossier Cuchet*.

p.7 "crossing points to England": Police report on movements of Landru family, 1914–15, 3 June 1919, Yvelines Archives, Carton 1373W2/788.

p.7 "from his bank account": 'Affaire Cuchet, Rapport de l'Inspecteur de la Police Brandenburger', 16 April 1919, Paris Police Archives, Carton JA 28, *Dossier Cuchet*.

p.7 "night in the farmhouse": Police report on movements of Landru family, 1914–15, 3 June 1919, Yvelines Archives, Carton 1373W2/788.

p.7 "directly to Paris by train": 'Affaire Cuchet' Rapport de l'Inspecteur de la Police Brandenburger', 16 April 1919, Paris Police Archives, Carton JA 28, *Dossier Cuchet*.

p.8 "farmer and his wife agreed": Police report on movements of Landru family, 1914–15, 3 June 1919, Yvelines Archives, Carton 1373W2/788.

p.8 "returned to her old apartment": Statement of Mme Jeanne Hardy, Gouvieux, 1 Aug 1919, Yvelines Archives, Carton 2U 769/2659.

p.8 "they were safe": Police report on movements of Landru family, 1914–15, 3 June 1919, Yvelines Archives, Carton 1373W2/788.

p.9 "real surname was Cuchet, not Diard": Statement of Mme Jeanne Hardy, Gouvieux, 1 Aug 1919, Yvelines Archives, Carton 2U 769/2659.

p.9 "relations with Landru, alias Diard": 'Disparition de Mme Cuchet et de son fils', Georges Friedman interview, 16 April 1919, Paris Police Archives, Carton JA 28, *Dossier Cuchet*.

p.9 "never set foot in her apartment again": 'Déposition de Mme Pelletier', 25 July 1919, Yvelines Archives, Carton 2U769/2608, *Dossier Cuchet*.

p.9 "island of New Caledonia": 'Disparition de Mme Cuchet et de son fils', Georges Friedman interview, 16 April 1919, Paris Police Archives, Carton JA 28, *Dossier Cuchet*.

p.10 "a letter to Mme Hardy": Statement of Mme Jeanne Hardy, Gouvieux, 1 Aug 1919, Yvelines Archives, Carton 2U 769/2659.

NOTES

Chapter 2: The Lodge at Vernouillet

p.11　"passed by the apartment": 'Audition de Mlle Marcelle Chaize' (Soeur Valentine), 20 July 1919, Yvelines Archives, Carton 2U 769, *Dossier Cuchet*.

p.12　"created 'havoc' by dossing down in the villa": 'Déposition de Mme Pelletier', 18 April 1919, Paris Police Archives, Carton JA 28, *Dossier Cuchet*.

p.12　"got the boy off his hands": Statement of Mme Jeanne Hardy, Gouvieux, 1 Aug 1919, Yvelines Archives, Carton 2U 769/2659.

p.12　"'great sorrow' through her own tears": 'Déposition de Mme Morin', 1919 (undated), Paris Police Archives, Carton JA 28, *Dossier Cuchet*.

p.12　"news about you as soon as possible": André Cuchet letter to Max Morin, 10 Sept 1914, Yvelines Archives, Carton 2U 769/2758. Max's letters to André were never found by the police.

p.13　"lamented to Max in early September": André Cuchet letter to Max Morin, 10 Sept 1914.

p.13　"enlist as an underage volunteer": 'Déposition de Mme Morin', 1919 (undated), Paris Police Archives, Carton JA 28, *Dossier Cuchet*.

p.13　"did not speak to me about him any more": 'Déposition de Mme Morin', 1919 (undated), Paris Police Archives, Carton JA 28, *Dossier Cuchet*.

p.13　the same unfounded news": 'Déposition de Mme Morin', 1919 (undated), Paris Police Archives, Carton JA 28, *Dossier Cuchet*.

p.13　"how to fire it if necessary": André Cuchet letter to Max Morin, 4 Oct 1914, Yvelines Archives, Carton 2U 769/2757.

p.14　"*Maman* does not want me to sign up": André Cuchet letter to Max Morin, 25 Oct 1914, Yvelines Archives, Carton 2U 769/2755.

p.14　"to give her final approval": 'Audition de Mme Oudry', 15 April 1919, Paris Police Archives, Carton JA 28, *Dossier Cuchet*.

p.15　"the short-term quarterly lease": 'Audition de Mme Oudry', 15 April 1919, Paris Police Archives, Carton JA 28, *Dossier Cuchet*.

p.15　"get my breath back": André Cuchet letter to Max Morin, 22 Dec 1914, Yvelines Archives, Carton 2U 769/2753.

p.16　"everything was rushed through": Jeanne Cuchet letter to Mme Morin, 4 Jan 1915, Yvelines Archives, Carton 2U 769/2760.

p.16　"such a visit was currently impractical": 'Réquisitoire Définitif', p.50, Yvelines Archives, Carton 2U772.

p.16　"wearing mechanic's overalls": 'Déposition de Mme Vallet, 1 Aug 1919, Yvelines Archives, Carton 2U 769/2676; 'Déposition d'Auguste Vallet', 1 Aug 1919, Yvelines Archives, Carton 2U 769/2670.

p.16　"a secret German agent": 'Déposition de Mme Picque', 15 April 1919, Paris Police Archives, Carton JA 28, *Dossier Cuchet*.

p.17　"the 'class' of 1917": *Le Journal*, 10 Jan 1915.

p.17   "I cannot avoid this destiny": André Cuchet to Max Morin, 20 Jan 1915, Yvelines Archives, Carton 2U769/2745.

p.17   "to convey his congratulations": André Cuchet to Louis Germain, 27 Jan 1915, Yvelines Archives, Carton 2U769/2744.

Chapter 3: The "Carnet Noir"

p.19   "a piece of his mind": 'Déposition de Mme Morin', no date 1919, Paris Police Archives, Carton JA 28, *Dossier Cuchet*.

p.19   "âge situation rapport": The first-known lonely hearts advert by Landru appeared in *L'Echo de Paris* on 15 March. Landru may have decided to place a second advert in *Le Journal* because it had a bigger circulation, with around 1 million readers throughout France.

p.20   "Accept my respectful sentiments, Buisson": *Le Matin*, 22 May 1933, serialisation of Louis Riboulet, Sam Cohen, *La Véritable Affaire Landru* (Paris, 1933).

p.20   "early months of the war": *Le Gaulois*, 17 Nov 1921.

p.21   "a wife who loves her husband must do": Riboulet, *Le Matin*, 22 May 1933.

p.21   "really counts for something": 'Déposition de Gaston Lavie', 29 Dec 1919, Yvelines Archives, Carton 2U769/3262, *Dossier Buisson*.

p.21   "he eventually scribbled": Riboulet, *Le Matin*, 22 May 1933.

p.21   "amounts to 8,000 francs": Riboulet, *Le Matin*, 17 May 1933.

p.22   "drink himself to an early death": 'Etat Civil de Mme Collomb', 7 May 1919, Paris Police Archives, Carton JA 28, *Dossier Collomb*.

p.22   "often staying the night": *L'Humanité*, 15 Nov 1921.

p.22   "imprisonment as an enemy alien": Report on Thérèse Rundinger, alias Mlle Lydie, 19 Nov 1919, Yvelines Archives, Carton 2U771/3972.

p.22   "another unknown address (8.00 pm)": 'Réquisitoire Définitif', p.298, Yvelines Archives, Carton 2U772; Riboulet, *Le Matin*, 29 May 1933.

p.23   "'intolerable sinuses'": Riboulet, *Le Matin*, 29 May 1933.

p.23   "decided to follow him": 'Audition de Monsieur Laborde-Line', 19 May 1919, Paris Police Archives, Carton JA 28, *Dossier Laborde-Line*.

p.23   "who soon loathed her": 'Audition de Monsieur Laborde-Line', 19 May 1919, Paris Police Archives, Carton JA 28, *Dossier Laborde-Line*.

p.24   "neglected nothing to find a position": Thérèse Laborde-Line letter to Vincent Laborde-Line, 27 July 1914, Yvelines Archives, Carton 2U 769/2869, *Dossier Laborde-Line*.

p.24   "came to Landru's attention": Thérèse used the name "Mme Raoul" in her small advert enquiring about work as a lady's companion and may have used it again if she replied to Landru's lonely hearts advert in *Le Journal*, 1 May 1915. Landru subsequently adopted "Raoul" as one of his aliases.

p.24   "now engaged to be married": 'Audition de Mme Tréborel', 20 May 1919, Paris Police Archives, *Dossier Laborde-Line*.

NOTES

p.24   "the friend later explained": 'Déposition de Monsieur Jean Rigaud', no date 1919, Paris Police Archives, Carton JA 28, *Dossier Guillin*.

p.25   "memory was sacred to him": 'Déposition de Monsieur Jean Rigaud', no date 1919, Paris Police Archives, Carton JA 28, *Dossier Guillin*.

p.26   "imminent departure for Australia": 'Interrogatoire Définitif', 7 Aug 1920, Paris Police Archives, Carton JA 28.

p.26   "'enjoying herself in the country'": 'Interrogatoire Définitif', 7 Aug 1920, Paris Police Archives, Carton JA 28, *Dossier Guillin*.

p.26   "forcing her out of his apartment": 'Audition de Monsieur Laborde-Line', 19 May 1919, Paris Police Archives, Carton JA 28, *Dossier Laborde-Line*.

p.26   "somewhere between France and Australia": 'Interrogatoire Définitif', 7 Aug 1920, Paris Police Archives, Carton JA 28, *Dossier Guillin*.

Chapter 4: The Villa Tric

p.27   "bartender and cleaning woman": 'Déposition de Mme Audouard', Le Havre, 1 May 1919, Yvelines Archives, Carton 2U769/3019, *Dossier Héon*.

p.27   "have a good gossip": Mme Dalouin letter to Bonin, 17 May 1919, Yvelines Archives, Carton 2U769/3058, *Dossier Héon*.

p.27   "intermediary not involved": *Le Journal*, 12 June 1915.

p.28   "apartment one late June or July day": In his *carnet* Landru first recorded a meeting with Berthe at Rue de Rennes on 28 August 1915. However, she made at least one visit to The Lodge at Vernouillet, which he quit at the start of August. He therefore must have met her for the first time between 12 June, the date of his lonely hearts advert in *Le Journal*, and the end of July.

p.28   "explained to Mme Dalouin": Mme Dalouin letter to Bonin, 17 May 1919, Yvelines Archives, Carton 2U769/3058, *Dossier Héon*.

p.28   "take a chance with him": Mme Dalouin letter to Bonin, 17 May 1919, Yvelines Archives, Carton 2U769/3058, *Dossier Héon*.

p.28   "about Berthe's 'morality'": *Le Gaulois*, 24 Oct 1919.

p.29   "she sailed for Tunis": Testimony of Mme Millot, *Journal des Débats*, 14 Nov 1921.

p.29   "a new pair of shoes": Riboulet, *Le Matin*, 16 May 1933.

p.29   "promised they could wed": Statement by Marie Lacoste, 16 Dec 1919, Paris Police Archives, Carton JA 28, *Dossier Buisson*.

p.29   "bearded, bowler-hatted *monsieur*": Testimony of Léocadie Leffray, *L'Echo de Paris*, 15 Nov 1921.

p.30   "funds had been cleared": *Le Journal*, 12 Nov 1921.

p.30   "know all about it by 10.00": *Le Petit Parisien*, 10 Oct 1915.

p.31   "the cobbler unlocked the gates": Interview with Pierre Vallet in report by Jules Hebbé, gendarme at Houdan, 16 March 1919, Yvelines Archives, Carton 2U770/3291.

p.31   "toilet, but no bath": Plan of the Villa Tric, May 1919, Yvelines Archives, Carton 2U770/3687.

p.31   "lived south of Paris": 'Audition de Monsieur Tric', 17 May 1920, Paris Police Archives.

p.32   "noted in his *carnet*": It was impossible to date Berthe's visit to the Villa Tric more precisely because Landru grouped all his notes for December 1915 on the same page in his *carnet*.

p.32   "returned to Paris in the meantime": *Le Gaulois*, 24 April 1919. In his memoir of the case, Brigadier Riboulet incorrectly stated that Landru bought the stove in Gambais in mid-December, on the same day that he leased the villa from Monsieur Tric in Melun, 90 kilometres away. See *Le Matin*, 16 May 1933.

p.32   "happily settled in Tunis": *L'Homme Libre*, 19 Nov 1921.

p.32   "Berthe's late daughter": 'Déposition de Mme Oger [*sic*]', 20 Nov 1921, Paris Police Archives, Carton JA 28, *Dossier Héon*.

Chapter 5: Madame Sombrero

p.33   "parked outside the front gates": Jean Monteilhet, witness statement, 6 May 1919, Paris Police Archives, reproduced in *Landru: 6h 10 Temps Clair, Les Pièces du Dossier* (Paris, 2013).

p.33   "seeing what he was doing": 'Audition de Marie Bizeau', 16 May 1919, Yvelines Archives, Carton 2U771/3716.

p.33   "white buskin boots": Riboulet, *Le Matin*, 18 May 1933.

p.33   "she had been with Monsieur Collomb": Statement by Victorine Pellat in 'Inspecteur Maury, Enquête générale', no date 1919, Paris Police Archives, Carton JA 28, *Dossier Collomb*.

p.34   "Anna reluctantly agreed": Statement by Victorine Pellat in 'Inspecteur Maury, Enquête générale', no date 1919, Paris Police Archives, Carton JA 28, *Dossier Collomb*.

p.34   "father of her little girl": The police were unable to locate either the daughter or Monsieur Bernard. Riboulet, *Le Matin*, 18 May 1933.

p.34   "typing pool where she worked": *L'Echo d'Alger*, 15 Nov 1921.

p.34   "her forthcoming marriage": 'Declaration de Mme Léone Gaujon', 4 Nov 1919, Yvelines Archives, Carton 2U770/3332, *Dossier Collomb*.

p.34   "less enthusiastic about it": 'Déclaration de Gaston Gaimond', 4 Nov 1919, Yvelines Archives, Carton 2U770/3331, *Dossier Collomb*.

p.35   "never read a book in her life": 'Déclaration de Mlle Lacoste', 16 Dec 1919, Yvelines Archives, Carton 2U769/3223, *Dossier Buisson*.

p.35   "my sister can take him": Riboulet, *Le Matin*, 22 May 1933.

p.36   "wasted his precious time": Riboulet, *Le Matin*, 2 June 1933.

p.37   "also in uniform": 'Déclaration de Mme Brissot', 18 March 1920, Yvelines Archives, Carton 2U770/3594, *Dossier Pascal*; 'Déclaration de Marcel

Léglise', 10 Feb 1920, Yvelines Archives, Carton 2U770/3568, *Dossier Pascal*.

p.37 "you old cow": Anonymous postcard, undated, Yvelines Archives, Carton 2U770/3490, *Dossier Pascal*.

p.37 "a minor offence, possibly soliciting": 'Pascal, Anne-Marie', Cours de Tribunaux, Toulon, 6 Nov 1912, Yvelines Archives, Carton 2U770/3583, *Dossier Pascal*. The note on the charge sheet is illegible. Annette paid a fine of 25 francs.

p.37 "in a blue jacket and grey, wide-brimmed hat": Riboulet, *Le Matin*, 30 May 1933.

p.37 "10 rue de la Fraternité, Toulon, Var": 'Réquisitoire Définitif', p.259. Several newspapers later incorrectly reported that Annette wrote this note just before she disappeared.

p.37 "Iris matrimonial agency": Riboulet, *Le Matin*, 30 May 1933.

p.38 "tailored, sombrero hat": Riboulet, *Le Matin*, 30 May 1933.

p.38 "doorbell at Villa Stendhal": Riboulet, *Le Matin*, 30 May 1933.

p.38 "right to love you as such": Riboulet, *Le Matin*, 30 May 1933.

p.38 "10 rue de la Fraternité, Toulon": "Déclaration de Marie-Jeanne Fauchet", 24 Jan 1920, Yvelines Archives, Carton 2U770/3560, *Dossier Pascal*.

p.39 "giving you a little kiss": Riboulet, *Le Matin*, 30 May 1933.

p.39 "wondering what had happened to him": "Déclaration de Marie-Jeanne Fauchet", 24 Jan 1920, Yvelines Archives, Carton 2U770/3560, *Dossier Pascal*.

p.39 "safe to come up": "Déclaration de Marie-Jeanne Fauchet", 24 Jan 1920, Yvelines Archives, Carton 2U770/3560, *Dossier Pascal*.

p.39 "next morning at Villa Stendhal": Riboulet, *Le Matin*, 30 May 1933.

p.39 "want to see me again": Riboulet, *Le Matin*, 30 May 1933.

p.39 "give her some money": "Déclaration de Mme Carbonnel", 10 Feb 1920, Yvelines Archives, Carton 2U770/3570, *Dossier Pascal*.

p.39 "refused to listen to such nonsense": 'Déclaration de Mlle Lacoste', 16 Dec 1919, Yvelines Archives, Carton 2U769/3223, *Dossier Buisson*.

p.40 "all noted in his *carnet*": Riboulet, *Le Matin*, 19 May 1933.

p.40 "promised to pay her back soon": 'Déclaration de Mme Paulière Moreau, 6 Nov 1919, Yvelines Archives, Carton 2U770/3341, *Dossier Collomb*.

p.40 "explained to a work friend": Riboulet, *Le Matin*, 18 May 1933.

p.40 "feelings towards her family": Statement by Victorine Pellat in 'Inspecteur Maury, Enquête générale', no date 1919, Paris Police Archives, Carton JA 28, *Dossier Collomb*.

p.40 "'Frémyet' would definitely be there": Statement by Victorine Pellat, no date 1919, Paris Police Archives, Carton JA 28, *Dossier Collomb*.

p.40 "decided she did not like him": Statement by Victorine Pellat, no date 1919, Paris Police Archives, Carton JA 28, *Dossier Collomb*.

p.41 "nest egg of 8,000 francs": 'Déclaration de Mme Paulière Moreau, 6 Nov 1919, Yvelines Archives, Carton 2U770/3341, *Dossier Collomb*.

p.41 "as soon as she returned to Paris": Statement by Victorine Pellat in 'Inspecteur Maury, Enquête générale', no date 1919, Paris Police Archives, Carton JA 28, *Dossier Collomb*.

p.41 "his return ticket, travelling alone": Riboulet, *Le Matin*, 18 May 1933.

Chapter 6: Lulu

p.43 "wagging his finger at Marie-Jeanne": 'Déclaration de Marie-Jeanne Fauchet', 24 Jan 1920, Yvelines Archives, Carton 2U770/3560, *Dossier Pascal*.

p.43 "the little dressmaking workshop": Riboulet, *Le Matin*, 30 May 1933.

p.43 "front-page essay on 9 March": Maurice Barrès (1862–1923) was too old for active military service.

p.44 "homesick soldiers at the front": Brigadier Riboulet report, 'Filleuls de guerre de la disparue', 24 Feb 1920, Paris Police Archives, Carton JA 29, *Dossier Jaume*.

p.44 "bolting to Italy in 1914": 'Réquisitoire Définitif', pp.213–14, Yvelines Archives, Carton 2U772, 'Déclaration de Léonie Barthélemy', 31 Jan 1920, Yvelines Archives, Carton 2U770/3483, *Dossier Jaume*.

p.44 "also disapproved of Louise": Henri de Laval letter to Louise Jaume, 24 March 1915, Yvelines Archives, Carton 2U770/3394, *Dossier Jaume*.

p.44 "for no apparent reason": 'Audition de Paul Jaume', 16 Feb 1920, Yvelines Archives, Carton 2U770/3419, *Dossier Jaume*.

p.44 "some time at the sister's home": 'Déclaration de Léonie Barthélemy', 31 Jan 1920, Yvelines Archives, Carton 2U770/3483, *Dossier Jaume*.

p.44 "crossed the Italian border": 'Audition de Paul Jaume', *op.cit.*

p.45 "seeking a divorce": Louise's delay in suing for divorce was not just because of her religious scruples. Under France's 1908 divorce law, she had to prove that she and her husband had not slept together for three years. This may explain why Paul Jaume was so adamant that he and Louise slept in different beds.

p.45 "until their next meeting": Riboulet, *Le Matin*, 25 May 1933.

p.45 "fortune teller in north-east Paris": Andrée must have met Landru on the evening of 11 March because she quit her job as a nanny on 12 March and failed to make her agreed rendezvous with her mother on 13 March. See Riboulet, *Le Matin*, 19 May 1933; '*Déclaration de Mme Collin [sic]*', 24 April 1919, Paris Police Archives, Carton JA 29, *Dossier Babelay*.

p.46 "Mme Colin later admitted": '*Déclaration de Mme Collin*', 24 April 1919.

p.46 "fetching her suitcase": Riboulet, *Le Matin*, 21 May 1933; '*Déclaration de Mme Collin*', 24 April 1919.

p.46 "she might be pregnant": '*Déclaration de Mme Collin*', 24 April 1919.

p.46 "her pretend uncle": Riboulet, *Le Matin*, 21 May 1933.

p.46   "Petit Casino music theatre": Riboulet, *Le Matin*, 21 May 1933.

p.46   "a soft holdall bag": Riboulet, *Le Matin*, 21 May 1933.

p.47   "the other side of Gambais": 'Audition d'Émilien Lecoq', 23 Jan 1920, Yvelines Archives, Carton 1373W2 856.

p.47   "note in his *carnet*": Riboulet, *Le Matin*, 21 May 1933.

p.47   "victorious Franco-British offensive": *Le Journal*, 17 April 1917.

p.48   "stolen them from an earlier fiancée": Marie Lacoste letter to Commissioner Dautel, 18 May 1919, Yvelines Archives, Carton 2U769/3168, *Dossier Buisson*.

p.48   "biscuits for the two of them": Riboulet, *Le Matin*, 30 May 1933.

p.48   "around an ornamental pond": 'Audition de Fernande Segret', 12 April 1919, Yvelines Archives, Carton 2U771/3829.

p.48   "gives me a lot of trouble": Riboulet, *Le Matin*, 30 May 1933.

p.49   "so look forward to giving you": Riboulet, *Le Matin*, 30 May 1933.

p.49   "pile in his shed": 'Déposition de Mme Lucienne Labure', 22 Jan 1920, Yvelines Archives, Carton 2U770/3453, *Dossier Jaume*.

p.49   "near the Gare du Nord": 'Déposition de Louise Lhérault', 18 Jan 1920, Yvelines Archives, Carton 2U770/3445, *Dossier Jaume*.

p.49   "the happiness I desire": Riboulet, *Le Matin*, 25 May 1933.

p.50   "his wife's funeral costs": 'Déposition de Marie Lacoste', 16 Dec 1919, Yvelines Archives, 2U769/3195, *Dossier Buisson*.

p.50   "did not mention the matter": Marie Lacoste letter to Commissioner Dautel, 24 April 1919, Yvelines Archives, Carton 1373W2/602.

p.51   "to sublet the property": Marie Lacoste letter to Commissioner Dautel, 18 May 1919, Yvelines Archives, 2U769/3168, *Dossier Buisson*.

p.51   "alone at the villa": Riboulet, *Le Matin*, 23 May 1933.

p.51   "impossible to tell what they were": 'Déclaration de Marie Lacoste', 16 Dec 1919, Yvelines Archives, 2U769/3195, *Dossier Buisson*.

p.51   "meddling younger sister": 'Audition de Marie Lacoste', 12 April 1919, Yvelines Archives, Carton 2U771/4695, *Dossier Buisson*; Riboulet, *Le Matin*, 23 May 1933.

p.52   "on a one-way ticket": Riboulet, *Le Matin*, 23 May 1933.

Chapter 7: Sacré Coeur

p.53   "break off their engagement": Riboulet, *Le Matin*, 25 May 1933.

p.53   "calling card slipped inside": Riboulet, *Le Matin*, 20 May 1933; 'Déposition de Mme Victorine Pellat', 8 May 1919, Yvelines Archives, Carton 2U770/3364, *Dossier Collomb*.

p.53   "enquiries about her disappearance": 'Déclaration de Gaston Gaimond', 4 Nov 1919, Yvelines Archives, Carton 2U770/3331, *Dossier Collomb*; Inspecteur Henry, 'Enquête générale', Paris Police Archives, Carton JA 28, *Dossier Collomb*.

p.54   "Landru had pretended to Anna": 'Déposition de Mme Victorine Pellat', 8 May 1919, Yvelines Archives, Carton 2U770/3364, *Dossier Collomb.*

p.54   "received any response": 'Déposition de Mme Victorine Pellat', 8 May 1919, Yvelines Archives, Carton 2U770/3364, *Dossier Collomb.*

p.54   "or to write to us": 'Déposition de Mme Victorine Pellat', 8 May 1919, Yvelines Archives, Carton 2U770/3364, *Dossier Collomb.*

p.55   "believe that he had killed Célestine": 'Audition de Marie Lacoste', 12 April 1919, Yvelines Archives, Carton 2U769/3157, *Dossier Buisson.*

p.56   "obviously up to no good": 'Déclaration de Marie Lacoste', 16 Dec 1919, Yvelines Archives, 2U769/3195, *Dossier Buisson.*

p.56   "hiring her own secretary": 'Déclaration de Marie Lacoste', 16 Dec 1919, Yvelines Archives, 2U769/3195, *Dossier Buisson.*

p.56   "overnight stay by Fernande": Riboulet, *Le Matin*, 24 May 1933.

p.56   "was working and could not come": Interview with Marie Lacoste, Inspector Belin report, 12 April 1919, Yvelines Archives, Carton 2U771/4695.

p.57   "to remove her furniture": 'Déclaration de Mme Lucienne Labure', 22 Jan 1920, Yvelines Archives, Carton 2U770/3453, *Dossier Jaume*; Riboulet, *Le Matin*, 25 May 1933.

p.58   "the shop as soon as possible": 'Audition de Mlle Jeanne Lhérault', 22 April 1919, Yvelines Archives, Carton 2U770/3445, *Dossier Jaume.*

p.58   "on the landing itself": 'Déclaration de Louise Lhérault', 18 Jan 1920, Yvelines Archives, Carton 2U770/3445, *Dossier Jaume.*

p.58   "it might still reach Louise": 'Déclaration de Louise Lhérault', 18 Jan 1920, Yvelines Archives, Carton 2U770/3445, *Dossier Jaume.*

p.58   "Louise's forwarded correspondence": 'Audition de Mlle Jeanne Lhérault', 22 April 1919, Yvelines Archives, Carton 2U770/3445, *Dossier Jaume.*

p.59   "on the train home": Riboulet, *Le Matin*, 31 May 1933.

p.59   "recently spent the night": 'Déclaration de Marie-Jeanne Fauchet', 24 Jan 1920, Yvelines Archives, Carton 2U770/3560, *Dossier Pascal.*

p.59   "name was 'Lucien Guillet'": 'Déclaration de Marie-Jeanne Fauchet', 24 Jan 1920, Yvelines Archives, Carton 2U770/3560, *Dossier Pascal.*

p.60   "would take place in February": Annette Pascal letter to Louise Fauchet, 14 Jan 1918, Yvelines Archives, Carton 1373W2/569.

p.60   "ticked her off half-jokingly": 'Déclaration de Marie-Jeanne Fauchet', 24 Jan 1920, Yvelines Archives, Carton 2U770/3560, *Dossier Pascal.*

p.61   "one can't live on promises": Annette Pascal letter to Louise Fauchet, 3 April 1918, Yvelines Archives, Carton 1373W2/571.

p.61   "before going to bed": Annette Pascal letter to Louise Fauchet, 3 Feb 1918, Yvelines Archives, Carton 1373W2/577.

p.61   "make me doubt your sincerity": Riboulet, 31 May 1933.

p.62   "other promising ventures in Brazil": 'Audition de Mlle Segret', 12 April 1919, Paris Police Archives.

NOTES

p.62   "protection from the bombs": Riboulet, *Le Matin*, 31 May 1933.

p.63   "we did not know what it was": Annette Pascal letter to Louise Fauchet, 21 March 1918, Yvelines Archives, Carton 1373W2/569.

p.63   "I'll keep you updated about everything": Annette Pascal letter to Louise Fauchet, 24 March 1918, Yvelines Archives, Carton 1373W2/569.

p.63   "I would be even unhappier": Annette Pascal letter to Louise Fauchet, 24 March 1918, Yvelines Archives, Carton 1373W2/569.

p.63   "her concierge recalled": 'Audition de Mme Joséphine Koestler', 21 April 1919, Yvelines Archives, Carton 2U770/3475, *Dossier Pascal*.

p.64   "luxurious modern taste": Annette Pascal letter to Louise Fauchet, 27 March 1918, Yvelines Archives, Carton 1373W2.

p.64   "dying of fear today": Annette Pascal letter to Louise Fauchet, undated, March 1918, Yvelines Archives, Carton 1373W2/570. The letter must have been written on 28 March because of references by Annette to earlier events.

p.64   "all the money I need": Annette Pascal letter to Louise Fauchet, 2 April 1918, Yvelines Archives, Carton 1373W2/566.

p.64   "kiss to Marie-Jeanne": Annette Pascal letter to Louise Fauchet, 3 April 1918, Yvelines Archives, Carton 1373W2/571.

p.64   "she told Louise": Annette Pascal letter to Louise Fauchet, 3 April 1918, Yvelines Archives, Carton 1373W2/571.

p.64   "green overcoat with fur trimming": 'Déclaration de Mme Carbonnel', 10 Feb 1920, Yvelines Archives, Carton 2U770/3570, *Dossier Pascal*.

p.65   "10 rue de la Fraternité, Toulon, Var": 'Réquisitoire Définitif', p.259.

p.65   "busy life one leads in Paris": Annette Pascal letter to Louise Fauchet, 5 April 1918 [re-dated 19 April], Yvelines Archives, Carton 1373W2/569.

p.65   "what has happened to me": Landru removed this note from the envelope containing the original letter, re-dated 19 April, which Mme Fauchet eventually received.

p.65   "the garden for burial": Dautel report on search of Villa Tric, 13 April 1919, Yvelines Archives, Carton 2U771/3690.

Chapter 8: The Fatal List

p.67   "the night with her": Riboulet, *Le Matin*, 31 May 1933.

p.67   "new automobile radiator": Police report of search of 76 Rue de Rochechouart, 10 May 1919, Yvelines Archives, Carton 2U771/3888.

p.67   "my thoughts are close to you": Landru letter to Fernande Segret, quoted in Riboulet, *Le Matin*, 3 June 1933.

p.68   "her mother had caused her": *Le Journal*, 23 Nov 1921.

p.68   "exit to my factory": Riboulet, *Le Matin*, 1 June 1933.

p.68   "supposedly to his office": Riboulet, *Le Matin*, 1 June 1933.

p.69   "Fernande could not hear them": Riboulet, *Le Matin*, 1 June 1933.

p.69 "they got back to Paris": 'Audition de Jeanne Falque', 2 June 1919, Paris Police Archives, reproduced in *Landru: 6h 10 Temps Clair, Les Pièces du Dossier* (Paris, 2013).

p.70 "he had negotiated": *Le Journal*, 3 Nov 1921.

p.70 "also rented space there": 'Audition de Romain Gamrat', 26 April 1919, Yvelines Archives, Carton 2U770/3606.

p.70 "of 26 per cent": 'Audition de Jeanne Falque', 2 June 1919, Paris Police Archives.

p.70 "with no means to pay": 'Déclaration de Mlle Yvonne Le Gallo', 26 March 1920, Yvelines Archives, Carton 2U770/3657, *Dossier Marchadier*.

p.71 "the sale of her furniture": 'Réquisitoire Définitif', pp.261–2, Yvelines Archives, Carton 2U772/unnumbered.

p.71 "at least one occasion": 'Réquisitoire Définitif', p.262, Yvelines Archives, Carton 2U772/ unnumbered.

p.71 "house in the country": *Le Petit Parisien*, 22 Nov 1921.

p.71 "'engagements' with other *messieurs*": *Le Petit Parisien*, 22 Nov 1921.

p.71 "cash from someone else": 'Audition de Mme Jeanne Falque', 2 June 1919, Paris Police Archives.

p.71 "to President Raymond Poincaré": *Le Gaulois*, 2 Jan 1919.

p.72 "live in the countryside": Riboulet, *Le Matin*, 27 May 1933.

p.72 "small tongs, iron grate": Riboulet, *Le Matin*, 27 May 1933.

p.72 "her future country home": *Le Petit Parisien*, 22 Nov 1921.

p.72 "acted as the villa's janitor": Inspector Belin report, 23 Jan 1920, interview with Pierre Vallet, Yvelines Archives, Carton 1373W2/841.

p.72 "1,800 francs in cash": Riboulet, *Le Matin*, 27 May 1933.

p.72 "desolate house": Another of Marie-Thérèse's prostitute friends saw her off at the station and recalled this scene. 'Déposition de Marguerite Delcourt', 28 March 1920, Yvelines Archives, Carton 2U770/3656, *Dossier Marchadier*.

p.73 "I had kept the memory": Landru personal memoir, September 1919, in 'Examen de Landru au point de vue mental', June 1920, Paris Police Archives, reproduced in *Landru: 6h 10 Temps Clair, Les Pièces du Dossier* (Paris, 2013).

p.73 "employer's house near the Rue du Rivoli": Marie Lacoste statement to police, 13 Feb 1919, Yvelines Archive, Carton 2U769/3143, *Dossier Buisson*.

p.74 "clear her furniture": Marie Lacoste statement to police, 13 Feb 1919, Yvelines Archive, Carton 2U769/3143, *Dossier Buisson*.

p.75 "where Gambais was located": Eugène Moreau, civil complaint, 2 Feb 1919, Yvelines Archives, Carton 2U770/3286, *Dossier Collomb*.

p.75 "from Moreau's lawsuit": Marie Lacoste, civil complaint, 3 Feb 1919, Yvelines Archives, Carton 2U770/3141, *Dossier Buisson*.

p.75   "some money to go away": Riboulet, *Le Matin*, 1 June 1933.

p.75   "she recalled tartly": Riboulet, *Le Matin*, 1 June 1933.

p.75   "nature of her business": 'Audition de Mme Jeanne Falque', 2 June 1919, 'Audition de Mlle Segret', 12 April 1919, Paris Police Archives.

p.76   "might well be a spy": Report by Jules Hebbé, 16 March 1919, Yvelines Archives, Carton 2U770/3291, *Dossier Collomb*. 'Enquête à Gambais', Procès-Verbal de la Gendarmerie de Houdan, 22 March 1919, Paris Police Archives.

p.76   "dubious tenant at the Villa Tric": Report by Inspector Belin, 12 April 1919, Paris Police Archives.

p.77   "by a young woman": 'Audition de Marie Lacoste', 12 April 1919, Yvelines Archives, Carton 2U769/3157, *Dossier Buisson*; 'Déclaration de Marie Lacoste', 16 Dec 1919, Yvelines Archives, 2U769/3195, *Dossier Buisson*.

p.77   "Lucien Guillet, 76 Rue de Rochechouart": Belin's version of this part of the story was corroborated by Marie Lacoste's testimony.

p.77   "three weeks to make the arrest": *Le Matin*, 18 Nov 1935.

p.77   "introduced himself as Lucien Guillet": 'Rapport de l'Inspecteur Deslogères', 4 June 1919, Yvelines Archives, Carton 2U771/5125.

p.78   "before about 11.30 am": Report by Inspector Belin, 12 April 1919, Paris Police Archives; Report by Inspector Belin, 26 March 1920, Yvelines Archives, Carton 2U770/3662.

p.78   "stark naked on the floor": Dennis Bardens, *The Ladykiller* (1972), p.83.

p.78   "to empty his pockets": 'Renseignements sur Landru', 12 April 1919, Yvelines Archives, Carton 2U771/3855.

Chapter 9: The Enigma of Gambais

p.81   "answering lonely hearts adverts": 'Renseignements sur Landru', 12 April 1919, Yvelines Archives, Carton 2U771/3855.

p.81   "Fernande along as a witness": 'Renseignements sur Landru', 12 April 1919, Yvelines Archives, Carton 2U771/3855.

p.82   "fell ill with food poisoning": 'Audition de Fernande Segret, 12 April 1919, Yvelines Archives, Carton 2U771/3829.

p.83   "adjoining the kitchen": Dautel report on search of Villa Tric, 13 April 1919, Yvelines Archives, Carton 2U771/3690.

p.83   "to put them to death": *Le Siècle*, 25 Nov 1921.

p.83   "prosecutor's office by noon": Dautel report on search of Villa Tric, 13 April 1919, Yvelines Archives, Carton 2U771/3690.

p.84   "'don't follow up', and so on": Riboulet, *Le Matin*, 29 May 1933.

p.85   "in trouble with the law": 'Audition de Gabriel Grimm', 17 May 1919, Paris Police Archives, Carton JA 30, *Dossier Général*.

p.85   "any headway with Landru": *Le Journal*, 15 April 1919.

p.86 "my respectful assurances": Landru to Moro, undated note, personal collection of Dominique de Moro Giafferri, reproduced in Dominique Lanzalavi, *Vincent de Moro Giafferri* (Ajaccio, 2011), p.77.

Chapter 10: Why Would I Have Killed Them?

p.87 "born on that day": G. Sinclair, '*Comment ils se sont découverts*', *France-Soir*, undated article, personal collection of Dominique de Moro Giafferri.

p.87 "a taste for fighting duels": Moro fought two duels in 1909 and 1910, against a Corsican politician and a regional newspaper editor, whom he accused respectively of insulting him and his mother's family. He lost the first and abandoned the second, with no one seriously injured. *Le Journal*, 9 July 1909, Lanzalavi, *Vincent de Moro Giafferri* (Ajaccio, 2011), p.77.

p.88 "on the street at 2.30 pm": *Le Journal*, 7 March 1912. Dieudonné was living in Paris in December 1911 but had gone to Nancy to work for a contractor. The prosecution argued that when he finished the job he returned to Paris, shot the bank messenger on 21 December, and then caught a train to Nancy in time to meet his friend for a drink at about 2.30 pm.

p.88 "she informed the press defiantly": *Le Journal*, 8 March 1912.

p.89 "an astonishing, prodigious man": *Landru: 6h 10 Temps Clair, Les Pièces du Dossier* (Paris, 2013), p.251.

p.89 "acquisition of the mass circulation daily *Le Journal*": Humbert was acquitted in May 1919. Humbert's friends accused the army of inventing the charges in revenge for a series of articles in *Le Journal* in 1916 that deplored the state of France's defences.

p.90 "'subsidence' in the cellar": 'Visite domiciliares: Villa des Lodges [*sic*] à Vernouillet', 19 April 1919, Paris Police Archives. *Le Gaulois*, 14 May 1919.

p.90 "yielded nothing of interest": Some bone fragments also examined by the laboratory were entirely of animal origin. '*Vernouillet, Examen des Os: Rapport Médico-Légal*', 5 July 1920, Yvelines Archives, Carton 2U771/4875.

p.90 "she remarked darkly": 'Déclaration de Mme Picque', 15 April 1919, Paris Police Archives, Carton JA 28, *Dossier Cuchet*.

p.90 "no reason to enquire further": Dautel interview with Émile Mercier, 15 April 1919, Paris Police Archives.

p.91 "we were not particularly worried": *Le Journal*, 16 April 1919.

p.91 "I was a mother": Mme Fauchet letter to Bonin, 18 April 1919, Yvelines Archives, Carton 2U 770/3542, *Dossier Pascal*.

p.91 "a fantasist who loved change": 'Enquête Générale', 14 June 1919, statement of Mme Colin, 24 April 1919, Paris Police Archives, Carton JA 29, *Dossier Babelay*.

p.92 "pleading pressure of work": *Le Journal*, 15 April 1919.

p.92 "he immediately rectified": *Le Matin*, 24 Nov 1921.

p.92 "putting Riboulet in his place": Riboulet, *Le Matin*, 3 May 1933.

p.93 "Lombroso [an Italian criminologist]": *Le Journal*, 28 April 1919. These photographs were later incorrectly described as showing Landru arriving at the court in Versailles during his trial in November 1921.

p.93 "missing women so far identified": By 27 April 1919, the police had identified nine of the ten women on the list in Landru's notebook. The tenth, Thérèse Laborde-Line, codenamed "Brésil", was identified in May 1919.

p.93 "you will find them": Reconstruction of Landru's interrogations on 27 April 1919 from *Le Journal*, *Le Petit Parisien*, 28 April 1919.

p.94 "not yet received a reply": *La Presse*, 27 April 1919.

p.95 "nothing more out of Landru": *Le Journal*, 28 April 1919.

p.95 "initial interview with Landru": *L'Ouest-Éclair*, 30 April 1919.

p.95 "staring perfectly well": Navières, 'L'affaire Landru'.

p.95 "to 'guarantee' Landru's rights": *L'Ouest-Éclair*, 30 April 1919. The same newspaper reported that Landru had been left at the Santé because he was meeting his lawyer.

p.96 "department of Seine-et-Oise": *Le Figaro*, 30 April 1919.

p.96 "Paris police laboratory he headed": For a dissection of Spilsbury's strengths and flaws, see Jane Robins, *The Magnificent Spilsbury and the Case of the Brides in the Bath* (London, 2010).

p.96 "from the wall of the oven": Gaston Bayle, a forensic chemist in the search team, told the press it was "very likely" that the blood stain was of human origin. *Le Journal*, 30 April 1919.

p.97 "as proved by the four roots": *Le Journal*, 30 April 1919. The newspaper mistakenly reported that more charred bits of haberdashery were found in the other locked shed.

p.97 "the sexton stated authoritatively": *Le Journal*, *Le Gaulois*, 30 April 1919.

p.97 "in less than three days": *Le Gaulois*, 30 April 1919.

Chapter 11: I Will Tell You Something Horrible

p.99 "People can judge for themselves": *Le Journal*, 21 May 1919.

p.99 "end of the Franco-Prussian War": In police and judicial documents, Marie-Catherine's maiden name was sometimes also spelt 'Remy', without an accent.

p.100 "did not reveal to *Le Journal*": Marie-Catherine told the police that she only got pregnant because Landru lied to her about his true age, implying that she did not realise he was about to perform his military service. 'Audition de Mme Landru', 7 May 1919, Paris Police Archives, Carton JA 30, *Dossier Général*.

p.100   "prey on the new recruits": The Ministry of War prosecuted Desclaves for his attack on the army but a civilian jury acquitted him.

p.100   "a skirt chaser": 'Audition de Mme Landru', 7 May 1919, Paris Police Archives, Carton JA 30, *Dossier Général*.

p.101   "the Tuileries gardens": 'Salon du Cycle et de l'Automobile (Palais des Machines)', *La Justice*, 17 Nov 1898.

p.101   "to manufacture the motorcycle": *Le Journal*, 31 May 1904.

p.101   "in custody at the Santé": *L'Echo de Paris*, 9 Nov 1921.

p.101   "an ambivalent diagnosis": Information on Vallon from http://psychiatrie. histoire.free.fr/pers/bio/vallon.htm

p.101   "had not yet crossed them": *Le Gaulois*, 22 Aug 1919.

p.101   "treated leniently by the court": A fourth psychiatrist, Dr Dubuisson, examined Landru in 1906. Dubuisson concluded that Landru was "unbalanced" and in an "unhealthy state which, while not madness, was no longer normal". *Le Gaulois*, 22 Aug 1919, quoting Dubuisson's report.

p.102   "any means for his projects": *Le Journal*, 31 May 1904.

p.102   "eastern edge of the Bois de Boulogne": Police report on the suicide of Julien Alexandre Sylvain Landru, 23 April 1912, Yvelines Archives, Carton 2U 771/4818. The prosecution at Landru's trial misdated the suicide as occurring in August 1912.

p.102   "Marie-Catherine told the police": 'Audition de Mme Landru', 7 May 1919, Paris Police Archives, Carton JA 30, *Dossier Général*. The police investigation of Julien Landru's later life and suicide was cursory. In the 1890s, Julien Landru got a manual job at a Paris publisher. He retired around 1905, when he and his wife moved to Agen, southern France, to live with their daughter and son-in-law. Julien's wife died in 1910, when he returned to Paris to live with Marie-Catherine and her children in an apartment on Rue Blomet.

p.102   "Marie-Catherine and her children, not him": 'Affaire Cuchet. Instruction', 13 Aug 1919, Paris Police Archives, Carton JA 28, *Dossier Cuchet*.

p.102   "'God, will he not have pity?'": *Le Journal*, 21 May 1919.

p.103   "under a false name": Police report on movements of Landru family, 1914–15, 3 June 1919, Yvelines Archives, Carton 1373W2/788.

p.103   "'gardening work' at The Lodge": 'Déclaration de Charles Landru', 14 April 1919, Paris Police Archives, reproduced in *Landru: 6h 10 Temps Clair, Les Pièces du Dossier* (Paris, 2013).

p.103   "the false name 'Frémyet'": 'Instruction', 13 Aug 1919, Paris Police Archives, Carton JA 28, *Dossier Cuchet*.

p.103   "belonged to Jeanne Cuchet": 'Commission Rogatoire', 18 Oct 1915, Pontoise, Paris Police Archives, Carton JA 28, *Dossier Cuchet*. 'Bulletin', 7 April 1916, Paris, 'Faux en écriture authentique et publique, 1915', Yvelines Archives, Carton 2U771/4862.

p.103   "disappearance of the typist Anna Collomb": In August 1916, Maurice was released early from the Cherche-Midi military prison in Paris. He was sent to the Somme, along with many other prisoners used as emergency reinforcements.

p.103 "a hotel south of Lyon": 'Declaration de Mme Léone Gaujon', 4 Nov 1919, Yvelines Archives, Carton 2U770/3332, *Dossier Collomb*.

p.103 "she was in southern France": 'Audition de Charles Landru', 4 Nov 1919, Yvelines Archives, Carton 2U770/3342, *Dossier Collomb*.

p.103 "forest near the village": 'Audition de Marie Landru', 6 Jan 1920, Yvelines Archives, Carton 2U769/3241, *Dossier Buisson*.

p.103 "withdraw Célestine's savings": Riboulet, *Le Matin*, 24 May 1933.

p.104 "forge Louise's signature": Riboulet, *Le Matin*, 24 May 1933.

p.104 "Annette Pascal and Marie-Thérèse Marchadier": 'Déclaration de Charles Landru', 14 April 1919, Paris Police Archives, reproduced in *Landru: 6h 10 Temps Clair, Les Pièces du Dossier* (Paris, 2013). Charles originally said he helped move four of the women's possessions and then increased the number to five. The correct figure was seven.

p.104 "formal interrogation by Bonin": *Journal des Débats*, 28 May 1919.

p.105 "his eyes filled with tears": *Le Journal*, 28 May 1919.

p.105 "Bonin asked Landru": After each interrogation with Landru, most or all of the transcript was leaked to the press. I have principally used the following newspapers to reconstruct dialogue: *Le Journal, Le Petit Parisien, Le Gaulois, Le Matin, Le Figaro*.

p.106 "first intervention in the case": *Le Journal*, 28 May 1919.

p.106 "this *insensibilité*, is significant": *Le Journal*, 28 May 1919.

p.106 "about 100,000 francs": *Le Journal*, 16 April 1919; 'Disparition de Mme Cuchet et de son fils', Georges Friedman interview, 16 April 1919, Paris Police Archives, Carton JA 28, *Dossier Cuchet*.

p.107 "(literally 'an affluence')": 'Audition de Mme Friedman', 16 April 1919, Paris Police Archives, Carton JA 28, *Dossier Cuchet*.

p.107 "informed about her affairs": 'Rapport de l'Inspecteur de Police Peretti', 2 July 1919, Paris Police Archives, Carton JA 28, *Dossier Cuchet*.

p.107 "'Fashionable House' shirt factory": 'Rapport de l'Inspecteur de Police Brandenburger', undated, Paris Police Archives, Carton JA 28, *Dossier Cuchet*.

p.107 "forced to borrow 1,000 francs": 'Rapport de l'Inspecteur de Police Peretti', 2 July 1919, Paris Police Archives, Carton JA 28, *Dossier Cuchet*; 'Déclaration de Mme Bazire', 28 July 1919, Yvelines Archives, Carton 2U 769/2613, *Dossier Cuchet*.

p.107 "had 'very few savings'.": 'Déclaration d'Albert Folvary', 26 July 1919, Yvelines Archives, Carton 2U 769/2605, *Dossier Cuchet*.

p.107 "most successful fraud of his career": 'Liste d'escroquéries 1913–1914', Yvelines Archives, Carton 2U771/4839. At Landru's trial, the prosecution reduced the total sum to just below 30,000 francs, without explanation.

p.107 "Marie-Catherine and her children": According to Marie-Catherine, Landru also took most of his late father's legacy when he fled Malakoff in April 1914, leaving her 500 francs. 'Affaire Cuchet. Instruction', 13 Aug 1919, Paris Police Archives, Carton JA 28, *Dossier Cuchet.*

p.108 "acted as Landru's minder": 'L'Affaire Landru', Auguste Navières du Treuil, Private Memoir, Personal Collection of Dominique de Moro Giafferri.

p.108 "his customary silence": *Le Figaro*, 24 July 1919.

p.108 "'Do you hear me – guillotined!'": 'L'Affaire Landru', Auguste Navières du Treuil.

p.108 "as poor old Landru, *monsieur le juge*": 'L'Affaire Landru', Auguste Navières du Treuil.

p.108 "handed down to his father": *Le Gaulois*, 3 June 1919, *Journal des Débats*, 4 June 1919.

p.108 "suddenly got his memory back": Maurice Landru interview, 27 July 1919, Yvelines Archives, Carton 2270/3317, *Dossier Collomb.*

p.109 "the proof of my crimes": *Le Gaulois*, 7 Aug 1919.

p.109 "she is sorry": *Le Journal*, 14 Aug 1919.

p.110 "making a fool of me": *Le Gaulois*, 21 Aug 1919.

p.110 "a mother to her": Louise Fauchet letter to Bonin, 9 June 1919, Yvelines Archives, Carton 2U770/3547, *Dossier Pascal.*

p.111 "Marie-Jeanne signed off helpfully": Marie-Jeanne Fauchet letter to Bonin, no date, Feb 1920, Yvelines Archives, Carton 2U770/3547, *Dossier Pascal.*

p.111 "thoughts and feelings expressed": Madame Zeegers letter to Bonin, 9 Jan 1920, Yvelines Archives, Carton 2U771/3905.

p.111 "completely unaware of this affair": Mlle Dutru letter to Bonin, 24 Feb 1920, Yvelines Archives, Carton 2U771/4016.

p.111 "has she been identified?": Mme Benoist letter to Bonin, 22 July 1919, Yvelines Archives, Carton 2U771/unnumbered.

p.111 "Mme Romelot began circuitously": Anseline Romelot letter to Monsieur Roux, Versailles, 19 May 1919, Yvelines Archives, Carton 2U772/5291.

Chapter 12: Conscience Recoils Before Such a Monster

p.113 "another psychiatric examination": *Le Gaulois*, 29 Aug 1919.

p.113 "'quite a lot of pain'": 'Examen de Landru au point de vue mental', 25 June 1920, Paris Police Archives, reproduced in *Landru: 6h 10 Temps Clair, Les Pièces du Dossier* (Paris, 2013).

p.114 "the purpose of his assignment": 'Audition de Charles Landru', 4 Nov 1919, Yvelines Archives, Carton 2U770/3342, *Dossier Collomb.*

p.115 "principal career at the Bar": Moro lost his seat in 1928.

p.115   "but only rarely": 'Audition de Mme Landru', 12 Dec 1919, Yvelines Archives, Carton 2U771/4823.

p.115   "brought to his office by the police": 'Landru, née Rémy, Marie-Cathérine, Procès-Verbal de première comparution', 18 Dec 1919, Yvelines Archives, Carton 2U770/3350, *Dossier Collomb.*

p.116   "'What are they guilty of and why?'": *La Presse,* 19 Dec 1919.

p.116   "woods near the village": 'Audition de Marie Landru', 6 Jan 1920, Yvelines Archives, Carton 2U769/3241, *Dossier Buisson.*

p.116   "Is that correct?'": 'Audition de Mme Landru', 10 Jan 1920, Yvelines Archives, Carton 2U769/3249, *Dossier Buisson.*

p.116   "an unconscious instrument": *Le Gaulois,* 11 Jan 1920.

p.116   "faking Célestine's signature": Marie-Catherine's lawyer was Moro's friend and fellow Corsican César Campinchi (1882–1941), another leading defence barrister.

p.116   "obey her husband": 'Audition de Mme Landru', 17 Feb 1920, Yvelines Archives, Carton 2U769/3250, *Dossier Buisson.*

p.117   "who had given them to me": 'Interrogation de Maurice Landru', 13 March 1920, Paris Police Archives, Carton JA 28, *Dossier Cuchet.*

p.117   "*'au moment de la chasse* '": "Interrogatoire de la femme Landru", 3 June 1920, Paris Police Archives, reproduced in *Landru: 6h 10 Temps Clair, Les Pièces du Dossier* (Paris, 2013).

p.117   "vanished at the villa": Based on Landru's notes in his *carnet,* the police concluded that Célestine Buisson had last been alive at the villa on the previous day, Friday, 31 August. At 10.15 on the morning of 1 September, Landru noted the time in his *carnet.* He next noted catching a train from Houdan to Paris later on the same day. The family may have come from Ézy-sur-Eure, 24 kilometres north-west of Gambais, where they had stayed in late 1914 and early 1915. A local woman recalled seeing Marie-Catherine and her daughters in Ézy in August 1917. 'Audition de Louise Lecomte', 10 Oct 1919, Yvelines Archives, 2U771/4802.

p.117   "the state of the investigation": *Le Gaulois,* 13 July 1920.

p.118   "his shoes all day and night": *Le Journal,* 13 July 1920.

p.118   "47 bits of teeth": 'Gambais, Examen des Os: Rapport Médico-Légal', 19 July 1920, Yvelines Archives, Carton 2U771/4898.

p.118   "in the garden": 'Gambais, Examen des Os', p.2, quoting from Bonin, 'Ordonnance' regarding examination of bone debris, 12 May 1919, Yvelines Archives, Carton 2U771/unnumbered, directly before 2U771/4877.

p.118   "(a point that the experts also did not make clear)": The report did not explicitly mention the discovery of any human bones or other human remains in the oven, which would have been compelling evidence that Landru had burnt some or all of his victims' corpses. However, the report did not refute the false rumour that part of a human toe bone had been recovered from the oven. *Le Figaro*, 30 April 1919.

p.118   "original corpses had been female": The female pelvis is larger and wider than a male pelvis.

p.119   "Landru's 'mental state'": 'Examen de Landru au point de vue mental', 25 June 1920, Paris Police Archives, reproduced in *Landru: 6h 10 Temps Clair, Les Pièces du Dossier* (Paris, 2013).

p.119   "the frontiers of madness": 'Examen de Landru au point de vue mental', pp.4–5.

p.119   "baby son in 1867": The loss of this baby boy was probably the reason why Landru's parents gave him the middle name 'Désiré', meaning 'Desired'.

p.119   "she was highly strung": 'Examen de Landru au point de vue mental', p.3.

p.119   "dizzy spells and disturbed vision": 'Examen de Landru au point de vue mental', pp. 6–7.

p.120   "its richness and variety": 'Examen de Landru au point de vue mental', p.8.

p.120   "the patriarchal principle": 'Examen de Landru au point de vue mental', p11.

p.120   "my ugly head": 'Examen de Landru au point de vue mental', p.12.

p.120   "responsible for his acts": 'Examen de Landru au point de vue mental', p.14.

p.121   "from the capital to Nancy": *Le Journal*, 5 Aug 1920.

p.121   "the case against Landru": I have been unable to identify Gazier's first name.

p.121   "any suggestion of madness": *Réquisitoire Définitif*, p.3, Yvelines Archives, Carton 2U772.

p.121   "'escapes us', Gazier noted tersely": *Réquisitoire Définitif*, p.162, Yvelines Archives, Carton 2U772.

p.122   "one's calling card at the *préfecture*": *Le Gaulois*, 3 Feb 1921.

p.123   "prisoners awaiting execution": *Le Gaulois*, 15 June 1921.

p.123   "he repeatedly adjusted": *L'Ouest*-**Éclair**, 24 Oct 1919.

p.123   "stronger pair was brought for him": *Le Figaro*, 28 Sept 1921.

p.123   "to keep up his strength": *L'Homme Libre*, *Le Rappel*, 27 Oct 1921, *Le Gaulois*, 29 Oct 1921, *Le Temps*, 30, 31 Oct 1921.

p.123   "leaving the shadow of a trace": *Le Gaulois*, 5 Nov 1921.

p.123   "keep an open mind": *L'Echo d'Alger*, 6 Nov 1921.

p.124   "everything will be resolved": *L'Echo d'Alger*, 6 Nov 1921.

Chapter 13: Chivalry No Longer Exists

p.127   "direct him to his bench": *Le Petit Parisien*, 8 Nov 1921.

p.127   "concealed in the bales": *Journal des Débats*, 9 Nov 1921. The cobbler received a two-year jail sentence.

p.127 "a profile of Landru": Colette's second husband, Henry de Jouvenel, was the editor of *Le Matin*.

p.127 "little birds gathered by the door": *L'Excelsior,* 8 Nov 1921.

p.128 "observe him discreetly": *Journal des Débats*, 9 Nov 1921.

p.128 "one reporter noted unkindly": *L'Excelsior*, 8 Nov 1921.

p.128 "as a personal souvenir": Godefroy's press cuttings are now held by the departmental archives for Yvelines.

p.129 "for the overnight editions": *Le Populaire*, 8 Nov 1921. The telephones were rented by the newspapers at a rate of 100 francs per day.

p.129 "his mind seemingly elsewhere": *L'Excelsior*, 8 Nov 1921.

p.129 "to Moro during the trial": Moro had also brought two assistant lawyers for this first day: Jean Baux, a close friend of Navières, and Marcel Kahn. Baux or Kahn attended most of the trial's sessions.

p.129 "an upright free man": Article 312, *Code d'Instruction Criminelle* (1808).

p.129 "jostling to take his picture": *L'Ouest-* Éclair, 8 Nov 1921.

p.130 "reading his enormous dossier": *Action Française*, 8 Nov 1921.

p.130 "snoring loudly": *Le Figaro*, 8 Nov 1921. The newspaper's cartoonist sketched Colette as she dozed.

p.130 "he must know by heart": *Le Figaro*, 8 Nov 1921.

p.130 "sententious phrases and melodramatic paragraphs": *Le Journal*, 8 Nov 1921.

p.130 "journalists covering the trial": On at least one occasion, a juror asked a reporter on a train for his opinion about whether Landru was guilty. *Le Siècle*, 13 Nov 1921.

p.130 "tailor's dummy in a shop window": *Le Matin*, 8 Nov 1921.

p.131 "the hearing to establish it": *Le Gaulois*, 8 Nov 1921.

p.132 "should begin without him": *Le Radical*, 9 Nov 1921.

p.132 "examination of the defendant": *L'Echo de Paris*, 9 Nov 1921.

p.132 "which were always the same": *Le Radical*, 9 Nov 1921.

p.132 "who had a daughter": *Le Petit Parisien*, 9 Nov 1921.

p.133 "easy to get down to business": *Le Gaulois*, 9 Nov 1921.

p.133 "nervously took the oath": *L'Excelsior*, 9 Nov 1921.

p.134 "worthy of her own": *Le Petit Parisien*, 9 Nov 1921.

p.134 "cash them in at a bank": 'Réquisitoire Définitif', pp.13–14, Yvelines Archives, Carton 2U772.

p.134 "'atoned' for his 'error'": *Le Gaulois*, 9 Nov 1921.

p.135 "uproar around the court was intense": *L'Ouest-Éclair*, 8 Nov 1921.

Chapter 14: Philomène's Dream

p.137 "the notebook until 1915": *L'Homme Libre*, 10 Nov 1921.

p.137 "the jurors' common sense": *L'Echo de Paris*, 10 Nov 1921.

p.138 "poor fist of defending himself": *Le Petit Parisien*, 10 Nov 1921.

p.138   "deep silence around the court": *L'Ouest-Éclair*, 10 Nov 1921.

p.139   "lengthen these exchanges": *L'Ouest-Éclair*, 10 Nov 1921.

p.139   "his mother's murder": *Requisitoire Définitif*, pp.2–3, Yvelines Archives, Carton 2U772/unnumbered.

p.139   "with such eagerness, Landru said severely": *L'Echo de Paris*, 10 Nov 1921, *Le Temps*, 11 Nov 1921.

p.139   "autumn of 1914": *L'Homme Libre*, 10 Nov 1921.

p.139   "after her husband's death": *Le Petit Parisien*, 10 Nov 1921.

p.139   "a modest nest egg": *L'Humanité*, 10 Nov 1921.

p.140   "live with her fiancé": *Le Petit Parisien*, 10 Nov 1921.

p.140   "to assure his future": *Le Petit Parisien*, 10 Nov 1921.

p.140   "on account of André": *Réquisitoire Définitif*, p.33, Yvelines Archives, Carton 2U772.

p.140   "his stiff white collar": *Le Petit Journal*, 10 Nov 1921.

p.140   "break off her engagement": "Disparition de Mme Cuchet et de son fils", Georges Friedman interview, 16 April 1919, Paris Police Archives, Carton JA 28, *Dossier Cuchet*; *Le Journal*, 16 April 1919.

p.141   "2–3 August at the villa": Statement of Mme Jeanne Hardy, Gouvieux, 1 Aug 1919, Yvelines Archives, Carton 2U 769/2659.

p.141   "from under her bonnet at the court": *Le Petit Parisien*, 10 Nov 1921.

p.141   "Philomène recalled": *Le Petit Journal*, 10 Nov 1921.

p.142   "the impression I had killed your sister": *Le Journal*, 10 Nov 1921.

p.142   "She had a heart, my sister": *Le Gaulois*, 10 Nov 1921.

Chapter 15: Her Private Life Does Not Concern Me

p.143   "make the murder counts stick": *Le Journal*, 10 Nov 1921.

p.144   "which he quickly stifles": *Le Populaire*, 9 Nov 1921. The commentator was the leading barrister Maurice Délépine (1883–1960).

p.144   "disarms his adversary": *Journal des Débats*, 9 Nov 1921.

p.144   "burst out laughing": *L'Intransigeant*, 8 Nov 1921.

p.144   "red and yellow dossiers": *Le Journal*, 11 Nov 1921.

p.144   "had been wiped out": *Le Populaire*, 11 Nov 1921.

p.144   "might have been my daughters": *Le Gaulois*, 11 Nov 1921.

p.144   "they were made of gold": *Le Gaulois*, 11 Nov 1921.

p.145   "we knew each other": *Le Gaulois*, 11 Nov 1921.

p.145   "probably from engine failure": "Maxime Henri Morin, classe 1916", Yvelines Archives, Carton 2U769/2621, *Dossier Cuchet*.

p.146   "Landru explained": *Le Journal*, 11 Nov 1921.

p.146   "this little lie proves nothing": *Le Journal*, 11 Nov 1921.

p.146   "matters beyond my station": *L'Ouest-Éclair*, 11 Nov 1921.

p.146   "what became of them next": *Le Gaulois*, 11 Nov 1921.

p.146   "in the back garden?": The neighbour could not identify the two women she saw picking flowers at The Lodge in the summer of 1915. 'Déposition de Mme Picque', 15 April 1919, Paris Police Archives, Carton JA 28, *Dossier Cuchet*.

p.147 "*Le Populaire* remarked unpleasantly": *Le Populaire*, 11 Nov 1921.

p.147 "the judge's intervention": *L'Ouest-Éclair*, 11 Nov 1921.

p.147 "between her and his wife": *Le Petit Journal*, 11 Nov 1921.

p.147 "reply to his last letter": 'Audition de Monsieur Laborde-Line', 19 May 1919, Paris Police Archives, Carton JA 28, *Dossier Laborde-Line*.

p.148 "the hearing ended at 5.25 pm": *Le Rappel*, 11 Nov 1921.

p.148 "delivers a poor speech": *Le Journal*, 12 Nov 1921.

p.148 "to be indulgent": *La Justice*, 11 Nov 1921.

p.148 "more deserving of pity than contempt": *Le Journal*, 12 Nov 1921.

p.149 "just the one head to offer you": *Le Gaulois*, 12 Nov 1921.

p.150 "savings to her fiancé": *Le Journal*, 12 Nov 1921.

p.150 "two or three steps beneath a canopy": *Le Gaulois*, 12 Nov 1921.

p.150 "Landru allegedly killed her": *Le Gaulois*, 12 Nov 1921.

p.151 "*Le Gaulois* remarked": *Le Gaulois*, 13 Nov 1921.

p.151 "the theatre of his exploits": *Le Journal*, 13 Nov 1921.

p.151 "better sight of the defendant": *Le Journal*, 13 Nov 1921.

p.151 "reasons you will understand": *Le Journal*, 13 Nov 1921.

p.152 "struck by her encounter": *Le Siècle*, 14 Nov 1921.

p.153 "her first communion": *Le Petit Parisien*, 13 Nov 1921.

p.153 "did not worry me at all": *Le Petit Parisien*, 13 Nov 1921.

p.153 "Mme Héon's furniture, that's all": *Le Journal*, 13 Nov 1921.

p.154 "an indeterminate shadow": *Le Journal*, 13 Nov 1921.

Chapter 16: You Accuse Me, You Prove It

p.155 "It would be superb": *Le Siècle*, 15 Nov 1921.

p.155 "dripped into the fire": *Le Journal*, 13 Jan 1921.

p.155 "soon be proclaimed": *Le Petit Journal*, 14 Nov 1921.

p.156 "about the little girl": 'Réquisitoire Définitif', p.137, Yvelines Archives, Carton 2U772; Anna Collomb, 'Enquête Générale', undated, Paris Police Archives, Carton JA 28, *Dossier Collomb*.

p.156 "the girl's probable father": *Le Journal*, 15 Nov 1921.

p.156 "lied about her age": *Le Petit Parisien*, 15 Nov 1921.

p.156 "on public holidays": *Le Journal*, 15 Nov 1921.

p.157 "would have been impolite": *Le Journal*, 15 Nov 1921.

p.157 "a singular interpretation": *Le Journal*, 15 Nov 1921.

p.158 "the bank documents": Godefroy was wrong. Landru drained all of Anna's savings with her written consent before she disappeared.

p.158 "obedience to her husband": *La Lanterne*, 15 Nov 1921.

p.158 "from Marie-Angélique's photograph": *Le Journal*, 15 Nov 1921.

p.158 "*messieurs les jurés*": *Le Temps*, 16 Nov 1921.

p.159 "fiancées that they can't find": *Le Journal*, 15 Nov 1921.

p.159   "the picture was deliberately sexual": *Le Petit Parisien*, 15 Nov 1921.

p.159   "under Landru's influence": *Le Journal*, 15 Nov 1921.

p.159   "tenderest of relations with her": *Le Journal*, 15 Nov 1921.

p.160   "was brought for her": *Le Petit Journal,* 15 Nov 1921.

p.160   "her fiancé owed her money": *Le Journal*, 15 Nov 1921. Mme Moreau said "before Christmas" but it is clear from the context that she meant 25 December.

p.160   "his refugee's allowance": *Le Figaro*, 15 Nov 1921. This was a pointless lie by Landru, who never claimed any refugee's allowance from Lille.

p.160   "murdered on 26 or 27 December": *Le Petit Parisien*, 15 Nov 1921.

p.160   "their baby girl Anna": 'État-Civil de Mme Collomb', Paris Police Archives, Carton JA 28, *Dossier Collomb*.

p.160   "Mme Leffray shouted": *L'Humanité*, 15 Nov 1921.

p.161   "the correspondent from *L'Humanité* lamented": *L'Humanité*, 15 Nov 1921.

p.161   "mistake her profession very easily": *Le Journal*, 16 Nov 1921.

p.161   "comfort her with kind words": *Le Journal*, 16 Nov 1921.

p.161   "the countryside delighted her": *Le Petit Parisien*, 16 Nov 1921.

p.162   "own documents to me": *Le Journal*, 16 Nov 1921.

p.162   "gave a start": *Le Petit Journal*, 16 Nov 1921.

p.162   "not unconnected with her disappearance": *Le Journal*, 16 Nov 1921.

p.163   "'I'm looking forward to it,'": *Le Journal*, *L'Excelsior*, 16 Nov 1921.

p.163   "thrown herself into the Seine": Riboulet, *Le Matin*, 21 May 1933.

p.163   "my daughter is no more!": *Le Petit Parisien*, 16 Nov 1921.

p.164   "a good heart and deserved pity": *Le Petit Parisien*, 16 Nov 1921.

p.164   "to keep on holding Landru's eye": *Le Gaulois*, 16 Nov 1921.

Chapter 17: Let Us Not Look for Tragedy

p.165   "jot down her first impressions": Mistinguett never filed any copy.

p.165   "Gilbert told the jurors": *Le Gaulois*, 17 Nov 1921.

p.165   "but you, you surpass him": *L'Echo de Paris*, 17 Nov 1921.

p.166   "I am sure your choice is made": *Le Petit Parisien*, 17 Nov 1921.

p.166   "a return and a single ticket": *Le Petit Parisien*, 17 Nov 1921.

p.166   "Célestine had vanished": Gilbert initially made an error, saying that Landru had noted the time as 10.15 in the evening. The time noted was 10.15 in the morning. Riboulet, *Le Matin*, 24 May 1933.

p.166   "10th or 11th of September": *Le Petit Journal*, 17 Nov 1921.

p.167   "the assets belonged to me": *Le Gaulois*, *Le Journal*, 17 Nov 1921.

p.167   "a great, big trunk like this one": *Le Journal*, 17 Nov 1921.

p.168   "inside his velvet glove": *Le Petit Journal*, 17 Nov 1921.

p.168   "as she referred to Landru": *L'Echo de Paris*, 17 Nov 1921.

p.168   "My sister was murdered": *La Lanterne*, 17 Nov 1921.

NOTES

p.169 "a superb pearl necklace": *L'Intransigeant*, 18 Nov 1921.

p.169 "I didn't say that either!": *Le Siècle*, 18 Nov 1921.

p.169 "submerged like shipwrecks": *Le Gaulois*, 18 Nov 1921.

p.169 "dream of such a success": *L'Intransigeant*, 18 Nov 1921.

p.169 "Gilbert's muddled pen portrait": *Le Journal*, 18 Nov 1921.

p.169 "any more than the others?": *Le Temps*, 19 Nov 1921.

p.170 "I cannot tell you at all": *Le Journal*, 18 Nov 1921.

p.170 "quietly and sadly": *Le Figaro*, 18 Nov 1921.

p.170 "turning towards the exit": *Le Journal*, 18 Nov 1921.

p.170 "One point, that's all": *Le Journal*, 18 Nov 1921.

p.171 "to notify me in advance": *Le Gaulois*, 18 Nov 1921.

p.171 "caused a sensation": *Le Journal*, 18 Nov 1921.

p.171 "judged in champagne": *Le Populaire*, 18 Nov 1921.

p.171 "puts them in a hangar": *Le Journal*, 18 Nov 1921.

p.172 "double the court's seating capacity": *L'Ouest-Éclair*, 19 Nov 1921.

p.172 "the Duke and Duchess of Valentinois": *Le Petit Journal, Le Petit Parisien*, 19 Nov 1921.

p.173 "45 Avenue des Ternes": *Le Petit Parisien*, 19 Nov 1921.

p.173 "further investigations immediately": *Le Petit Parisien, L'Homme Libre*, 19 Nov 1921.

p.173 "Landru remarked dismissively": *Le Journal*, 19 Nov 1921.

p.174 "in another hand to read '19 April'": Annette Pascal letter to Louise Fauchet, 5 April 1918 [redated 19 April], Yvelines Archives, Carton 1373W2/569.

p.174 "fetched a much higher price": *La Lanterne, L'Echo de Paris*, 19 Nov 1921.

p.175 "'Murderer!'": *Le Petit Journal, Le Journal*, 19 Nov 1921.

p.175 "a loud 'mezzo-soprano' voice": *Le Petit Journal*, 19 Nov 1921.

p.175 "his hands around her neck": "Déclaration de Mme Carbonnel", 10 Feb 1920, Yvelines Archives, Carton 2U770/3570, *Dossier Pascal*.

p.175 "the feminine attraction to horror": *Le Gaulois*, 19 Nov 1921. Geley, who was a qualified medical doctor, also believed in reincarnation.

p.176 "like a compass needle": *Le Journal*, 20 Nov 1921.

p.176 "'psychological studies'": *Le Gaulois*, 20 Nov 1921.

p.176 "presenting myself to the police?": *Le Gaulois*, 20 Nov 1921.

p.177 "her career as a prostitute": *Le Journal*, 20 Jan 1921.

p.177 "they were open for business": *Le Journal*, 20 Jan 1921.

p.177 "gasps from the audience": *Le Gaulois*, 20 Jan 1921.

p.177 "a nuisance to her": *Le Figaro*, 20 Jan 1921.

p.177 "'not to betray their sentiments' about the case": *Le Journal*, 20 Nov 1921.

p.178 "a swirl of flowing robes": *Le Gaulois, L'Ouest-Éclair*, 20 Nov 1921.

p.178 "followed by Navières": *Le Journal*, 20 Nov 1921.

p.179   "a generous concession": *Le Journal*, 20 Nov 1921.

p.179   "potential to cause trouble for the defence": After Lagasse's death, Moro acknowledged that Lagasse had had the right to finish the questioning of witnesses, as the older and therefore more senior lawyer. Lanzalavi (2011), p.75.

p.179   "adjourned till Monday": *L'Excelsior*, 20 Nov 1921.

Chapter 18: You Cannot Live With the Dead

p.181   "the 'wretched, emaciated' defendant": *Le Journal*, 22 Nov 1921.

p.181   "sleeps like a baby": *L'Echo d'Alger, 20 Nov 1921, quoting L'Éclair*.

p.181   "sold her furniture": Godefroy's announcement overstated how much the prosecution knew about Berthe's movements after she left Marcelle's apartment on 8 October 1915. It is likely that Berthe stayed for a few nights at a hotel on Rue de Rennes, as Godefroy stated. She then moved to the Hotel de l'Union near the Gare Saint-Lazare, where she stayed for at least a week, before moving again to 45 Avenue des Ternes. Curiously, *La Presse* reported a fortnight before Landru's trial that Berthe had gone to "a room on Avenue des Ternes". The newspaper did not give a source for its information. *La Presse*, 27 October 1921.

p.181   "one of your victims": *Le Journal*, 22 Nov 1921.

p.182   "wanted her name in the press": Juliette Auger letter to Gilbert, 15 Nov 1921, Paris Police Archives, Carton JA 28, *Dossier Héon*.

p.183   "deeply shocked by his comment": *Le Journal, Le Petit Parisien*, 22 Nov 1921.

p.183   "a marble headstone for Marcelle's grave": 'Déclaration de Mme Oger [*sic*]', 20 Nov 1921, Paris Police Archives, *Dossier Héon*.

p.183   "lived at Avenue des Ternes": *Le Journal*, 22 Nov 1921.

p.183   "gaps in the investigation": *Le Journal, Le Gaulois*, 22 Nov 1921.

p.183   "I never received a reply": *L'Excelsior*, 22 Nov 1921.

p.184   "bring us cakes": *L'Excelsior*, 22 Nov 1921.

p.184   "gentle with her": *Le Petit Journal, L'Excelsior*, 22 Nov 1921.

p.184   "used her blood": *L'Excelsior, Le Figaro, Le Rappel*, 22 Nov 1921.

p.185   "had supposedly vanished": *L'Ouest-Éclair*, 22 Nov 1921.

p.185   "testify at Landru's trial": Adrienne Poillot letter to Bonin, 20 March 1920, Yvelines Archives, Carton 2U770/3652.

p.186   "the bailiff's error": *Le Journal, Le Temps*, 22 Nov 1921.

p.186   "disappointment from the audience": *Le Journal*, 22 Nov 1921.

p.186   "Yvonne shot back": *L'Humanité, Le Figaro*, 22 Nov 1921.

p.186   "rackety life than anyone else": 'Déclaration de Mlle Yvonne Le Gallo', 26 March 1920, Yvelines Archives, Carton 2U770/3657, *Dossier Marchadier*.

p.186   "only visit to Gambais": Mme Jeanne Falque, 'P.V. de M. Tanguy, Commissaire de Police', 2 June 1919, Paris Police Archives.

p.186   "around their apartment": *Le Journal*, 23 Nov 1921.

p.187   "an occasional female tenant": *Le Petit Journal*, 23 Nov 1921.

p.187   "through her tears": *L'Excelsior, Le Journal*, 23 Nov 1921.

p.188   "are indeed human bones": *Le Gaulois*, 24 Nov 1921.

p.188   "to send him to the guillotine": *L'Intransigeant*, 21 Nov 1921.

p.189   "'from head to toes'": *Le Temps*, 23 Nov 1921.

p.189   "could not have committed these crimes": *Le Gaulois*, 23 Nov 1921.

p.189   "'False hypotheses,' Landru remarked": *Le Journal*, 24 Nov 1921.

p.190   "smells that are normal,'": *Le Journal*, 24 Nov 1921.

p.190   "'to find the corpses'": *L'Intransigeant*, 24 Nov 1921.

p.190   "my supposed victims": *Le Journal*, 24 Nov 1921.

p.190   "phosphate of lime": *Le Journal*, 24 Nov 1921.

p.191   "heavy package in the water": *Le Gaulois*, 24 Nov 1921.

p.191   "I was moving out": *Le Journal*, 24 Nov 1921.

p.191   "her original witness statement": 'Déclaration de Mme Picque', 15 April 1919, Paris Police Archives, Carton JA 28, *Dossier Cuchet*.

p.191   "told him to go away": Dautel interview with Émile Mercier, 15 April 1919, Paris Police Archives.

p.191   "ladies who visited his house": *Le Matin*, 24 Nov 1921.

p.192   "of burning flesh": *Le Figaro*, 24 Nov 1921.

p.192   "alleged murders on the charge sheet": *Le Journal*, 24 Nov 1921.

p.192   "scandal-mongering and imaginative hindsight": *Le Journal*, 24 Nov 1921.

p.192   "the villa from Paris": *Le Journal*, 24 Nov 1921.

p.193   "13 April and 25 April": *Le Matin*, 24 Nov 1921.

p.193   "'search' ('fouille') several times": Dautel report on search of Villa Tric, 13 April 1919, Yvelines Archives, Carton 2U771/3690.

p.193   "made during the second": *Le Journal*, 24 Nov 1921.

p.193   "summoned to testify": *Le Journal*, 24 Nov 1921. The four diggers were never formally summoned.

p.193   "to produce material proofs": *La Justice*, 24 Nov 1921.

Chapter 19: A Veritable Puzzle

p.195   "at being Landru,' they explained": *Le Petit Parisien*, 24 Nov 1921.

p.195   "decapitated head of a sheep": In September 1929, Bayle was assassinated outside the Palais de Justice by a criminal he had helped to convict. *Le Petit Parisien*, 17 Sept 1929.

p.195   "as the vulgar expression goes": *Le Journal*, 25 Nov 1921.

p.195   "somewhat grumpy silence,' Moro declared": *L'Excelsior*, 25 Nov 1921.

p.196   "confuse the two professions": *Le Journal*, 25 Nov 1921.

p.196   "Dr Paul's deposition": *L'Excelsior*, 25 Nov 1921.

p.196   "stands up again and smiles": *Le Petit Parisien*, 25 Nov 1921.

p.197 "impassive, mysterious face": *Le Figaro*, 25 Nov 1921.

p.197 "the real and the certain": *Le Temps*, 26 Nov 1921.

p.197 "deliver 'in all conscience'": *Le Populaire*, 25 Nov 1921.

p.197 "to a young woman": *Journal des Débats*, 26 Nov 1921.

p.197 "'industrial' enterprises at the villa, Landru said": *Le Journal*, 25 Nov 1921.

p.198 "washed away rapidly": *Le Journal*, 25 Nov 1921.

p.198 "in the summer of 1918": *L'Echo de Paris*, 26 Nov 1921. The prospective subtenant, a man called Lambert, had not gone to the police until after Landru's arrest nine months later, casting some doubt on his story.

p.198 "could not testify in person" Jean Monteilhet, witness statement, 6 May 1919, Paris Police Archives, reproduced in *Landru: 6h 10 Temps Clair, Les Pièces du Dossier* (Paris, 2013).

p.199 "get his name in the papers": *Le Petit Parisien*, 26 Nov 1921.

p.199 "interruption to his labours": *Journal des Débats*, 27 Nov 1921.

p.200 "'Till Monday, *messieurs*'.": *Journal des Débats*, 27 Nov 1921.

Chapter 20: You Have Death in Your Soul

p.201 "Le Journal reported in dismay": *Le Journal*, 29 Nov 1921.

p.201 "looked down at his script and began": *L'Echo de Paris*, 29 Nov 1921.

p.201 "a criminal Charlie Chaplin": *Le Journal*, 29 Nov 1921.

p.202 "utterly uninterested in Godefroy": *L'Excelsior*, 29 Nov 1921.

p.202 "*L'Excelsior* remarked": *L'Excelsior*, 29 Nov 1921.

p.202 "terrible events in Vernouillet and Gambais": *L'Ouest-Éclair*, 29 Nov 1921.

p.202 "as packed as in the gallery": *Le Petit Journal*, 29 Nov 1921.

p.202 "fascinated by Landru": *L'Excelsior*, 30 Nov 1921.

p.203 "settled on his forehead": *Le Gaulois*, 29 Nov 1921.

p.204 "adjourned for the day": *Le Petit Parisien*, 29 Nov 1921.

p.205 "'beyond scientific certainty'": *Le Journal*, 30 Nov 1921.

p.205 "with a feline *politesse*": *Le Petit Parisien, Le Journal*, 30 Nov 1921.

p.206 "Terrible words!": *Le Journal, L'Ouest-Éclair*, 30 Nov 1921.

p.206 "charged with felony": *Le Journal*, 30 Nov 1921.

p.207 "reproach your silence": *Le Journal*, 30 Nov 1921.

p.207 "you will reply, *Non!*": *L'Ouest-Éclair*, 30 Nov 1921.

p.207 "he shook the hand of his *avocat*": *Le Petit Parisien*, 30 Nov 1921.

Chapter 21: Do You Feel Nothing in Your Hearts?

p.209 "one reporter grumbled": *L'Echo de Paris*, 1 Dec 1921.

p.209 "sentenced to death": *La Lanterne*, 1 Dec 1921.

p.209 "remarked sourly to one of his guards": *Le Petit Parisien*, 1 Dec 1921.

p.210 "your famous thesis?": *Le Petit Journal*, 1 Dec 1921.

p.210 "human or animal matter": 'Gambais, Examen des Os: Rapport Médico-Légal', 19 July 1920, Yvelines Archives, Carton 2U771/4898, pp.3–4.

p.210 "I do not believe it": *L'Ouest-Éclair*, 1 Dec 1921.

p.211 "observed with distaste": *Le Journal*, 1 Dec 1921.

p.211 "budged from their story": *Le Petit Journal*, 1 Dec 1921.

p.211 "the alleged corpse": *Le Journal*, 1 Dec 1921.

p.211 "Landru was sane": *L'Ouest-Éclair*, 1 Dec 1921.

p.211 "with all his heart": *Le Journal*, 1 Dec 1921.

p.211 "the words of his barrister": *Le Journal*, 1 Dec 1921.

p.211 "secrets of Landru's house?": *L'Ouest-Éclair*, 1 Dec 1921.

p.212 "to start a new life": *L'Ouest-Éclair*, 1 Dec 1921.

p.212 "until the very end": *L'Ouest-Éclair*, 1 Dec 1921.

p.212 "an artist's pet monkey": The artist was the well-known painter and sculptor Aimé Morot (1850–1913).

p.213 "Look to yours": *Le Journal*, 1 Dec 1921.

p.213 "I have killed no one": *Le Matin*, 1 Dec 1921.

p.213 "shouted above the din": *L'Ouest-Éclair*, 1 Dec 1921.

p.213 "all around the courtroom": *Le Rappel*, 1 Dec 1921.

p.214 "hear the verdict": *La Presse*, 11 June 1922. The article concerned Gilbert's reasons for not allowing photographers in court during the trial of Mme Bessarabo, accused of murdering her husband.

p.214 "his emotion or his nerve ": *L'Excelsior*, 1 Dec 1921.

p.215 "you shameless scum!": *Le Journal*, 1 Dec 1921.

p.215 "your head sliced at the neck": *Le Journal*, 1 Dec 1921.

p.215 "looked on helplessly": *Le Figaro*, 1 Dec 1921.

p.216 "until the morning": *Le Petit Journal*, 1 Dec 1921.

p.216 "my final protest": *Le Petit Journal*, 1 Dec 1921.

Chapter 22: A Terrible Doubt Came to You

p.217 "complained to his guards": *Le Petit Parisien*, 1 Dec 1921.

p.217 "column for *La Presse*": *La Presse*, 3 Dec 1921.

p.217 "washed their hands of the case": *L'Echo d'Alger*, 2 Dec 1921.

p.218 "*Psst! Montez-vous?*": *Le Journal*, 6 Dec 1921.

p.218 "to sign his appeal for clemency": *La Lanterne*, 6 Feb 1922.

p.218 "for the coming battle": *La Lanterne*, 17 Feb 1922.

p.218 "collect his latest submission": *La Lanterne*, 20 Feb 1922.

p.218 "to be brave": *Le Petit Parisien*, 23 Feb 1922.

p.218 "listened carefully to his points": *Le Figaro, La Lanterne, Le Matin*, 24 Feb 1922.

p.219 "Deibler had guillotined": As a young man, Deibler had assisted at a further 96 executions under his grandfather and father.

p.219 "would be erected": The street is now called Rue Georges Clemenceau.

p.219 "the bedrooms upstairs": *Le Journal*, 26 Feb 1922.

p.219 "sensed that I understood": The full text was published by *Le Matin*, 9 March 1922.

p.220 "an innocent man to have courage": Auguste Navières du Treuil, 'L'Affaire Landru', Personal Collection of Dominique de Moro Giafferri.

p.220 "bowler-hatted executioners": *Le Journal*, 26 Feb 1922.

p.221 "a music hall in north-west Paris": *L'Echo d'Alger*, 27 Feb 1922.

Chapter 23: The Signpost

p.225 "I am taking with me": *La Presse*, 13 Sept 1922.

p.225 "grunted *'adieu'*": Moro interview with Henri Martin, reproduced in Lanzalavi (2011), p.84.

p.225 "something more than pebbles": *Le Petit Parisien*, 18 Dec 1922.

p.226 "another private collector": *Le Petit Parisien*, 29 Jan, 30 Jan, 20 Feb 1923. I have not been able to establish what happened to the oven.

p.226 "Landru-themed restaurant": *Paris-soir*, 4 Nov 1930.

p.226 "his other fiancées": *Paris-soir*, 4 Nov 1930, 2 Dec 1934.

p.226 "Britain and the United States": Landru's brand was also retroactive. George Smith, Britain's "Brides in the Bath" murderer, who was hanged in 1915, became known in France as the "English Landru".

p.226 "Welles's script": Chaplin possibly first heard about Landru in the autumn of 1921, shortly before the trial, when he visited Paris to promote his film *The Kid*.

p.227 "she still called 'Lucien'": Fernande's last known stage appearance was in a light opera called *Le Roi d'Amoir*, which closed after six performances. *La Lanterne*, 19 Nov 1922.

p.227 "in the freezing water": Some accounts of Fernande's suicide suggest she left a short note in her room, saying she still loved Landru but was suffering too much. Pierre Darmon, *Landru* (1994), p.291.

p.227 "did not live with me": *Le Matin*, 8 Aug 1924.

p.228 "on the other side of the cemetery": *Le Matin*, 1 May 1927.

p.228 "moved to Clichy": *Le Matin*, 2, 3 March 1933.

p.228 "journalists and blackmailers": I have found no trace of Marie-Catherine or Maurice in public records and newspapers after 1933.

p.228 "Bonin was only 43": *Le Matin*, 14 April 1922.

p.228 "transferred four years earlier": *L'Express du Midi*, 14 Nov 1924.

p.228 "none of them remotely true": See Belin's interviews in *Le Matin*, 18 Nov 1935, 23 Dec 1937.

p.228 "cracked open *l'affaire Landru*": *L'Ouest-Eclair*, 23 Sept 1931.

p.229 "has never been seen since": see Note on Sources, p.287.

p.229 "this astonishing and shocking case": *Le Petit Parisien*, 25 Sept 1922.

p.229 "any doubt in the case": *Le Matin*, 12 March 1922, quoting interview by Godefroy in *L'Éclair*.

p.229 "stellar career at the Paris Bar": Moro's next client was Mme Bessarabo, who had put her husband's corpse on the overnight sleeper to Nancy. He lost the case in June 1922, after Mme Bessabaro's daughter denounced her. Moro managed to save Mme Bessarabo from the guillotine, on the grounds that the murder was a *crime passionel*. She was sentenced to 20 years with hard labour.

p.229 "even beyond the grave": Information from Dominique de Moro Giafferri, March 2017.

p.229 "three-page private memoir": Auguste Navières du Treuil, 'L'Affaire Landru', Personal Collection of Dominique de Moro Giafferri.

Chapter 24: The Road to Gambais

p.231 "the importance of facts": Monteilhet's professional scruples may explain why he declined to identify Landru formally when he was shown Landru's police mug shots in May 1919.

p.232 "cast-net in the pond": Jean Monteilhet, witness statement, 6 May 1919, Paris Police Archives, reproduced in *Landru: 6h 10 Temps Clair, Les Pièces du Dossier* (Paris, 2013).

p.232 "directed operations from the bank": *Le Temps*, 11 May 1919.

p.234 "appear in the *carnet*": 'Réquisitoire définitif', p.299, Yvelines Archives, Carton 2U772.

p.234 "had not been established": 'Liste des femmes ayant été en correspondance ou en relations avec Landru', Paris Police Archives, Carton JA 30, *Dossier Général*.

p.234 "her fiancé's country house": Mme Dalouin letter to Bonin, 17 May 1919, Yvelines Archives, Carton 2U769/3058, *Dossier Héon*.

p.234 "identified as Landru": 'Audition de Marie Bizeau', 16 May 1919, Yvelines Archives, Carton 2U771/3716.

p.235 "29 March 1918": Mme Bizeau or her husband may have noted the date in order to make sure he was paid for the job.

p.236 "after Annette's disappearance": Mme Bizeau said she saw Landru for the last time in November 1918 in the garden of the Villa Tric.

p.237 "pouring out of his chimney": *Le Journal*, 24 Nov 1921.

p.237 "sneered at the women": *Le Journal*, 24 Nov 1921.

p.238 "at work in the kitchen": Three women in the hamlet of Boulay testified at Landru's trial about foul smoke wafting across the fields one winter's evening from the villa. They could not remember the month or the year. *Le Petit Parisien*, 24 Nov 1921.

Chapter 25: The Road to Vernouillet

p.241 "fields behind the house": The area behind The Lodge is now built-up.

p.241 "are reproduced identically": 'Interrogatoire Général', 3 Aug 1920, Paris Police Archives, Carton JA 28, *Dossier Cuchet*.

p.242 "who may have been married": I cannot find Pierre Capdevieille through census and genealogical records.

p.243 "added to the mournful list": 'Réquisitoire définitif', 4 Dec 1920, pp.2–3, Yvelines Archives, Carton 2U 772/4907.

p.243 "volunteer for the army": *Le Gaulois*, 11 Nov 1921.

p.243 "it was pointless": André Cuchet letter to Maxime Morin, 25 Oct 1914, Yvelines Archives, Carton 2U 769/2755.

p.243 "this is *maman* who says so": *Le Journal*, 11 Oct 1914. The letter was possibly a piece of propaganda, designed to stoke hatred of the Germans as France's casualty rate increased.

p.243 "speaking little or no English": US Department of Homeland Security, Yearbook of Immigration Statistics (2008).

p.244 "business trips to America": 'Audition de Mme Oudry', 15 April 1919, Paris Police Archives, Carton JA 28, *Dossier Cuchet*.

p.245 "the 'poor weather'": Jeanne Cuchet letter to Mme Morin, 4 Jan 1915, Yvelines Archives, Carton 2U 769/2760; 'Réquisitoire Définitif', p.50, Yvelines Archives, Carton 2U772.

p.245 "dated 20 January 1915": André Cuchet to Maxime Morin, 20 Jan 1915, Yvelines Archives, Carton 2U769/2745.

p.246 "André's final letter to Max": *Le Journal*, 24 Nov 1921.

p.246 "Landru probably used a gun": Riboulet, *Le Matin*, 5 June 1933.

p.248 "purpose of his visit": 'Déclaration de Landru, Charles, dit Frémyet, Charles, 14 April 1919, Paris Police Archives, Carton JA 28, *Dossier Cuchet*, reproduced in *Landru: 6h 10 Temps Clair, Les Pièces du Dossier* (Paris, 2013).

p.248 "'gardening work' ('*jardinage*')": 'Cuchet: Instruction', report by Brigadier Riboulet, 13 Aug 1919, Paris Police Archives, Carton JA 28, *Dossier Cuchet*.

p.248 "and had had to flee": 'Audition de Gabriel Grimm', 17 May 1919, Paris Police Archives, Carton JA 30, *Dossier Général*.

p.250 "because she was a prostitute": Outside the court Moro was a champion of women's rights, addressing a suffragettes' rally one evening during the trial. *Le Rappel*, 19 Nov 1921.

Afterword: From the Quai de la Pinède to the Jardin des Plantes

p.251 "come into harbour": *Le Journal*, 29 Oct 1927.

p.251 "led by Moro in the National Assembly": The campaign was led in the press by the investigative journalist Albert Londres.

p.251 "to write this book": Eugène Dieudonné letter to Moro, 21 July 1930, reproduced in Lanzalavi, (2011), p.48.

p.252 "could offer was 'hypotheses'": *Le Journal*, 24 Nov 1921.

p.252 "'*le grand Moro*'": See Robert Badinter's memoir of Moro in Lanzalavi, (2011) pp.9–12.

Note on Sources

The surviving original documents on the Landru case are held today by the Archives de la Préfecture de Police in north-east Paris and the Archives départmentales des Yvelines near Versailles.

There are two major gaps in the combined collections. The court transcript (*procès-verbal*) of Landru's trial was either lost or stolen at some point before the Second World War. I have relied instead on the extensive newspaper coverage of the trial to reconstruct the key exchanges, many of which were published verbatim. Most of the dialogue in this book was reproduced in very similar form in various newspapers.

The second gap is more intriguing. Landru's infamous *carnet* and a significant body of other material disappeared from the Paris police archives before the liberation of France in 1944, when the absence of these documents was first noticed. It was assumed that the material had been removed during the German occupation, probably by the Nazis, and perhaps transported to Berlin. However, there are strong circumstantial grounds for believing that the *carnet* and other correspondence were taken about a decade earlier.

In 1933 Brigadier Louis Riboulet, one of the main detectives in the case, published a ghostwritten memoir, *La Véritable Affaire Landru*, which was also serialised by *Le Matin* newspaper. Riboulet used extensive extracts from the *carnet* and also quoted at length from the same correspondence that was later discovered to be missing from the case files. The coincidence is striking, since none of this material ever surfaced before or after in print.

The need to rely on Riboulet's memoir as the only available source for the *carnet* presents an obvious dilemma. Riboulet was biased in favour of the prosecution and keen to portray himself in a favourable light. I have nonetheless assumed that Riboulet's extracts from the *carnet* were accurate, because leading figures at the trial who had also seen the notebook were still alive in 1933 and in a position to correct any distortions: notably, Godefroy, Moro, Navières and Gilbert.

Like Riboulet's book, my case is not objective. I have made selective use of the *carnet* (as reproduced by Riboulet) and the surviving case material in the police and judicial archives. Based on these documents, I have drawn my own conclusions about the credibility and importance of various witnesses.

A number of key prosecution witnesses struck me as unreliable or even liars: in particular, Jeanne Cuchet's sister Philomène and brother-in-law Georges Friedman, the three detectives Riboulet, Dautel and Belin, and the three psychiatrists who pronounced Landru mentally fit to stand trial. Conversely, I thought the testimony of several witnesses who did not appear at the trial merited close attention. They included Mme Hardy, Jeanne Cuchet's inquisitive neighbour in La Chaussée, and Jeanne's friend and probable lover Pierre Capdevieille.

I treated one other witness in a manner that may seem too harsh. Fernande Segret wanted a starring role in the case and that is how she appears in most books on *l'affaire Landru* – centre stage, in the full glare of the limelight. Yet Fernande was a self-styled "survivor", unlike Landru's victims. This book is about their tragedy, not Fernande's, which reached its *dénouement* many years after the events described in these pages.

Select Bibliography

Primary Sources

Archives de la Préfecture de Police, Pantin, Paris
Affaire Landru: Cartons JA 28 – JA 33.

Archives départementales des Yvelines, Montigny-le-Bretonneux
Affaire Landru: Cartons 1373W2, 2U767, 2U768, 2U769, 2U770, 2U771, 2U772.

Personal Collection of Dominique de Moro Giafferri, Paris
Auguste Navières du Treuil, "*L'affaire Landru*", private memoir, undated.

Sam Cohen, Louis Riboulet, *La Véritable Affaire Landru* (Paris, 1933, serialised in *Le Matin*)
Extracts from Landru's notebook (*carnet*).

Miscellaneous correspondence to and from Landru.

Bibliothèque Nationale, Paris
Newspaper Collection, available online at:
http://gallica.bnf.fr/html/und/presse-et-revues/presse-et-revues

Main newspapers consulted:
L'Action Française
Comœdia
L'Echo d'Alger
L'Echo d'Oran
L'Echo de Paris
L'Excelsior
Le Figaro
Le Gaulois
L'Homme Libre
L'Humanité
L'Intransigeant
Le Journal
Le Journal des Débats Politiques et Littéraires
La Justice

La Lanterne
Le Matin
L'Oeuvre
L'Ouest-Éclair
Paris-Soir
Le Petit Journal
Le Petit Parisien
Le Populaire
La Presse
Le Radical
Le Rappel
Le Siècle
Le Temps

Secondary Sources

Books in English

Bardens, Dennis, *The Ladykiller: The Crimes of Landru, the French Bluebeard,* P. Davies, London, 1972.

Le Queux, William, *Landru: His Secret Love Affairs,* Stanley Paul & Co., London, 1922.

Mackenzie, F.A. (editor), *Landru,* Geoffrey Bles, London, 1928.

Wakefield, Herbert Russell, *Landru, The French Bluebeard,* Duckworth, London, 1936.

Books in French

Belin, J., *Commissaire Belin. Trente Ans de Sûreté Nationale,* Bibliothèque France-Soir, Paris, 1950.

Béraud, Henri, Bourcier, Emmanuel & Salmon, André, *L'Affaire Landru,* Albin Michel, Paris, 1924.

Bernède, Arthur, *Landru,* Jules Tallandier, Paris, 1931.

Biagi-Chai, Francesca, *Le cas Landru à la lumière de la psychoanalyse,* Imago, Paris, 2007.

Darmon, Pierre, *Landru,* Plon, Paris, 1994.

González, Christian, *Monsieur Landru,* Scènes de Crimes, Paris, 2007.

Jaeger, Gérard, *Landru: bourreau des coeurs,* L'Archipel, Paris, 2005.

Lanzalavi, Dominique, *Vincent de Moro Giafferri: Défendre l'homme, toujours*, Ajaccio, Albiana, 2011.

Masson, René, *Landru, le Barbe-Bleue de Gambais*, N'Avouez Jamais, Paris, 1974.

Michal, Bernard, *Les Monstres,* Bibliomnibus, Paris, 2014.

Sagnier, Christine, *L'Affaire Landru,* Editions de Vecchi, Paris, 1999.

Yung, Eric, *Landru: 6h 10 Temps Clair*, Editions Télémaque, Paris, 2013.

Acknowledgements

In Paris, Dominique de Moro Giafferri kindly shared his memories of his grandfather, Vincent de Moro Giafferri, and made available his private collection of material on the Landru case. I am extremely grateful to him. I would also like to acknowledge my debt to Dominique Lanzalavi's fine biography of Moro, based on the same collection, which contains much previously unpublished information on Landru's defence barrister.

My friend Laurence Soustras helped me with many tricky translations of French words and phrases, including some obscure early twentieth-century *argot*. All errors in French are of course my own. I thank her as well for being so interested in the story and giving me a French perspective on *l'affaire Landru*.

I am grateful to the staff of the Archives de la Préfecture de la Police in Paris and the Archives Départmentales des Yvelines, which together hold all the surviving case files on Landru, as well as most of the photographs reproduced in this book. The rest of my research would have been impossible without online access to the Bibliothèque Nationale's magnificent newspaper collection. Lastly in France, I thank the many family historians whose research on their ancestors, posted online, gave me crucial biographical information about Landru and his victims.

In Britain, I am grateful to my copy editor Linne Matthews, who saved me from numerous errors and inconsistencies and helped me tell a fiendishly complicated story as clearly as I could. At my publisher Pen & Sword, many thanks to Laura Hirst, who supervised the production, to Emily Robinson, who organised the publicity, and to my commissioning editor Jonathan Wright.

Various friends were enormously helpful at different stages of research, writing and editing. Mark Redhead put me straight about how to start the story and was always ready with encouragement and advice. Sarah Helm read an early draft of the first two chapters and made me realise I had to write them again. Nick Hindley cast his expert psychiatrist's eye on the murky issue of whether Landru was clinically insane. Amelia Blacker and Paul Unwin helped me narrow an original longlist of more than fifty images down to the pictures you see in this book.

As ever, I owe huge thanks to my agent Jane Turnbull for all her support and tireless editorial advice as I inflicted her with more drafts and redrafts of the manuscript than I care to admit.

Finally, I cannot thank enough my partner Tess and our daughter Hannah, who have been endlessly supportive and patient while I laboured over *l'affaire Landru*.

Index

INDEX